The Musical Lives of Charles Manson

The Musical Lives of Charles Manson

The Beatles, the Beach Boys, and the Invention of the Sixties—or, No Sense Makes Sense

Nicholas Tochka

BLOOMSBURY ACADEMIC
NEW YORK • LONDON • OXFORD • NEW DELHI • SYDNEY

BLOOMSBURY ACADEMIC
Bloomsbury Publishing Inc, 1359 Broadway, New York, NY 10018, USA
Bloomsbury Publishing Plc, 50 Bedford Square, London, WC1B 3DP, UK
Bloomsbury Publishing Ireland, 29 Earlsfort Terrace, Dublin 2, D02 AY28, Ireland

BLOOMSBURY, BLOOMSBURY ACADEMIC and the Diana logo are trademarks of
Bloomsbury Publishing Plc

First published in the United States of America 2026

Copyright © Nicholas Tochka, 2026

For legal purposes the acknowledgments on p. 226 constitute an extension of this copyright page.

Cover design by Louise Dugdale
Cover image: raisbeckfoto/Getty Images

All rights reserved. No part of this publication may be: i) reproduced or transmitted in any form, electronic or mechanical, including photocopying, recording or by means of any information storage or retrieval system without prior permission in writing from the publishers; or ii) used or reproduced in any way for the training, development or operation of artificial intelligence (AI) technologies, including generative AI technologies. The rights holders expressly reserve this publication from the text and data mining exception as per Article 4(3) of the Digital Single Market Directive (EU) 2019/790.

Bloomsbury Publishing Inc does not have any control over, or responsibility for, any third-party websites referred to or in this book. All internet addresses given in this book were correct at the time of going to press. The author and publisher regret any inconvenience caused if addresses have changed or sites have ceased to exist, but can accept no responsibility for any such changes.

Library of Congress Cataloging-in-Publication Data
Names: Tochka, Nicholas author
Title: The Musical lives of Charles Manson: the Beatles, the Beach Boys, and the invention of the sixties -or, no sense makes sense / Nicholas Tochka.
Description: [1.]. | New York, NY: Bloomsbury Academic, 2026. | Includes bibliographical references and index. | Summary: "Nicholas Tochka analyzes the role of rock music in the life of Charles Manson, the Family, and the August 1969 Tate-LaBianca killings, which also gives larger insights into Sixties counterculture. Did the guitar-playing guru personify the violence that the rock counterculture had inflicted on American society? Or did his music diagnose the dehumanizing effects of that society's broken institutions? For nearly five years, commentators debated the meaning of Charles Manson and the Tate-LaBianca killings. The key thread linking these narratives was rock music"– Provided by publisher.
Identifiers: LCCN 2025025041 | ISBN 9781501384561 hardback | ISBN 9781501384554 paperback | ISBN 9781501384585 pdf | ISBN 9781501384578 epub
Subjects: LCSH: Rock music–Social aspects–United States–History–20th century | Manson, Charles, 1934-2017 | Beatles–Influence | Beach Boys–Influence | Rock music–1961-1970–History and criticism
Classification: LCC ML3918.R63 T62 2026 | DDC 781.660973/09046--dc23/eng/20250730
LC record available at https://lccn.loc.gov/2025025041

ISBN: HB: 978-1-5013-8456-1
PBK: 978-1-5013-8455-4
ePDF: 978-1-5013-8458-5
eBook: 978-1-5013-8457-8

Typeset by Deanta Global Publishing Services, Chennai, India
Printed and bound in the United States of America

For product safety related questions contact productsafety@bloomsbury.com.

To find out more about our authors and books visit www.bloomsbury.com and sign up for our newsletters.

For John Bryning, and L. S. Witt.

Guard grimly your veracity / With desp'rate pertinacity.
  —Advice from *It Happened in Boston?* (1967) by Russell H. Greenan

Contents

List of Illustrations	viii
A Note on Obfuscation	ix
Prologue: Who Are These People?	1
1 March 1967 to October 1967: or, Disenchanted Seekers	7
2 November 1967 to March 1968: or, Man's Son	37
3 April 1968 to September 1968: or, A Group of Beatle Addicts	71
4 October 1968 to July 1969: or, Rumor's Children	103
5 July 1969 to December 1969: or, The Love and Terror Cult	141
6 December 1969 to February 1972: or, Child of the State	175
Epilogue: The Invention of the Sixties	219
A Note On Reading *No Sense Makes Sense*	223
Acknowledgments	226
Notes	227
References	258
Index	265

Illustrations

1. Peace.
   As drawn on the Helter Scelter door, *c.* October 1969. Realized by the author.

2. Inkblot.
   After the 1921 series by Hermann Rorschach. Realized by the author.

3. "The Hanged Man."
   After an illustration (allegedly) by Norman Greene for *Harper's* (March 1970), based on an image by Pamela Colman Smith (1909). Realized by the author.

4. Barker Ranch, Death Valley.
   After a photograph by Vernon Merritt for *Life Magazine* (December 1969). Realized by the author.

5. Exhibit 228.
   Cover of *The Beatles* (1968), designed by Richard Hamilton.

6. Manson analyzes the White Album.
   After a description by Charles Manson in *Rolling Stone* (June 25, 1970). Realized by the author.

7. "Who Are These People?"
   Photographer unknown, from the front page of the *Los Angeles Free Press* (February 6–12, 1970).

8. "Secret Pictures."
   Realized by the author.

A Note on Obfuscation

No book can be entirely objective. And this despite objectivity—or at least, a kind of seriousness—constituting an essential feature of the nonfiction genre. So let us say from the start: this book is not objective. It examines how certain countercultural practices and postwar generic conventions, as well as non-rational logics and even occult knowledges, related to a shift in how some Americans (not all, by any means) apprehended and experienced reality at a particular point in time (from about the mid-1960s to the early 1970s). And it perhaps suggests something about the consequences of that shift for those of us alive today.

Because the aim here is not mere historiography, the materials have been presented in the form of a historical paraethnography, albeit without some of the usual scholarly apparatus, for reasons suggested throughout. Such an approach has been necessary because so few potential interviewees today remain; many met death by violence decades ago. But the characters and events depicted herein are real, and the author—that is, me—accepts responsibility for any unintentional similarities to fictitious persons or incidents. Only in rare instances, noted in the text, has obfuscation been required.

Prologue
Who Are These People?

ONCE A GROUP OF YOUNG PEOPLE, at least four, committed a series of brutal murders in Los Angeles. A charismatic leader had brainwashed them. He had quite literally worked to "deprogram" their minds, erasing the moral convictions and social aptitudes that from birth parents, teachers, television shows, books, or films had inculcated in them. And then, he filled their now-emptied heads with new convictions, some quite perverse. Submit. Death is life. *No sense makes sense.* He accomplished this mostly through drugs and sex. He also used rock music.

The leader suffered from what experts would call delusions of grandeur: he believed himself to be a very powerful person, and to enjoy special relationships with other very powerful people. He at least had a clinical form of narcissism, they agreed, if not outright paranoid schizophrenia. One of the delusions made him believe that he would become a famous singer. He would record and sell records, touring the United States and beyond, sharing his message through song. Several industry veterans in Los Angeles, including the drummer of the Beach Boys, a singing group from Hawthorne, California, had encouraged his musical ambitions. This had worsened the delusions.

Another delusion made the charismatic leader believe that even bigger recording artists than the Beach Boys had been secretly communicating with him through song lyrics. The Beatles, an English musical recording group, had prophesied that a race war between Black Americans and whites would soon begin. So the leader needed to secret his followers away somewhere in Death Valley, California. There they would remain, in a system of caves deep underground, as Black Americans exterminated white Americans, and as their group grew to 144,000 souls. At that point the leader would emerge with his followers to rule the Blacks—and the rest of the world. John Lennon, Paul McCartney, George Harrison, and Ringo Starr had hinted at this prophecy on a double album released in November 1968 titled *The Beatles*, which most people called the White Album because of its plain white packaging. The Christian

Bible confirmed the scheme's basic contours. It also confirmed that the Beatles really were prophets.

The war would be called Helter Skelter, after a song on the White Album by Beatle Paul. But before the leader could hide his followers in the desert, the violence had to begin. That's why the group had committed those murders in Los Angeles. To jumpstart Helter Skelter. Black Americans, you see, had been dragging their feet on getting the apocalypse going.

~

To borrow a phrase: All this happened, more or less.

Race, sex, violence, drugs, and of course, rock music: small wonder the story of the Manson Family murders has from the beginning served as a kind of urtext for narrating the Sixties and its consequences for the United States.[1] Members of the group committed several other murders, too, some allegedly related to drug deals. Their last confirmed murder had to do with snitching, which is prison slang for informing the authorities about criminal activities. But it's the preceding sequence of events—about brainwashing and bottomless pits, the Beatles and the Beach Boys—that figures most prominently in retellings. These events generated what may be the most complex mythos centered on a single person in maybe two thousand years.

And this, despite making no sense.

The story never really made much sense.[2] In the days following what came to be known as the Tate-LaBianca murders, competing interpretations of what had happened—and what it *meant*—ran rampant. Journalists so quickly flooded the market with tales weird and macabre that, in early 1970, lawyers representing Charles Watson filed a brief requesting his trial be moved from Los Angeles. Known in Manson's commune by the nickname Tex, Watson stood accused of murder in the first degree; he would soon be convicted of killing seven people across those two nights in August 1969. One hundred and fourteen samples of media coverage submitted to the court described drug use, orgies, occult rituals, sadomasochism, even snuff films. The legal brief noted that only the Kennedy assassination six years earlier had rivaled coverage of the Tate-LaBianca murders in sheer number of press items. All these uncorroborated claims had no doubt leached into the pool of potential jurors, lawyers for Watson argued, contaminating their minds.

The judge denied the request, and ruled that the trial would remain in California. "Sensational events," he reasoned, "cannot be accurately portrayed in prosaic terms."[3] In the true-crime bestseller *Helter Skelter: The True Story of the Manson Murders* (1974), prosecutor Vincent Bugliosi would echo this conclusion. "It was admittedly bizarre, but from the first moment I was assigned to the case, I'd felt that for murders as bizarre as these the motive itself would have to be almost equally strange," Bugliosi wrote, "not something you'd find within the pages of a textbook on police science."[4]

Five decades later, new accounts of the Manson Family murders continue proliferating, their authors (and readers) complicit in ensuring a robust afterlife for the story and its characters. In a way that makes good sense. After all, didn't this moment, as our most sober commentators periodically remind us, help end the Sixties? If we are ranking eschatological fantasies of the postwar American psyche, only Mick and Keith at Altamont can vie with Charlie and the Girls at Cielo Drive for most fructuous. And the Stones rate, as always, at best a distant second.

But why should this story have commanded such a prime position in the imaginations of so many Americans? For sure, an innate perversity of the American character, observable in its most pathological form among a certain generation, goes a long way toward answering this question. We may need to dissect this perversity, examining its constituent parts in sociological and historical detail. But here's the real question: Why has a story seemingly so resistant to rational explanation appeared to explain so much?

~

Listen: There are just so many different iterations of the story of Charles Manson and the Tate-LaBianca murders. Over the course of my research, I have consumed firsthand accounts and memoirs, newspaper and magazine articles, sociological works both major and minor, police interviews, court transcripts, music recordings, biographies, even histories. I have pitted alternative accounts against official ones, cross-referencing contrasting stories and compiling discrepancies. My collection of Mansonalia bristles with bits of colored paper. Trust me: my research folders overflow.

Over the past three decades, a group of revisionists has demanded we reject the "so-called Helter Skelter story."[5] First in this body of work was *The Manson File: Myth and Reality of an Outlaw Shaman* (1988) by Nikolas Schreck, now in its third edition. Several key revisionists cultivated personal relationships with Charles Manson, even visiting him in the Protective Housing Unit of the California State Prison at Corcoran before his death in 2017. Others work anonymously, populating listservs and blogs devoted to parsing the case. A few, such as George Stimson, webmaster of an early site called Access Manson, have at various points entered the inner circle of what remains of Charlie's commune. (Stimson's partner, Sandra Good, was the commune member better known as Blue.) In 1997, the *New York Times* ran an article about Access Manson headlined, "History Rewritten by Losers."[6] Succinct, if a bit uncharitable.

The history these revisionists have been rewriting is the basic story outlined in prosecutor Vincent Bugliosi's *Helter Skelter*. Told and retold, cut up and repackaged and reissued and reprinted, Bugliosi's tale is the one you encountered in my opening paragraphs. Pick up the *New Yorker* or *LA Times* or almost any trade book and you'll find a version of this narrative. It's been transformed into an award-winning television series, several made-for-TV movies, a podcast, comic books, even an opera. It narrates events from March 1967 to March 1971, with short forays into the tawdry and pathetic early life of "Charles Milles Manson (1934–2018)." It revolves around the Beatles, and the Manson Family's exegetical readings of their White Album. Sun-kissed drummer Dennis Wilson of the Beach Boys, producer (and son of Doris Day) Terry Melcher, and professional friend-to-the-stars Gregg Jakobson feature, too.

That's not all. There's an early counter-history, *The Family: The Story of Charles Manson's Dune Buggy Attack Battalion* (1971) by erstwhile Beat and folk-rocking Fug Ed Sanders, the countercultural founder of *Fuck You: A Magazine of the Arts*. An inspiringly psychedelic experiment in shoe-leather reporting, this account relates—with a bracing absence of editorial discretion—every lead, clue, rumor, story, and theory that Sanders turned up over an obsessive eighteen months' worth of research. Then there are the memoirs by commune members: Tex, but also Susan Atkins (known as Sadie Mae Glutz), Lynette Fromme (Squeaky), Dianne Lake (Snake), and Paul Watkins (Little Paul). And finally we have the fictionalized or semi-fictionalized accounts: from pulpy sci-fi retellings featuring the Manson Family as aliens to exploitation slasher remakes to bigger-budget exercises both serious and artistic.

So many iterations of the same basic story exist, with new ones emerging every year. We might ignore them; you could close this book.[7] But if we decide to pay attention, we should because the particularities of the true-crime stories that authors choose to narrate matter. "These collective obsessions are often dismissed as exploitative, sensationalistic, and distasteful," writes Rachel Monroe. "But the murder stories we tell, and *the ways that we tell them*, have a political and social impact and are worth taking seriously. Lessons are embedded within their gory details. *When read closely*, they can reveal the anxieties of the moment, tell us who's allowed to be a victim, and teach us what our monsters are allowed to look like."[8]

Something similar could be said of the stories we tell about rock. Heroes and villains populate the written worlds of rock's histories and hagiographies, individuals whom we have collectively decided to believe can exercise real effects on society through their music. In our romantic emplotments of their lives, rock has the capacity to change the world, to start revolutions—to free us from the shackles of the present and to prefigure future utopias. This approach most often results in our narratives taking the form of "a drama of self-identification symbolized by the hero's transcendence of the world of experience, his victory over it, and his final liberation from it."[9] Think legends of the Holy Grail, or the Gospel stories. Perhaps this explains why, in the true-crime stories we tell about Charles Manson, rock music—not only the group's exegetical readings of Beatle lyrics and albums, but also their own music-making, and its alleged roles in brainwashing followers before connecting them to Hollywood stars like Dennis Wilson and spurring them to murder—has so rarely taken center stage. But how else might this story be narrated? That's the question.

Now because I believe virtually everything I read, the following chapters draw on all sorts of sources and stories, some less reliable than others. I plan to draw on these sources unashamedly, without irony, maybe promiscuously.[10] But also advisedly. (Unlike many authors, I'm no Manson groupie.) And in the service of a higher ideal: the truth about the musical lives of Charles Manson.[11]

HERE'S THE THING: Nothing that has been written thus far has come close to explaining it. But it can be explained. The most important thing to say is that you should not take too literally what is written in this book. And I ask only that you recall the ambience of the late Sixties—perhaps the most turbulent and chaotic time in America in the last fifty years.

Special care should be exercised in exploring this period, "an era in which no reality can be approached," as one eyewitness noted, "unless it is read in multiple ways."[12] Given our source material, an approach that admits multiple readings seems not only sensible, but essential. For pure empiricism, by virtue of its method, unfairly excludes metaphysics. Such an approach also features an even more salutary attribute: a historically accurate sensitivity to how certain Americans—including most of the protagonists in this book—experienced this period.

To some Americans, the nature of reality itself seemed, from about 1964 or so, to become radically plastic, unstuck: open to interpretation and contestation, imagining and reimagining. Reality became malleable within certain parameters, and through particular modes of expression. So too did truth. And with consequences for us today. Because if ours is a world often opaque and requiring interpretation, an untrustworthy world that demands we dig beneath the surface of things in order to understand what is *really happening*, a world that we must decode, struggling to break through the veil of signs and countersigns that mask *what is actually going on*, then ours is also a world inherited. Ours is a world constructed, and so also a world not entirely of our own making. (After all, if I make my world, then surely you must be making your worlds, too.) And if ours is a world invented, as so many have claimed (and in so many ways) over the past half century: can we say it's an invention of the Sixties?

1

March 1967 to October 1967

or, Disenchanted Seekers

"AND WE SLEPT IN THE PARK and we lived on the streets and my hair got a little longer and I started playing music and people liked my music and people smiled at me and put their arms around me and hugged me—I didn't know how to act."

So said Charles Willis Manson: or Charlie to fellow travelers in the labyrinthine California underground. So said Charlie in a jailhouse interview to a journalist at the short-lived countercultural rag *Tuesday's Child* sometime in early 1970.[1] Manson had spent nearly seventeen of his thirty-two years in jails, prisons, or group homes for wayward children. Released from the federal penitentiary on Terminal Island in late March 1967, the ex-con had slim prospects. He had learned to play guitar and had written some songs; he told the prison psychologist he hoped to make a living selling them.

By most accounts, Charlie netted a few coins here and there during his early days of freedom, humming and strumming on the streets. Sometimes a bar owner would let him play, and he would "pass the hat." His rough ex-con act worked a charm. Charlie exuded outlaw credibility; it was part of his schtick. When patrons proved too tight, he wasn't above a cheap bluff.

"I just got out of prison, and me and my two partners had come by this place to rob it," Charlie would holler. "I talked my partners into letting me try to earn a few honest dollars instead of robbing the place. Now if some of you bastards don't put a few dollars into this empty hat, so that I ain't a liar, I don't know how long I can keep my two partners from walking through that door with their shotguns."[2] (So said Charlie to Nuel Emmons about fifteen years after that particular hustle had ended.)

Much had changed since Manson was sentenced in July 1961. While the court dropped charges for violating the Mann Act (the small-time pimp had crossed state lines with two women), a federal fraud charge (for cashing a thirty-something-dollar US Treasury check) stuck. So Charlie didn't know how to act. Because those six years, as anyone will tell you, had transformed the United States. The shifting of the tectonic plates underlying the American experiment, plates which had only just begun twitching in the fat, anxiety-ridden years following the Second World War, now ground ever louder, with shocks of deep rock here and there erupting at the surface. So Manson learned.

"I went to Frisco when I got out of the prison," Charlie said, "and I went up to the head gangster and I told him, 'Yeah, I just got in town, I want to work at one of your clubs.' He got a whole bunch of nightclubs and he said, 'Yeah, what do you want to do?' I said, 'I've been practicing guitar in prison and I'm pretty good and I want to play and sing.' He said, 'Let's hear what you can do, dig?' So I did a few songs for him and he said, 'Charlie, that's nice but, man, Bing Crosby's been gone. You know Frank Sinatra's nothing anymore, that's not what they're playing.' I said, 'What do you mean?' He said, 'Come on, smoke this. Come on to the Avalon ballroom.'"

So said Charlie about thirty-five years after the fact to some jailhouse hanger-on. "And I got a sports coat on and sports shoes, and my mind is running around in a '59 Oldsmobile 88 and all that, so the Grateful Dead come out and I never seen anything like that. I was on the Island. Twenty years behind in Washington State. And when those guys started playing and a strobe light came on, I freaked out, man, I jumped and ran out of that place."

"I said, '*God*.' I threw my guitar over a cliff, man. I said, '*That's it*, that's the end of *that*, man.'"[3]

~

Man's potential for making the leap, for transcending this world, first revealed itself fully, some would say, in a rectangular patch of land in San Francisco called the Haight in the early heady days of Nineteen-Sixty-Seven. That year began with the Human Be-In: a Pow Wow and Peace Dance, a Gathering of the Tribes, with "the two radical scenes"—the political types and the freaks, mutually distrustful—"for the first time beginning to look at each other more closely."

A beginning.

"A new concert of human relations being developed within the youthful underground must emerge, become conscious and be shared," a spokesperson told the *Berkeley Barb*, "so that a Revolution of form can be filled with a Renaissance of compassion, awareness and love in the Revelation of the unity of all mankind." The park grounds "will hold fifty thousand people, and an endless number of sounds, scents, and sights. Beads, bells, flutes, incense, flags, symbols, cymbals, drums, feathers, flowers. And words. Words kept short. Words painting a picture of a free loving society to come."[4]

Keeping words short pushed experience to the fore, enabling a congress between the cerebral and the sensual, the political and the bodily.* Bands played. The Diggers distributed free food. Countercultural sages and activists alike spoke. The thirty-thousand or so attendees listened and danced, and communed as one: as *a group*.

Reports in the national press seeded visions of the Gathering far and wide, though not everyone got it. Here an unimaginative historian might interpolate a song lyric about the growing divide between the progressives and the staid conservatives, the countercultural vanguard and their critics. Something is happening, the young seemed to be saying to their elders, but you don't know what it is. Do you? No one ever agreed on what *it* really was. Its political component had multiple origins: in movements for free speech, civil rights, and peace. Its cultural component did, too: in movements for the emancipation of literature, art, drugs, and sex. And of course, the division between these distinct components, never as clear-cut as their architects sometimes imagined, had already begun blurring before fully disintegrating into a politics of experience.[5]

And where did *the music* fit into all this? As young white people began populating the Haight-Ashbury neighborhood just south of the panhandle jutting out from the Golden Gate Park, a few made art, some formed bands, others held dances. And many embarked on experiments in living—no longer simply making do with reality, but making *real life* rollick and gambol and *sing*.

~

Singer Paul McCartney, a member of the Beatles, looms large on the wall of a coffeehouse in *The Free People* (1969), a collection of photographs chronicling those halcyon days in the Haight. A boy in shadow sits before Brother Paul, pensive and unshaven, doe-eyes peering beatifically into the lens at the end of the photographer's camera; at another table, a girl slumps over, hand cradling downy head.[6]

---

* A collage accompanying coverage in the *Berkeley Barb*, for instance, nestled the hairy among the serious, with a bare-bottomed young woman and a fist-raising Black activist bracketing the scene. On the following page, the Community for New Politics advertised "an Orgy . . . in the name of Peace." (Then, next to the headline "Human Be-In Prelude to Revolution?" on page three, readers viewed a photograph showing a painted slogan in tall block letters that, before the authorities pulled it down, had greeted commuters along the Bayshore Highway: "LBJ KILLED JFK.")

The images in this book speak for themselves. They show hairy beards, bell-bottom jeans, bare-chested young men on beaches, motorcycles, and so many huntress-lithe young women, breasts bared (nary a bra in sight), captured by the photographer's eager lens. A short essay by a man named Peter Marin prefaced the collection. Peter had been a "former Visiting Fellow at the Center for the Study of Democratic Institutions," the dust jacket informs us, and now works as "a writer and poet." His primary goal has become "finding a sensible way to live with my friends." A modest aim, deserving of praise.

"Freedom is for me as much the feeling of *particular* moments as it is a quality of person," writes Marin, "and it is from my memory of such moments that I construct for myself an image of free *people*." We Americans live in a contingent world, an order ever-shifting, and so the sensitive writer must take especial care in making his observations, Peter suggests, as "to pretend to speak about it authoritatively would be silly, irresponsible." Unconsciously or not, Marin's prose seems to model contingency. His writing becomes dense and layered through fragments, snatches of poetry and imagistic scenes, moments rendered in rough, quick strokes.

We live in grace, Peter proposes, but also fear, "and the underside of 'freedom' is an inexplicable sense of bondage and isolation." We experience good sex, and feeling good. The world promises music, and art, and the lightness that comes from a self-discovery acquired by learning to live through playacting at life. But we experience violence and ugliness, too, a world of ignorance and loneliness. We wallow in a shallowness wrought by our privilege, by that unexamined safety net of the affluent. (A white, comfortable Marin assumes the same background for his readers.)

Society proves a disorienting ground against which this dialectic of self-knowledge and trauma plays out. "It is not merely that society has proved imperfect or corrupt," writes Marin, "it is, put simply, that 'social reality' seems to have disappeared altogether. What has coherence in the culture or makes sense? . . . Indeed, there no longer seems to be any kind of reality to confront; instead, one drifts in a limbo and constructs a world from one's imagination—as if one fathered and mothered oneself."

Adrift, free to make reality fit oneself, to make one's self: "the young seem forced in the vacuum to improvise, to find their own ways back to wisdom or joy. But how can they handle that? There are ways that lead back and through the self, ways to find in oneself and others what is missing in the world. But they take patience and time and privacy—and where can the young find those?"[7]

So many ways to make a start. A discreditable notion occurs to me, that we could cast off our obligations to begin, slipping imperceptibly into the story midstream. But that can't work. Heavy burden, heavy sin.[8] So we proceed, once again from the start.

On the twenty-first of March, Charles Manson walked out of prison a free man. Terminal Island's penitentiary housed some eight hundred souls; it sits on a small block of land by California coast south due south from downtown Los Angeles, so to leave you must drive over a bridge or take a short ferry ride. For hours he sat beside a battered valise and guitar case, unsure about reentering the world.[9] At last a man in a truck, recognizing the paralysis, offered a ride. Here's the full story: born to a fifteen-year-old girl named Kathleen Maddox in 1934, Charles Manson had spent over half his troubled life in state institutions. His most recent stint came after a parole violation. For cashing a stolen check in late 1959, Manson had received a suspended ten-year sentence; a judge reinstated the sentence in early 1960 after he was arrested for violating the Mann Act, originally called the White-Slave Traffic Act of 1910. Manson always had stupid luck in committing federal crimes, which carried stiffer penalties. Had he committed the same crimes at the state level, authorities would have sequestered Manson from law-abiding society for no more than seven years—not seventeen.

Charlie learned a lot over those seventeen years. He entered prison a racist and a misogynist, and remained both. But he also took correspondence courses and flirted with different belief systems, from Norman Vincent Peale's Power of Positive Thinking to Dale Carnegie's How to Win Friends and Influence People to L. Ron Hubbard's Dianetics. He learned guitar, too. A Depression-era gangster (and ex-FBI Public Enemy No. 1) named Alvin "Creepy" Karpis had taken pity on Little Charlie, his amiably shiftless cellmate. "I decide it's time someone did something for him and to my surprise, he learns quickly," Karpis later recalled in a memoir crafted disarmingly in the present tense. "He has a pleasant voice and a pleasing personality although he's unusually meek and mild for a convict."[10]

In September 1963, an official noted Manson had become "something of a fanatic at practicing the guitar." A year later, he remained "emotionally insecure and tends to involve himself in various fanatical interests."[11] He acquired enough skill to begin playing at prison variety shows, either on his steel-string guitar or a communal drum kit. In May 1966, a staff member noted "he has been spending his free time writing songs, accumulating about 80 or 90 of them during the past year, which he ultimately hopes to sell following release." Three months later: "He has come to worship his guitar and music." Musical aspirations now formed the core of his post-release plans—or at least, that's what Manson told the parole board.¹²

Along the way, Charlie also became what people call a hardened criminal. At the time, many Americans believed that boys needed some hardness to their personality. Otherwise, you grow up to be a wimp and a mark, and that's no way for a man to be. But that adjective, "hardened," warns of the moral atrophy accompanying criminal activities. The criminal risks a metaphorical thickening of an emotional armor plating the soul, the stiff carapace inuring normal persons to feelings of guilt about those they hurt. Hardened: the word describes well the men who taught Charlie to con people and "turn out" girls, but also to "keep his word" and uphold strict norms of fraternal conduct, this perverse admixture of cruelty shot through with a code of honor making life "inside" livable.

You don't want a hardened criminal getting too comfortable in your home. That's why after a hot meal, a shower and a shave, and a good night's rest, the wife of the truck driver had him put Charlie out.¹³ If this stranger in a strange land initially felt ill at ease, he at least had that magpie collection of skills and dispositions, not to mention the good luck to be ejected into a San Francisco on the cusp of the Summer of Love, a place where a guy with a guitar and a good rap just had to knock, and doors would open.

~

Open any history of the Sixties and find any number of explanations for the relatively rapid shifts in consciousness taking place in the United States between the 1950s and early 1967. Sexual, technological, and economic revolutions liberated certain people (in certain places) from the bonds of drudgery, childbearing, wage labor. A mass culture renaissance exploded, heard most spectacularly in rock 'n' roll's transubstantiation into rock. Then there's the revelation of mind-altering substances such as marijuana and LSD.

Beatles John and George first ingested LSD in April 1965, dosed by a posh dentist after a dinner in London.¹⁴ Neither dared try the hallucinogen again until later that year. A two-week concert tour in the United States, the one that began in those handsome tan jackets and dark slacks at Shea Stadium, concluded in California on the last day of August. You can hear recordings from the Los Angeles concerts on *The Beatles at the Hollywood Bowl* (1977), one of my favorite records as a child, though the sound quality is atrocious. This was the Fab Four's penultimate stand—not the one marred by the protests and death threats inspired by John's offhand comment that the Beatles were "bigger than Jesus."

"The second time we had it was in L.A.," Lennon told *Rolling Stone* in 1971. "We were on tour in one of those houses, Doris Day's house or wherever it was we used to stay, and the three of us took it, Ringo, George and I. Maybe Neil and a couple of the Byrds—what's his name, the one in the Stills and Nash thing, Crosby and the other guy, who used to do the lead. McGuinn. I think they came, I'm not sure, on a few trips."

But not the Byrds' producer, and son of Doris Day, Terry Melcher. No one remembers him. There is clear evidence that actor Peter Fonda attended. He kept whispering, "I know what it's like to be dead," which John then used in a song.[15] (And for the record, John misremembered: Zsa Zsa Gabor owned that big house, as bright as any sun, the one at 2850 Benedict Canyon Drive, which other musicians, from Herman's Hermits to Jimi Hendrix, later rented. The ghost of Lennon used to visit the house, its final owner claimed, before it was demolished in the 1990s.)

John's second trip led to "a thousand" more over the next few years. "You see, I got the message that I should destroy my ego and I did, you know. I was reading that stupid book of Leary's [*The Psychedelic Experience*]; we were going through a whole game that everybody went through, and I destroyed myself. I was slowly putting myself together round about Maharishi time. Bit by bit over a two-year period, I had destroyed me ego."[16]

~

Ego nearly destroyed Brian Wilson, too. In an effort to keep pace with the musical experimentation of the Beatles, Brian had begun investing huge amounts of himself and his band's capital into increasingly complex studio recordings. And during the first half of 1966, Brian succeeded in getting the Beach Boys to complete recordings for what proved to be their defining album.

Pet Sounds took longer to conceive and record than any album to that point. The Beatles' first album, *Please Please Me*, famously recorded over just twelve hours, cost £400; *Pet Sounds*, released forty months later, took nearly three months, and cost $70,000. Session musicians laid down most of the backing tracks at United Western and Gold Star Studios in Hollywood. The Beach Boys, of course, performed their own soaring harmonies. "We'd pray together, and we prayed for light and guidance through the album," Brian told a journalist at the time. "We kind of made it a religious ceremony."[17] On hearing *Pet Sounds*, Beatle Paul went straight home and confected "Here, There, and Everywhere" (1966). A kind of creative one-upmanship ensued, the story goes, with *Pet Sounds*

(1966) begetting *Sgt. Pepper's Lonely Hearts Club Band* (1967), and *Sgt. Pepper's* begetting Brian Wilson's psychological breakdown over the failed recording of his never-completed masterpiece, *SMiLE*.[18]

At least, that's the story many of us have been repeating for years; its roots can be traced to contemporary interviews with Brian.[19] And in truth, the fortunes of the Beatles and the Beach Boys did begin diverging at this point. The Beatles had two, if not three, deeply creative forces driving them to evolve and grow with each record, as well as a manager who allowed them full creative rein. The Beach Boys had one visionary, the increasingly homebound Brian, and a few plucky young men (cousin Mike, brother Carl, and soon, Al Jardine) entrusted to translate these visions on stage, as well as a patriarch, Murry, whose ineptitude as a manager was outstripped only by his cruelty as a father. There was a handsome younger brother, too, sun-kissed Dennis, whom Brian nicknamed "dumb angel."

As the fortunes of the two groups diverged, phenomena associated with each seemingly converged. A kind of propinquity—of moments, and of sense—ensued. But you would need to look closely to see this. The concordances could be discerned only through the careful excavation of lyrics and recordings, by reading between the lines, through the parsing of tone, and especially voice.

~

"The voice was that of a young girl. But except for occasional giggles—'And Sharon went through quite a few changes [laughs], quite a few changes'—it was flat, emotionless, dead. It was as if all the human feelings had been erased. *What kind of creature is this?* I wondered."

The reel-to-reel then stopped. "O.K., now we're going to get you something to eat," said Sadie's lawyer, "including some ice cream."

"Though the tape cleared up some mysteries," prosecutor Bugliosi summarized, "many remained."[20]

This exchange between Bugliosi and commune member Susan Atkins can be found in the first part of the true-crime classic *Helter Skelter*. At this point, a note on that qualification, true: "The very notion of true crime," suggests one commentator, "proceeds as if 'crime' itself were assumed to be a fictional thing, such that the word 'true' must be added to bend it toward fact; the line between crime fact and crime fiction is in play from the start."[21]

Our book, at least in part, aims to consider the significance of true crime as one among many postwar genres concerned with making truth claims about the relationship between the individual and society. By uncritically invoking

Bugliosi's archetypal work, has that line been in play from the start here, too? If so, that should have been noted earlier. There's really no good reason for our narrative, on this point, to have remained silent.

~

"I been silent so long now it's gonna roar out of me like floodwaters and you think the guy telling this is ranting and raving my *God*; you think this is too horrible to have really happened, this is too awful to be the truth!" says Chief Bromden, the supposedly schizophrenic narrator of Ken Kesey's 1962 novel *One Flew Over The Cuckoo's Nest*.

"But, please. It's still hard for me to have a clear mind thinking on it. But it's the truth even if it didn't happen."[22]

~

Happenstance and propinquity: for the historian, these paths lead straight to ruin. The conscientious author relies on proper sources. In describing Charlie's exit from Terminal Island, I drew from a book compiled by Nuel Emmons in the early 1980s. Emmons did time with Charlie on drug charges at McNeil Penitentiary in the early 1960s; they became reacquainted after the con-turned-freelance writer ("an honest career") sent Charlie a letter in 1979. At some point, Manson agreed to allow Emmons to craft a memoir in his voice.

"The material for this first-person narrative has been assembled from many interviews," wrote Emmons in prefatory notes, "corroborated by his correspondence with me and with others, despite numerous obstacles. Even after Manson had agreed to cooperate, he was not always willing to do so, and I listened to hours upon hours of repetitive complaints about how rotten the prisons and the prison system were . . . With the exception of [several] limited occasions, I had to make mental notes until I could record them on tape or in writing. I spent many hours in the prison parking lot, writing down names and specific phrases that typified Manson's speech and his ideas. I frequently had to go over events with Manson several times to confirm details and *correct the misperceptions created by other accounts*. In some cases it was impossible to corroborate Manson's version of the facts, but the purpose of this book is, above all, to record that version."[23]

The publisher titled the book *Manson in His Own Words*; its subtitle read: *Destroying a Myth: The True Confessions of Charles Manson*.

~

Manson often used a keyword, slipped into his rap here and there, punctuating a (purposely?) disordered patter at significant moments in interviews from the 1980s and 1990s. It's a keyword we've encountered several times.

Changes. And I was going through changes. Some pretty heavy changes.

This countercultural phrase has fallen out of common usage. Today you'd be hard-pressed to find someone "going through changes." It refers to a shift in consciousness, whether due to external circumstances (stressors such as money problems, police harassment) or internal ones (revelatory experiences with drugs or sex, or even encounters with new ideas or kinds of people). It implies a passage from one state of being to another. Two parts explanatory to one part exculpatory, the expression also suggests you have come to shed the conventions of straight society, to *see through them*.

"Hang your fear at the door and join the future," as the Human Be-In press release concluded. "If you do not believe, please wipe your eyes and see."[24]

As CHARLIE STRUMMED ON A WARM APRIL MORNING, some scruffy mutt came nosing around his case full of coins. Its prim owner cried out: she thought Charlie had raised a foot to the dog. He let her think he had. Charlie and Mary, that's her name, somehow got talking, and an invitation to crash on her couch for the night turned into weeks.[25]

Mary Brunner—Mother Mary, who twelve months later gave birth to the commune's first child, Michael Valentine, day-to-day known as Pooh Bear, and who thirty-six months later would testify against another commune member, Bobby Beausoleil, at the Hall of Justice in Los Angeles—had two degrees and a steady job in the library system on the University of California's Berkeley campus. Vincent Bugliosi will later describe Mary as "singularly unattractive."[26] Then again, the prosecutor had argued, invoking a kind of everyday, commonsense misogyny that rarely merits examination, maybe Charlie *targeted* lonely hearts and broken women.[27] How lonely had Mary felt? God only knows. How broken?

Charlie stayed on the couch each night. He played music and rapped to the young hip passersby in Berkeley and the Haight each day. One day Charlie saw a "big black man" tailing a girl and intervened. "Hey," he greeted her, "I've been looking for you—where you been?" The suspicious man (a would-be pimp?) walked off. The sixteen-year-old white runaway, Darlene, now moved into Mary's apartment, too. When the two began sleeping together, Mary complained. "Are you sure you're treating her well?" But who was Mary to say? Hadn't she rebuffed Charlie? And Darlene brought home other lovers, too, scruffy boys and young men.

Then one day while Mary tidied, Charlie began strumming a few hummed lines. His narrator had "found a girl to love and trust," but their relationship could not be consummated: to her, *sex* was a dirty word. So the narrator "searched on," finding a "wayward waif without a home of her own," someone who "shared my must for lust."

"I am a man torn!" the poor narrator beseeched, "wanting the girl I love to ease my struggling mind and be my love—sharing my lust with some of her own!"

"Gee, Charlie, coming from you those lyrics were almost nice," Mary allegedly responded. "You didn't say, 'I want to fuck you,' like you normally do. Though you implied it."

"Some of your class and uppity culture is rubbing off on me," Charlie laughed.

"I doubt that."[28]

With Mary and Charlie's relationship blossoming, Darlene at some point left. Mary kept her job, and the two traveled in her car up the coast to the Pacific Northwest, through the beautiful redwood forests of Northern California. Soon Charlie decided to call on several recording studio contacts, and his parole officer approved a trip south to Los Angeles. The contacts didn't materialize, but no matter. Charlie traveled and passed the time, exploring the beach towns dotting the California coast. That's how he came to Venice, "a smaller version of Haight-Ashbury: pot, acid, and people wandering in search of something."[29]

Lynette Fromme had come to Venice searching for something, too. But now she found herself sitting on a curb, miserable, her face clouded (Charlie allegedly inferred) by "a combination of hurt, anger, and sadness." Approaching the eighteen-year-old, he sat down and caught her eye. A few months on the outside had made him comfortable engaging young women in conversation.

Here's the line he used:

"I am the God of fuck."[30]

~

Fucking, taking drugs, exploring the outer limits of reality: "In the sixties and seventies, countless individuals pursued intense and sometimes shattering hedonic, pharmacological, and esoteric experiences," writes one historian. "Many of these 'spiritual virtuosi' had good reasons for launching raids on the ineffable and returning with novel goods, either to answer their own existential questions, to test and disseminate alternative belief systems, or to provoke new ways of thinking and relating to the world."[31]

Sex and psychedelics provided such virtuosi with two key tools, though popular accounts sometimes err, I think, in assigning them too much weight. Each worked alongside many other "building blocks" for tinkering with our minds, for shifting our perceptions and *experiences* with social reality itself: cheap paperbacks about UFOs and astral projection and ESP and the Tarot, not to mention comic books, Beat poetry, high-minded science fiction, the non-rational world of the Twilight Zone, the orcs and elves of Middle Earth.[32]

In his contemporary account of the problem, Theodore Roszak explained how "the leading mentors of our youthful counter culture have, in a variety of ways, called into question the validity of the conventional scientific worldview."[33] They do so, he claimed, to undermine the technocracy, the regime of expertise that, rather than making life more livable, has "enmeshed [the public] in a gargantuan industrial apparatus which it admires to the point of idolization and yet cannot comprehend."[34]

Faced with this unfeeling Father, small wonder young people had begun cultivating techniques and practices for remaking themselves, for gaining access to the grounding reality of experience itself. To the above list of building blocks we can add lyrics, album cover art, songs, sounds. To fucking and drug-taking we can also add the close listening practices of the rock counterculture, its ecstatic dancing and its ritualized forms of consumption, as well as a gnostic impulse toward the exegetical interpretation of works by certain rock musicians.

But the problem has not yet been properly presented. To overcome this Father, we need to diagnose His "peculiar power" over us, a power Roszak located in the realm of myth: "the myth of objective consciousness." "There is but one way of gaining access to reality—so the myth holds—and this is to cultivate a state of consciousness cleansed of all subjective distortion, all personal involvement," Roszak noted. "What flows from this state of consciousness qualifies as knowledge, and nothing else does . . . At every level of human experience, would-be scientists come forward to endorse the myth of objective consciousness, thus certifying themselves as experts. And because they know and we do not, we yield to their guidance."[35]

What if we refused to submit to those so-called experts? Though let's take care not to not uncritically valorize all those who dissent from the myth of the rational and the objective. After all, how many who launched "raids on the ineffable" ever attained the status of virtuoso? For each person who summited the peaks of the self, how many others have fallen?

~

Falling into the depths of herself, Susan Atkins absorbed the sounds of the room as they penetrated the wooden box and began washing over her, searching out each small opening in her soft outer layer before burrowing under the elastic skin. Though the High Priest didn't like the girls taking drugs, Susan had ingested a tablet infused with lysergic diethylamide-25 before disrobing and climbing into a casket for the Topless Witches Revue.[36]

Susan had been working at a bar in North Beach when the agent there brought her and a few other go-go dancers to meet Anton LaVey at the Black House on 6114 California Street, a few blocks north of Golden Gate Park. This headquarters of the Church of Satan—its foyer housed a human skeleton, its living room, a taxidermized wolf, its backyard, a mangy half-dead real-life lion—creeped her out. Founded in the Fourth Month of Year One of *Anno Satanis* (better known as 1966), the Church of Satan emerged from an eclectic group of thirty-something iconoclasts who had been attending a Magic Circle led by LaVey.[37] To grow the group, LaVey advertised events in the pages of San Francisco's underground newspapers: Friday night rituals, one-off spectacles such as The Madness of Logic (a satire on America's "media-led society"), and now these topless shows.

Few younger people came.* LaVey hated drugs (in one ceremony, he ritualistically stamped on an LSD tablet). He delighted in hierarchy and order. And while the bared breasts at the kitschy horror nights titillated journalists, the Topless Witches Revue ran only briefly, alienating most members of the Church.[38] By then, Susan was long gone: "half dead" from drug use and untreated venereal diseases, she allegedly spent the waning days of the Summer of Love in the hospital.[39]

---

* Writing in the underground *LA Free Press* (August 4, 1967), Nat Freedland adopted a bemused tone about the prophet with the "Yul Brynner shaven scalp": "Any man who is a priest of Satan and lives in a house done in psychedelic Charles Addams with a pet lion can't be all bad.... The way he describes black magic, it's sort of like Ayn Rand with hexes" (p. 9). After attending one of LaVey's lectures, Arthur Johnston in the *San Francisco Express Times* (September 4, 1968) responded with a bit more bite: "'Any illusion is no longer reality,' LaVey said. He looked like Wagner's Mephistopheles: bald head, trim pointed beard, self-confident, brashly cynical. 'We are totally against drugs. We believe in material things.' The audience, composed of Your Mothers and Your Fathers, and an unexpected overflow of barefoot onlookers, listened attentively to the Satanic star of *Rosemary's Baby*; Mia Farrow's phantom stud. ('dominating male, leather avail. seeks chick who digs tannis root')." Johnston amusingly titled the article, "the devil as a liberal" (p. 10).

Time may tell just who has fell, and who's simply been left behind. But Atkins had, by her own account, a broken upbringing. When people say that, they mean the normal, straight line of development from birth to adolescence to healthy maturity has been interrupted, quite literally snapped, in Susan's case, by instances of abuse, the death of one parent, then serious neglect by the surviving one.

But not all seekers come from broken homes. Another young woman who soon entered the orbit of Charlie's growing group, Patricia Krenwinkel, had been a girl scout and a junior member of the Audubon Society. That is what her father, Joseph Krenwinkel, told the court at her sentencing for first-degree murder in February 1971, portraying the now twenty-three-year-old as an "exceedingly normal child, very obedient."[40] (Finding little else to flesh out the portrait, Vincent Bugliosi and later chroniclers mention obesity in early adolescence, homeliness, and an excess of body hair resulting from an endocrine condition, suggesting a susceptibility to coercion due to poor self-image.) After dropping out of Spring Hill College in Alabama in late 1966, Patty moved back to California. She met Charlie, Lyn, and Mary around July 1967.[41]

A final seeker, Leslie Van Houten, had not just been a girl scout, but had been elected Homecoming Queen, too. (In postwar American narratives, invoking a veneer of normalcy does not necessarily obscure a person's difficult past, but may cast their brokenness in sharper relief.) Prison psychologist Clara Livsey would later reveal the pain hidden behind a self-image of "the Van Houten family as supernice": the adoption of two Korean orphans supplanting Leslie as the baby of the family, an authoritarian mother and overindulgent father, the inevitably messy divorce, the teenager's pregnancy and abortion at age fifteen.[42] Leslie soon after discovered *The Psychedelic Experience* and became fascinated by the esotericism of P. D. Ouspensky. She next joined a group called the Self Realization Fellowship.[43]

Leslie then enrolled in secretarial school, one story goes, in order to train for service in the Fellowship, a philosophical organization that raised consciousness in members through meditation and yoga. (If you think this was some fringe operation, know that Elvis Presley attended Fellowship seminars, as did Beatle George Harrison.) But restless Leslie soon relocated to San Francisco, entering a kind of group marriage relationship with two other young women and a young man that most people called Cupid.[44]

"I didn't have any ambitions or goals," Leslie later said of this time with Bobby Beausoleil, "just to find the truth and try to live in tune with the earth was my main objective."⁴⁵

~

Objectively speaking: "All persons and events depicted herein are real. Any similarity to fictitious persons or events is purely coincidental." I have borrowed this disclaimer from Robert Cohen's 1967 cult film *Mondo Hollywood*. It applies here and now in precisely the same spirit as it did there and then. When it comes to the truth, you can never be too careful.

~

Careful readers will know that Lynette Fromme remembered her initial meeting with Charlie differently. In her recent memoir, she recalls having just left her family home for the second time. She sought ideas: "existentialism, transcendentalism, disestablishmentarianism . . . talk of Buddhism, reincarnation, timelessness, and universality." She wanted to experience the arcane knowledge embodied by the Beats who once haunted the coffeehouses of Venice Beach, those "gems of true character [so] unlike the frightened shadows who cheerlessly admitted to being our parents."* Here's the encounter with Charlie as narrated by Fromme:

"Name's Charlie," Charlie opened. "In San Francisco they call me 'The Gardener.'"

The wiry man seemed "both big and small," Fromme writes, "with a two-day beard and [he] reminded me of a fancy bum, elegant." Lyn remained aloof until Charlie accurately guessed that her father had kicked her out. (The term for this trick, employed by mediums and fortune tellers, is "cold reading.") She then burst open completely, speaking to Charlie about her hopes, dreams, fears, and anxieties. The Gardener's response shook the green eighteen-year-old.

"Don't want out and you're free. The want ties you up. Be where you are. You got to start some place."⁴⁶

Emmons reported Charlie remembering a slightly different exchange, and though the gist remains the same, the circumstances differ slightly. Lyn recalled a van filled with Darlene and a few other young people, but in the Emmons book,

---

* In certain genres, writing too well discredits you. Members of the Manson research community sometimes fault Fromme for sounding "too literary." Among authors—all covering roughly the same ground, the same stories, the same events and theories—her crystalline prose stands out for its evocative, at times allegorical, style.

there's only Charlie—Darlene has split.⁴⁷ The account in Emmons provided the basis for Jess Bravin's biography, *Squeaky* (1997), which Jeff Guinn seems to draw on in his authoritative biography, *Manson* (2013), interleaving the bare facts related above with insights from an imaginatively psychoanalytic retelling in *The Manson Women* (1979) by prison psychologist Clara Livsey (who never met Fromme).

Whither that other, crude come-on?

Because of its vulgarity, I almost didn't mention it before, but you can find that line on page thirty-four of a 1971 book by Ed Sanders. Unless you purchased for an exorbitant sum the first edition of *The Family: The Story of Charles Manson's Dune Buggy Attack Battalion*, there's a good chance your paperback relates the obscene pickup line on a different page. (After the Process Church of the Final Judgment, a Scientology splinter group, sued the publisher, most of the first run got pulped.⁴⁸)

"Every assertion in every sentence of this book," claimed Sanders (on page seven of the collectible first edition), "is based upon information received from official documents, court records, trial transcripts, taped and written interviews with witnesses to events described herein, personal observation, maps, photos and public officials." Over the course of eighteen months, the poet had become "a data addict," Sanders promised, compiling "about 10,000 pages, literally, of data."⁴⁹

But should we trust Sanders? "I'd like to say that author is a fucking liar," Charlie allegedly told Nuel Emmons. "As are a lot of other writers."⁵⁰

CHARLIE KEPT NO SECRETS, not from Lyn and not from Mary, and not from the other seekers and dropouts they met along their way. At some point Mary left her library job for good. Then Charlie, Lyn, and Mary's little dog bundled into the ex-librarian's car, and all four relocated to Mendocino, just a few hours' drive north of San Francisco.

Mary rented a post office box so her family (and Charlie's parole officer) could keep in touch. Lyn quailed at the depth of her housemates' intimacy; it intimidated her. "Mary made small dinners in the cabin while Charlie talked with the dog, and then with his guitar," she later recalled, "private conversations, venturing out on chords, repeating sequences, and fingering single strings—his body bowed over it, his face blank, as if listening to its confidences." As we know, Charlie had left prison with dozens of songs, and his plan remained to sell them. The lyrics "sounded faux folk-and-freedom," Lyn thought at the time, too "sappy" or even "vacuous."⁵¹

The foursome traveled, exploring nature and visiting neighbors. In her memoir, Lyn recalled rustic homes "furnished with antiques or cleverly salvaged scraps of natural, nearly edible materials, instruments of art and music, colorful quilts, weavings and embroideries, dried flowers, clay vessels, incense, candles, and books galore."[52] The middle-class inhabitants tended to be older than the disenchanted seekers swarming the Haight they'd left behind; more philosophically and artistically mature as well. They loved hearing Charlie's stories about the joint: about the characters he'd met, the food, solitary confinement, the everyday rhythms of doing time.[53] The stories must have titillated them. And they eagerly absorbed Charlie's raps:

"Ego is made up of thoughts. It's a big collection of thoughts. *Whose* thoughts? Where'd you get those thoughts? Do you even know what you're thinking?"[54]

~

To know what you're thinking, in one sense, represents a simple proposition. The perceptions of a normal individual align with their experiences of the world. Experts called this being sane, having "mental integrity." The self-image of an especially healthy, normal person should also align with how others in their social world perceive them. Experts called that successful alignment "identity": a one-to-one affinity between two like things (the internal image, and the external one).[55]

In the years just before Charlie laid his rap on those middle-class Mendocino dropouts, experts had hyper-focused on these problems of alignment between self and society. What material conditions promoted proper alignment? How did individuals maintain their mental integrity? Develop into sane adults? Which basic needs must human beings satisfy to survive? To thrive—to achieve self-actualization? What kinds of social structures engendered conformity? Or threatened de-individualization?[56]

While experts had only recently begun asking these questions, we can view them as the late-stage symptoms of a longer process through which the West learned that not only did a person have a mind, but that the healthy individual must do everything in their power to keep from losing it. We might trace the beginnings of the history of that process back to Freud.[57] Freud revealed that we all have hidden interiors, interiors just begging to be plumbed by expert-talkers endowed with the power of retrieving truths from deep within the inky blackness of that repository the Austrian called our unconscious.

Along the way, other minds also became available: for tweaking and liberating, but also for controlling and damaging. Consider the salivating, animal mind of Pavlov, with its attendant anxieties about human autonomy; or the mythic, archetypal mind of Jung, and its esoteric relationship to the collective. And what about the ameliorable mind, open to improvement through advances in pharmacology, therapies, mass-market self-help guides?

This plastic mind made possible so many new phenomena in the 1950s and 1960s. It helped invent encounter therapy, for instance, where members of a group at places such as Synanon (founded in California in 1958) verbally attacked and broke one another down in order to rebuild healthy persons from the ground up. We've already mentioned L. Ron Hubbard's *Dianetics: The Modern Science of Mental Health* (1950) in another context, as well as Norman Vincent Peale's *Power of Positive Thinking: A Practical Guide to Mastering the Problems of Everyday Living* (1952).[58] We'll soon examine Eric Berne's transactional analysis, introduced to a mass audience in *Games People Play* (1964), which described how we flit between three ego states—The Adult, The Parent, The Child—as we act out pre-scripted (and often dysfunctional) "mind games" with one another.

All this to say: by the time June 1967 arrived, the constituent elements of Charlie's rap had become well established in mainstream American thought. You might have hated the Red Communists for brainwashing American GIs in Korea, using mind control to treat our boys like Pavlov's curs. Your wife might have been taking little yellow pills to pep up (just as I sometimes take little white pills to calm down). You might have filled the shelves of your bookcase with self-help books. If you're the more literary type, you probably would have been reading authors who invariably placed at the center of their fictional worlds individuals confronting the problem of free will.[59]

"Call me Jonah," author Kurt Vonnegut opened his apocalyptic *Cat's Cradle* (1963). "My parents did, or nearly did. They called me John." "Jonah—John—if I had been a Sam, I would have been a Jonah still—not because I have been unlucky for others, but because somebody or something has compelled me to be certain places at certain times, without fail. Conveyances and motives, both conventional and bizarre, have been provided. And, according to plan, at each appointed second, at each appointed place, this Jonah was there."[60]

~

Poor Jonah: The waters compassed me about, *even* to the soul: the depth closed me round about, the weeds were wrapped about my head. I went down to the bottoms of the mountains; the earth with her bars *was* about me for ever: yet hast thou brought up my life from corruption, O LORD my God.[61]

So speaks Jonah, son of Amittai, who had been fleeing by boat to Tarshish when the Lord called down a tempest, compelling the crew to cast into the sea this disobedient messenger. God had directed the man to bring a prophecy to the wicked city of Nineveh. Only after that famous, harrowing ordeal in the belly of the great fish would Jonah do so. And at last, faced with God's wrath, the citizens of Nineveh made themselves abject before the Lord:

And God saw their works, that they turned from their evil way; and God repented of the evil, that he had said that he would do unto them; and he did *it* not.[62]

~

Did it *not* give parents hope, the possibility that their own wayward children might turn from evil ways? Turn to the back pages of any underground newspaper from this period and you will find notices from worried mothers, begging their lost children to at least phone home. Here's another major context for making sense of our narrative: youthful rebellion, a "generation gap," the exploration of alternatives to the nuclear family.

What happened after a young person disavowed the obligations laid for them by well-meaning parents, rejecting the socially sanctioned paths so lovingly scripted by their class background, skin color, gender, and upbringing? If they repented, would society take them back? Surely—following such a disavowal of one's duty, and after suitable consequences—this person could experience the grace of forgiveness? After all, that particular narrative arc affirms the social compact in ways mere compliance never could.

In one of the first book-length treatments of dropouts, *Hippies in Our Midst* (1968), Delbert Earisman addressed this question in a roundabout way. Some of what Earisman saw in the public parks and crash pads of New York City troubled him. There is the pathetic violence of exploitation that always trails vulnerable children and teenagers in America (these "thousands of plump white rabbits surrounded by wounded coyotes").[63] There also seems to be a new kind of psychedelic violence. At one place, a young Black man named Al describes a bad trip where he felt as if nails had been driven into the palms of his hands, an LSD-induced stigmata.

But there's also silliness, so much play. After all, many of these hippies are just kids. Earisman watches two girls sprinkling sand and murmuring love spells in Tompkins Park. "The sand was a magical sand, a mixture of sand from holy places like the backyards of Bob Dylan and Timothy Leary," he reports. "They wouldn't tell me what the spell was supposed to accomplish because if they told it wouldn't work."[64]

And different people have different commitments. Men must commit to growing out hair and beards, he noted, while young women can more easily put on (and take off) countercultural costumes. Earisman also distinguished the "summer hippies," who commuted home to New Jersey each night, from those who now permanently occupied the underground.[65] "In a way, the summer hippie may turn out to be one of the most influential members of the hippie community," Earisman posits, "for if he moves back into the world of straight society while keeping his hippie values he may do a lot to leaven (or taint or corrupt, depending on your point of view) the society in which he lives."[66]

A year later and writing on the opposite coast, Dr. David E. Smith reached different conclusions. "It is often said that young people who involve themselves in what can be called the psychedelic movement are going through a 'phase' and will become 'straight' again," Smith wrote in *Clinical Pediatrics*. But this might not be the case. Both heavy LSD users and individuals committed to "the psychedelic subculture," Smith claimed, show evidence of "profound alterations in psychosocial functioning," which he proposed to call "psychedelic syndrome." An essential incompatibility between the values of the psychedelic underground, emphasizing communalism and love, and those of the dominant straight culture, with its ethics of individual competition and violence, exacerbated the situation.

"So long as they remain in the psychedelic subculture their *psychedelic syndrome*, with its characteristics of nonviolence and magical beliefs, is actually respected," Smith concluded. "They cannot be called mentally ill by the standards of their community—only by the standards of ours." And not only that, but get this: "Becoming *straight* [again] can cause severe psychologic[al] problems, and be a much more difficult process than most adults predict."[67]

~

Predictions, sooner or later, make fools of us all, and so all interpretive acts—reading the tea leaves on a saucer, or the lines on a lover's hands, or the cards of the Tarot—require a degree of hardheadedness in addition to humility.[68] The professional knows to take care in allowing for multiple interpretations; it is only the amateur who, and safely in hindsight, argues that objectively correct, literal readings of a phenomenon could have been possible in the first place.

Attempt a literal reading, and sometimes you can quickly get into trouble. "Your home is where you're happy," Charlie sang in an early song. "It's not where you're not free!" Listening with today's ears, knowing what we now know, picturing "the Manson girls" skipping into court singing this song in 1970, and it becomes difficult to recall its origins at the penitentiary on McNeil Island. (Don't forget that a prisoner's hatred is just a love song speeded up on the warden's gramophone and made incomprehensible even to the prisoner.[69]) But listen again to the lyric—as a faux-folk-and-freedom jailhouse lament, not a blandly repetitive sop about communalism: "As long as you've got love in your heart—you'll never be aloooone!"

Should we even try to take lyrics literally? Consider that from the beginning, rock's critics saw themselves as exegetes.[70] In a virtuoso explication of "Soul Kitchen" from the Doors first album, for instance, critic Paul Williams focused on three words, a repeating mantra, from a track even the band members themselves considered "inconsequential."

"'Learn to forget'—what power that phrase has!" wrote Williams. "It's possible to get stoned for days by listening to this song... for a while it will seem the one truth available to us." He has already noted in this review one fact of the rock song, that its "truth is totally accessible to anyone listening to the song," though he failed to mention that the listener needs to know *how* to listen. Williams helpfully modeled the proper interpretive mode in a lengthy (444 words) discourse on sex and desire before returning to his main point: "'Soul Kitchen,' as I was saying before those parenthetical thoughts interrupted, is a catalyst with more potential for generating truth—in my opinion—than anything since middle Faulkner."

And this line, *learn to forget*, holds more power than an explicit, literal statement ever could. According to Williams, that's a key property of rock as a genre. "'Folk' basically demands a relationship between all words and ideas in a song, unless nonesense words [*sic*?] are used," Williams wrote, "whereas rock may be as totally non-cognitive without being nonesense [. . .]." Rock allows the lyricist to "slip" a phrase (such as "learn to forget") into a seemingly anodyne ditty. And because the genre works at a subliminal level, "a phrase like 'learn to forget' can actually become your whole body, can sink into your soul on a more-than-cognitive level." With such a song, there's one "further advantage, common in rock, that you can't hear all the words, so that *you can pretty much contextualize as you like*."[71]

On the road in 1967, around the same time this review appeared, Lyn laughed at the adjective "too-much" in the title of Charlie's "Ego Is A Too-Much Thing," hearing the teenybopper slang for "amazement" or "delight" as a few years out of date.⁷² But not his other keywords, such as ego, ego trips, even ego death (and incidentally, all having to do with the self and its proper management). "For the first time in my thirty-three years of life," as Charlie confirmed with Emmons, "I was current with fads and lifestyles."⁷³

Here's what Charlie sang, in the cabin and to the friends that the threesome, now lovers, made as they traveled the coast: "Your ego is a too-much thing / It'll make you fool yourself—you'll think you're somebody else / Look out for the trouble it brings." And the group continued to travel, and they kept encountering like-minded souls. At some point, they returned to San Francisco. And they decided to live free.

"Prison walls make for a bitter, ugly world, but they also make a person really able to appreciate nature: the clean fresh air, the free-flowing rivers, the unconquerable force of ocean waves. Driving up the coast that summer, I really got caught up in thinking no one should ever be confined or controlled by other people."⁷⁴

And: "Freedom, love, and music were our thing, and understanding—each willing to honor the feelings and thoughts of others—tightened our circle."⁷⁵

CHARLIE'S VOICE DRIFTED DOWN THE STAIRS. Susan stood transfixed, for several minutes letting the sounds wash over her. She had been living in some kind of group marriage arrangement, monogamous, but unsavory in other ways; her man, Bob, had just gotten picked up for dealing drugs.

Here's how Susan described what happened next in her memoir, *Child of Satan, Child of God* (1977). She outlines the encounter twice, on pages 1–8 and then again on pages 80–1; the two accounts, as the best stories do, demonstrate several small discrepancies. (You'll find a similar antinomy at the beginning of this chapter, for instance, as well as in the opening chapters of the Book of Genesis.) Because it's more compellingly crafted, I'll draw on Susan's first version here.⁷⁶

"I gasped for breath and felt the dampness of perspiration across my lower back," Atkins wrote. "The hallway was darkening in the late afternoon. Faintly I heard music. 'Someone's singing,' I thought. I exhaled noisily, then stood still and listened. Somebody was singing upstairs. Delicate guitar patterns formed around the voice. I wondered. 'No one here plays like that.'"[77]

Susan walked up the stairs ("my short skirt swishing barely audibly back and forth across my thighs," her ghostwriter leers) and entered the upstairs room, its air heavy with incense and the sickly-sweet smell of marijuana, where Charlie played. He played beautifully; he sang softly. Two girls perched on either side of him, as other girls ringed 'round. Susan danced slowly to the song, "The Shadow of Your Smile," a saccharine ballad made famous by crooner Tony Bennett.

Charlie stared deep into her eyes; she thought he could read her mind. Someone put on *The Doors* (1967), and then *Surrealistic Pillow* (1967) by Jefferson Airplane. Then Susan put on "another Doors record."* She and Charlie danced, moving as one, mirroring each other and melting together, at one point seeming to pass through one another. Charlie whispered.

"That's right. That's good. Yes. In reality—in your God-self—there's no repetition . . . Everything is new. Let it be new . . . You are beautiful. You are perfect . . . You must always be free."[78]

Then Charlie departed with the girls.

~

"The girls" now comprised Mary and Lyn, as well as that other young woman, Patricia Krenwinkel. The group traveled in a shared Volkswagen bus, which Charlie had acquired in trade for an upright piano, gifted to him by a man named Dean Moorehouse.[79] They broke bread together; they made love together. They traveled, meeting Charlie's former friends, mostly small-time crooks. They met a prison psychologist from his time inside who harped with Charlie about "the new culture." "The Beatles' music has a lot of the subliminal in it," Manson told him. "You would know about that."[80] And they lived as a family.

In experimenting with communal living, the group had entered a long American tradition of seeking out alternatives to mainstream arrangements. Writing in *Escape to Utopia* (1959), Everett Webber had surveyed these experimental communities, examining the structures and values of such

---

* The Doors released their eponymous first album, *The Doors*, in January 1967. Their second album, *Strange Days*, came out in late September 1967; Atkins checked in with her parole officer in San Francisco on November 10, 1967. This would suggest that the meeting occurred sometime in October. This seems to confirm that Manson's upcoming recording session in Los Angeles—sometimes dated September 11 (i.e., 9/11)—may have occurred on November 9 (11/9). Or later? (See Sanders, *The Family*, p. 43 and Wells, *Coming Down Fast*, p. 90; we'll soon discuss this recording date in Chapter 2.) Then again, perhaps Susan simply muddled the timeline in her memoir.

celebrated places as Oneida, Icaria, Fruitlands, and Brook Farm. But he ended that book on a note of pessimism. The very many "leveling contrivances" of the postwar United States—government subsidies, social security, welfare benefits, and so on—had made the revival of communes unlikely. "The song," Webber concluded, "is surely done."[81]

Webber could not have been more wrong. Just eight years later, another historian estimated that nearly two thousand communes had sprung up across thirty-four states in the preceding years.[82] In contrast to earlier movements, many of these groups settled west of the Mississippi River. A man named Lou Gottlieb founded one of the earliest revival communities, Morningstar, in 1966; an offshoot, Morningstar East, soon appeared outside Taos, New Mexico. A wealthy dropout bought the land for nearby New Buffalo, which survived nearly two decades; another cashed in IBM stock to purchase land for Lorien, named after Tolkien's land of the elves. "All over the West, boys whose fathers worked in air-conditioned twenty-story office buildings were discovering how to grow wheat," wrote Elinor Horowitz at the time, "and girls whose mothers never dreamed of making bread were finding mystical joy in learning to knead and to bake."[83] These people were "rediscovering for themselves the natural creative energies of their being," as one documentary put it. "They are seekers: seekers of a more meaningful human experience."[84]

What had caused the revival? Robert Houriet toured over one hundred such groups in 1968 and 1969. Their members, he concluded, shared "an intense reaction against a fragmented, commercialized society whose institutions— from the family on up to the community—had, they were convinced, lost vital, unifying vision." But the problem could not be fixed easily; it was systemic. "Somewhere in the line of history, civilization had made a wrong turn, a detour that had led into a cul-de-sac."

These groups aimed to "drop out and go all the way back to the beginning," the sociologist proposed, "keeping to the main road and to the central spirit and consciousness that modern man had lost along the way."[85] Houriet's dropouts are contemplative, philosophical: in fact, all they seem to do is sit around and talk. Few members used hard drugs, he reported, though marijuana and LSD were common. And nearly all sexual partnerships remained monogamous, if short-lived. Even at the group marriage commune he visited, Harrad West—so named for the scandalous 1966 novel by George Rimmer—all the household members seemed to *do* was talk: about themselves, what they were *feeling*, what they *should* have been feeling, how to *overcome* what they had been feeling.

Certain mainstream depictions—prurient photo spreads in the less reputable corners of the print world, softcore film sequences in the growing psychsploitation genre—suggest that many outside observers remained as aroused as they were horrified by this phenomenon.[86] Yet as another commentator wrote, albeit with a dash of skepticism at the end, "communes are for experiments for the recovery of human potential. In their eclectic gathering of cultural bits and pieces—combining Zuñi ceremonials and yoga meditation disciplines with Buckminster Fuller's geodesic domes and Esalen-developed group-sensitivity techniques—they frequently look like a class project in a freshman anthropology project."[87]

Beyond a bit of skinny-dipping and some stoned fondling here and there, it seemed, there's not a real, honest-to-god sex-and-drugs orgy to be found. Instead, freedom. A life not scripted by your background. A family of your own choosing.

~

Choose to begin anew, learn to forget. Two days after their initial meeting, Susan saw Charlie again. A drug bust had emptied the house where she had been staying. So they walked to the pad where Charlie's group crashed. Learn to forget. "You've got to love yourself," Charlie said, as Susan observed herself in a floor-length mirror. The reverie continued. "When you were a little girl, did you ever want to make love to your father?"

"You've got to be free of all your inhibitions and your fears." Learn to forget. "They're weighing you down. They're choking you. You've got to break free." Learn to forget.

Another song by the Doors, Susan later recalled, came, unbidden, into her mind. Break on through to the other side. They made love. "I must live in the now," Susan thought afterward.[88] So she joined the group, just at the conclusion of the Summer of Love.

~

"There's not enough love," another teenager had told Delbert Earisman back in New York. "If we had had enough love in our homes, if the parents uptown had given us more love, maybe we wouldn't have to come down here. All of this, the sex, the drugs, the be-ins, all of it is a way to try to have a kind of universal love because we haven't been able to learn to love as individuals."[89]

~

At least seven individuals now cohered into one group. Two other young women who were living with Susan, Barbara and Ella Jo, had joined, too. What alchemy, that process through which a collection of individuals become a purposeful, coherent tribe.

It's unfortunate that so few firsthand descriptions of the formation of this commune exist, other than the narrations by Susan and Lyn. As others have noted, it would have made for a remarkable case study.[90] So thought Dr. David E. Smith, who published his own firsthand impressions around the time of the group's trial. Known as Doctor Dave to denizens of the Haight, Smith had founded the Haight-Ashbury Free Clinic in June 1967. A specialist in addiction and the use of psychedelics, Dr. Smith also helped found the *Journal of Psychoactive Drugs*. (Recall that we benefited from his medical expertise on the so-called psychedelic syndrome just a few pages ago.)

Smith also got to know Charlie, Lyn, Mary, Pat, and Susan. But the timeline that Dr. Smith gives for his acquaintance with the group in *Love Needs Care: A History of San Francisco's Haight-Ashbury Free Medical Clinic* (1971) cannot possibly be correct. He writes that "Manson went to Los Angeles and thereby missed the Summer of Love," and that "when the summer was over, he moved to Berkeley"—almost the exact opposite of events.[91]

Yet Smith also claimed to have a remarkably nuanced understanding of the group's psychology—and Manson's techniques for indoctrination. "When a potential female family member came to him, he would give her acid and initiate her sexually," Smith wrote in *Love Needs Care*, "lecturing in the mystical terms so long used to reinforce the hallucinogenic experience." The young women, in Smith's telling, seem to be preternaturally submissive, empty vessels. "The girls either never realized the price they paid for his protection or were too blinded by the immediate rewards. They never complained of mistreatment or resisted him."[92]

Another psychologist at the clinic believed Charlie to be "a paranoid-schizophrenic with an encapsulated psychosis." (His followers, this Dr. Dernburg thought, "were probably not psychotics but hysterical women who were prone to broad swings of emotion and who required constant stimulation to compensate for their underlying depressions"—and their "extreme submissiveness . . . an exaggerated manifestation of the wish for protection and nurturance seen in so many young people in the Haight-Ashbury.")[93]

Sex and drugs, suggestive hints of prostitution and armchair diagnoses of mental illnesses, but nowhere in the account does Smith mention—not once—the music-making that, in the retrospective accounts of the commune members themselves, seems to have been their primary activity during the period that the doctor would have known them. But Doctor Dave does explain why the group spent so much time at the clinic. Apparently, Manson's parole officer, Roger Smith, liked meeting him there.[94] To distinguish Roger Smith from David E. Smith, we can invoke the commune's nickname for him. The commune called him Jubal.

~

Jubal comes from Robert Heinlein's science fiction masterpiece, *Stranger in a Strange Land* (1961). The story depicts the return of a Mars-born human being, Michael Valentine Smith, to Terra (a latter-day Earth). Jubal Harshaw, a recurring figure in Heinlein's universe, functions as Michael Valentine's advocate and protector.

As Martians do, Michael Valentine can slow his body's resting heart rate to almost nothing. He can also commit suicide on command by "discorporating" himself. He brings other Martian practices to Terra: water-sharing rituals that bind people as "water brothers," mortuary cannibalism, and an easygoing attitude toward sexual expression in groups. Before rival cultists strike him down, he founds a Church of All Worlds.

Heinlein's book became a countercultural hit in the United States, even introducing a Martian word, *grok*, into everyday speech. In its simplest, most literal sense, *to grok* means "to drink." Figuratively speaking, to drink in the Martian sense means to imbibe so deeply, to understand something or someone so intuitively, that you absorb and fully grasp its essence. But it doesn't end there, as Terra's leading linguist explains. This term encompasses "a hundred other English words, words which we think of as antithetical concepts."

"'Grok' means *all* of these," says Dr. Mahmoud. "It means 'fear,' it means 'love,' it means 'hate'—proper hate, for by the Martian 'map' you cannot hate anything unless you grok it, understand it so thoroughly that you merge with it and it merges with you—then you can hate it. By hating yourself. But this implies that you love it, too, and cherish it and would not have it otherwise."[95]

CHARLIE AND LYN, at some point in their travels, came to an intractable disagreement over some small factual point or other. "He seemed to think that a large part of history was hearsay," Lyn writes. This is how she remembers the exchange that followed:

"Someone said that someone said that someone told them that someone said," Charlie winked.

"It's people who know what they're talking about," Lyn thought. "It's years of research."

"I don't have anything against it," Charlie replied, as if reading her mind. "I just look at it for what it is."[96]

~

We can decide to just look at it for what it is, too. Facts and stories and interpretations, contradictions and impossibilities: all suffuse the corpus of accounts narrating the creation of this loose-knit group. If the verbatim quotations from this literature sometimes seem to run too long in our text, know that this represents a conscious choice, this paraethnographic thick description.[97]

Because in the late 1960s, the interpretations, critiques, and methods of commentators on the counterculture and countercultural participants alike began converging.[98] What would we gain by considering the knowledge held by these twentieth-century nomads to be an important form of social expertise? After all, these seekers critiqued the American order from a point outside or above it; they attempt to peel back the surface layers of society, as ethnographers do, in order to analyze what is really going on.

But of course, experts do not merely describe reality. They also shape it. And they do so by framing problems in particular ways. In proposing that we can only understand the world in terms of truth and untruths, and by locating these truths in *experience*, our seekers began making reality accessible in new ways. If they say that "no sense makes sense," or that sanity is really madness, or that love is hate, what choice do we have but to work within these frames?

~

Frames matter. We cannot step outside them, of course, and this has consequences for the stories we tell about our worlds. "We are like sailors who must rebuild their ship on the open sea, never able to dismantle it in dry-dock and to reconstruct it there out of the best materials," philosopher Otto Neurath famously wrote in his classic articulation of this quintessentially modern problem. "Where a beam is taken away a new one must at once be put there, and for this the rest of the ship is used as support. In this way, by using the old beams and driftwood the ship can be shaped entirely anew, but only by gradual reconstruction."

We could imagine a compendium of metaphors that might provide plausible alternatives to Neurath's sailors. In one we are like bakers rolling out dough thin and elastic before folding it lengthwise and crosswise and lengthwise again to form flaky, delicate layers. We only have so much flour and butter, so many eggs, with which to work. In this way, the dough builds up through evermore fragile tiers without ever expanding beyond its original, constitutive elements. In another metaphor we are like a father brushing a young child's neglected curls, forcing the comb hopelessly into the matted hair until we take shears to the knots. We subtract and deform our object in frustration. Through hot tears and shame we act in confronting something unable to be disentangled.

~

That certain phenomena became so entangled in the first place, I have sometimes thought while researching this book, almost beggars belief. (Entangled? Or exhibiting a kind of occult tensegrity?) Consider just one final example.

"Someone has just got to do a [film] version of that book *Stranger in A Strange Land*," Dennis Wilson told an interviewer in August 1969, "and I think I know someone who has the rights to it anyway—he wanted Paul McCartney to play the role of the Martian. That is a fantastic book."[99]

~

A final metaphor, from another fantastical book, this one relating the story of the baron who went to live in the trees. Shunning his noble family, feeling cruelly used by his parents, a young nobleman takes to the world of the trees. He learns to eat, sleep, and make his home among the branches, traveling from larch to walnut to elm to oak by means of purpose-built mechanisms and his own wit. He refuses to ever again touch the ground.

The young baron disciplines himself as an expert arborist, cutting and pruning to promote each tree's health, "able to make love for his arboreal element become, as happens with all true loves, a pitiless and painful love, which wounds and cuts back to enhance growth and give shape."

Imagine the healthy story to be such a tree: shorn of its deadwood and secondary branches, remaining all trunk and leafy crown and thick, rising boughs. In pursuing this metaphor we can now reveal a secondary motivation for the shaping of our own story to this point, a motivation scarcely less important than the primary one, a motive described in figurative terms by the young baron as follows. "Certainly he was always careful, in pruning and trimming the trees, *to serve not only the interest of the owner of the tree but also his own*, that of a traveler who has to make his paths more passable; so he worked in a way that the branches he used as a bridge between one tree and another were always saved, and *gained strength from the suppression of the others*."[100]

~

And now Charlie traded the Volkswagon bus for a larger, yellow school bus. The group had the bus painted black, to avoid contravening local laws. And now Charlie and the girls embarked on a more permanent move south, to Los Angeles.

2

November 1967 to March 1968

or, Man's Son

"You know what, man, I wrote a lot of these songs and I'm just singin' 'em, you know, and I ain't even for*gotten* the ones I wrote."[1]

Picture Charlie peering back at Gary Stromberg, seated in the control room. Charlie through the looking glass. A few of the girls came along to this test session at Universal; you can hear snippets of their smiling, laughing crosstalk on various recordings released over the past few decades.

"Forget we're even here, man," Stromberg says over the intercom. "I ain't even here, baby—you're all by yourself out there. What are you nervous about? Just blow your soul, man."

"Well look here, let me explain something to *you*," Charlie goes. "I wrote about a couple hundred songs, you know? Are you listening? And then I forgot—and I started making 'em up as I go. You know? And then—I, uh. I forgot the other songs that, you know—I mean, I got 'em all written down and all *that*, man. But uh, I'll give you an example, man, I'll try to stick to a song that'll make you some money."

Charlie laughs. The magnetic tape captures his fingers stretching out to feel through a few chords. Retrospective accounts often describe Manson sounding nervous at this first recording session, ill at ease before the microphone and unable to take direction. But on the full demo, recorded sometime in the middle of November in the year Nineteen-Sixty-Seven, the truth seems to be a bit more complicated. Charlie raps and does his schtick, running through a handful of originals. He tries a couple two or three times, each iteration at some point pulling apart before grinding to a halt.

"I'm having a hard time going with a spon*taneous* song, man," he says after one false take, "because I'm *on point*." The rest of the demo consists of improvised Charlie songs and standards: "Shadow of Your Smile," but also "Swamp Girl" and

"Invisible Tears" and "The Girl From Ipanema" and "Remember Me" and a few others.

Still feeling out chords, Charlie laughs again. "This song is for the youngsters." He slips into an original, "Your Home Is Where You're Happy," preserved for posterity, so to speak, on a few feet of Ampex-brand tape.

~

There's little overtly spiritual on these demos beyond some free-association wordplay. "Fear of need *is* need, baby." "You can't be*long* to nobody." "Be in*sane*—be in*sane*—*be* insane, having a name." (There are jokey improvisations about monkeys, drums, and Chinese restaurants, too.)

But that song "for the youngsters" does demonstrate the rough-and-ready philosophical pretensions found on several more fully realized tracks. "Your home is where you're happy / it's not where you're not *free-eee*." This recording swings and moves, unlike the hymnlike unison singing of "the girls" captured by news cameras outside the Los Angeles Hall of Justice three years later. And it's jazzier than a recorded version that turned up on an album, *LIE: The Love and Terror Cult*, released in March 1970.

Listeners would have encountered this song's message in mainstream pop songs. "You can have a castle," Charlie croons, "and diamonds for all to see." Money can't buy you love, so rely on your own personal, inner strength. And true peace comes when you *learn* to be free.

> So burn all your bridges /
> leave the old life behind—
> You can do what you want to do /
> because you're strong in your mind.

The song breaks up at this point during the first take, frustrating Charlie.

Sometime in the next two years, the songwriter will revise that lyric: "leave the old life behind" becomes "leave *your whole life* behind." In the 1967 demo, we can imagine an ex-con singing to himself. Give up your dreams of wealth and power, make a clean break from that old life of crime and avarice, and you will at last free yourself, becoming an honest man. Directed to potential recruits for a cult, the revised injunction—*leave your whole life behind*—of course begins to seem sinister.

Did Manson's songs function as instruments of indoctrination at this point—tools of brainwashing? We could search for more evidence. Hidden within the lengthy improvised sections found elsewhere on the tape, where Charlie vamps on one or two or three chords, still more suggestive textual clues emerge. "The more you love / the less you have to worry"—repeated *ad infinitum et ad nauseum* (which means into the infinite, and until emesis). That demand recurs and then disintegrates, collapsing on one word—*love, love, love, love, love*—before reaching an ecstatic apotheosis: "With *no* thought patterns in your *mind*."

Or consider another mantra, this perverse koan: "You can be when you cease to be / and then you can see when you *seeeee*—the sound of one hand clapping! It's the sound of one hand clapping—it's the *sound* of one hand clapping; it's *the* sound of *one hand* clapping—"

This, too, then abruptly stops. The tape captured all this and more for Gary Stromberg and his colleagues at Universal.

~

Universal Studios might have tapped newcomer Richard Pryor to play Black Jesus in *The Second Coming of Christ*, a film Stromberg pitched around this time.[2] Pryor could have caught the eye of executives after his star turn as Black nationalist Stanley X in the teensploitation film *Wild In The Streets* (1968), a farce featuring a twenty-something singer using the power of rock to take control of the US government. (Imagine that.)

A long panning shot would have established the opening scene. The hot heat rising from the asphalt at first obscures our vision. Clang, clang, irons clang, as a jump cut presses the viewer face-to-face with five young men, their inky skin slick with sweat, walking single file under the bored gaze of white prison guards in short sleeves. This is modern slavery. But it's a form of slavery, the camera wants to suggest, that ennobles rather than deforms the spirit. (A facile idea, easy to suggest if it's not your flesh that's being ennobled.)

At a short remove from the chain gang, a Christ-like Black hippie swats a buzzing horsefly. He beckons his flock to follow, so many plump white rabbits. The camera tightens in on him as another follower jogs up and begins complaining, using a caricatured jive argot that won't be reproduced here.

"You want us to do *nothing*?" the white follower asks. "We're just going to *leave* them?"

The Christ-like hippie seems weary; he removes a red sash from his afro-style hair and mops his brow.

"You know the way out is not only through the door," the leader raps. "You have to keep faith."

The white follower's eyes narrow. Later in the film we learn his background in a series of flashbacks: from activist at an Ivy League university in New England to community organizer, shepherding voter registration in Mobile, to dropping out and letting his straw hair grow long and blonde in the hot Southern sun, to joining this ragtag group of disciples. We see him debating the bombings perpetrated by a group of activists in the north; in another scene, we see him reading the Black Panther community newspaper. As the follower drops back, the camera keeps this sullen white Judas in frame; he's kicking at rocks a few steps behind the leader.

"The way out," the Black Christ murmurs again, "is not only through the door."[3]

~

"You know, everybody's stuck in the realities that are already made, and locked in the realities that have already perpetrated those realities," Charlie later said, describing his association with Stromberg. "You know? It's like, when I got out I went to Universal Studios, and this Hebrew producer told me he wanted me to help him write the music for a movie about the Second Coming of Christ."

"He told me that he wanted me to play music with a guy from South Africa, and another guy from Africa, and I said, 'Man, my uncle would *shoot* me for doing something like that.' I said, 'No, no, no—I don't play music like that.' So then he blackballed me from the music system, and he burned all my music up, because I wouldn't go along with his trip, see?"[4]

That story seems to be true, more or less. Stromberg passed on recording an album; the singer-songwriter may have been too green, or perhaps the songs just weren't there, or his voice, guitar playing, or image just didn't make the cut. But Stromberg did hang with Charlie and the girls: visiting them on their black school bus, taking them out for meals. And he did talk with Charlie about a film where Christ returns to earth as a Black man in the American South. And it may not have stopped there.[5]

"For a long period of time," Charlie told Nuel Emmons, "I had the run of Universal." He met a few "bigwigs," and got invited to drug- and sex-fueled parties with "not-so-straight idols of the movie world." Manson and the group didn't exactly fit in. They used LSD and marijuana rather than opiates and cocaine, and "had long ago chucked our inhibitions about sex, but chains, whips, torture and other weirdness were not part of our routine." If the account in Emmons is to be believed, Charlie even began a sexual relationship with a higher-up at Universal, one "Mr. B," cuckolding the executive in his handsomely appointed home.

"My association with Universal eventually ended with nothing accomplished," Charlie said, and Emmons reported. "My second recording session never materialized, nor did the Second Coming of Christ flick get off the ground."[6]

~

These failures represent the ground against which a key theory about the motive for the Manson Family murders rests: the Charlie-as-frustrated-artist hypothesis. Frustrated by individuals who did not, or would not, recognize his talents, Manson snapped and, driven into a homicidal spiral of violence, directed his slave-like followers to punish the gatekeepers, the "beautiful people," who had stifled his creative ambitions.

There's no reason this theory might not be true. But in its contours we should recognize a powerful parable about artistic self-expression. Everyone has a fundamental, human need to be recognized, this hypothesis claims, to *express* themselves. Bottle up those energies, deny human beings those avenues for actualizing their creative selves, and some of them just explode. Allow free expression, a drive inherent in the human species, and you empower people to maintain healthy senses of self, and consequently an overall healthy social equilibrium.

Perhaps this has brought us too far into the realm of mere speculation. To return to properly historical questions: What ambitions did Manson harbor for his musical career at this point? How should we characterize Manson's reaction to the rejection by Universal?

Sanguine—not sanguinary. Charlie believed that Stromberg wanted to move ahead with an album, but others felt he needed time to work out arrangements and put together a band.[7] At least, that's what Manson allegedly told Emmons.

~

Though Nuel Emmons might be lying—or worse. Consider that in just ten years the ex-con-turned-author had somehow transitioned from armed robbery to serious drug trafficking to journalism—and maybe also, according to one Manson researcher, snitching, as a federal informant.

And consider that over the final two decades of his life, Manson repeatedly disavowed *Manson in His Own Words*. He even told one prison pen pal that Emmons was a "cheat, and only lying to himself."[8]

FOLLOWING THE SOUNDS OF SOFT FEMALE VOICES, the fourteen-year-old ascended the staircase winding up the side of the dilapidated home at the end of Topanga Canyon Lane. "Charlie, we found Dianne," a red-haired girl called out. "She's here!"[9]

Dianne Lake had lived a peripatetic life before arriving at this notorious house. Following canonical practice, we will call it the Spiral Staircase; it sat among a collection of ramshackle cabins filled with artists and dropouts, in a low-lying floodplain, teeming with wildlife, called the Snake Pit. Some "trippy broad" back in San Francisco, "pumped up about devil worship and other satanic activities," had invited Charlie and the group to park their bus out back. "In looking back," a reflexive Charlie said (*in his own words*), "I think I can honestly say our philosophy—fun and games, love and sex, peaceful friendship for everyone—began changing into the madness that eventually engulfed us in that house."[10]

The Spiral Staircase functioned as a crash pad of sorts for all kinds of people. In her memoir, Dianne described these people as "drifters, drug users, musicians, and devil worshippers." She had crashed there a few months earlier with a couple and their infant as an adolescent live-in nanny.* Now as many as forty people camped in and around the Spiral Staircase each night. When Charlie's group first moved in, Susan recalled, they found a scene where records by the Doors, Bob Dylan, and Jefferson Airplane constantly played, providing a soundtrack for the acid-fueled inhabitants who projected impromptu light shows on the bare, peeling walls.

That first night Susan had felt as one with those people. "I love them so much that I want to die for them," she thought to herself, "but they will not know that." She sought out Charlie, finding him incandescent in a flowing white robe, holding a pan of warm water. As a crowd gathered, he knelt and washed her feet. She then washed an onlooker's feet. People began making love. She began making love. "My God," she screamed internally. "I'm making love to myself." Any sense of self evaporated. "Who am I?" she thought. A voice answered: "You're everyone."[11]

A house of magic, or at least illusions. How had the red-haired girl known to call Dianne by name? Lyn took her hand, leading Dianne into a room "where a

---

* And as teenaged live-in lover to both husband and wife. Lake's parents had first moved the family to the Hog Farm, a loose collective headed by Hugh Romney, better known as Wavy Gravy, before emancipating Dianne. According to Lake' memoir (p. 97), here's what happened: Romney thought that, as "jailbait," Dianne brought too much heat to the collective. What Romney meant by this misogynistic term was that the teenager attracted attention from men attracted to girls, which might bring subsequent attention from police or welfare officers. It's remarkable how often one person's liberation depends on another's exploitation. Rather than place checks on the freewheeling group that might preclude unwanted advances on minors, Romney told the fourteen-year-old to leave.

bunch of people were sitting in a circle, and in the middle of the floor sat a small man playing the guitar. There were girls surrounding him, singing along to his soulful music of songs I'd never heard before." Freckled Lyn waited until the singing stopped, and then introduced Dianne to the group.[12]

~

"Only one town is built on magic," intones the narrator at the beginning of *Mondo Hollywood* (1967), "and that town is Hollywood."

Director Robert Cohen began shooting *Mondo Hollywood* in 1965. He had gotten his start in filmmaking by having the good fortune to be the first American to record footage of Mao's China. After selling excerpts to the National Broadcasting Company, Cohen cobbled together the rest for his first feature-length documentary, *Inside Red China* (1957). The ex-Navy man became a specialist of sorts on communism, next completing *East Germany* (1959), then *Committee on Un-American Activities* (1962) and *Inside Castro's Cuba* (1963). When his agent pitched the idea for a film about Hollywood, Cohen had been traveling the college lecture circuit with these films. Almost immediately, people began coming out of the woodwork, you might say, to tell their stories.

So we meet the dissolute failson of a millionaire businessman from Long Island and his vegetarian pet monkey. Why did he move to Hollywood? Because it's where television shows and films are made, it's "the cultural and ideological capital of the world." There are countless beauticians and hairdressers, too; beauty is big business. We meet an entrepreneur who wants to market body paint as clothing; we meet Jay Sebring, ex-boyfriend of Sharon Tate and hairdresser to the stars. He commands US$300 for styling hairpieces and counts Frank Sinatra, Dean Martin, and Rock Hudson among his clientele.

While the characters could be seen as simply demonstrating the overweening weirdness of Los Angeles, Cohen uses them to ventriloquize what he wants us to understand as an emergent philosophical ethos: "Living fully," as a champion skydiver and motorcycle enthusiast says, "is intensified by nearly dying."

What else does Cohen's coterie of weirdos explain? A struggling musician, hairy Bobby Jameson, caterwauls into a microphone, then pontificates on the beach next to Gail, his stunning girlfriend. (By the film's release, she would be living in Topanga Canyon with a toddler, Moon Unit, and a new beau, Frank Zappa.) "After I'd been in Hollywood a few years, with people telling me I was going to be a star," Bobby says, "it almost drove me crazy—I couldn't write or sing anymore, I didn't know who I was . . . This society is a propagandized machine: if you believe in it, you are a robot. It makes you *believe* you are free, like a hypnotized robot: if you believe in it you are not free!" Gail nods.

Then there's a Canadian actor who dresses up in horror drag for dinner theater about vampires and monsters; there's a nice middle-class African American family; there's Richard Alpert, later Baba Ram Dass; there's a herd of living fossils, film stars from the silent era, at a tea club. There's Vito Pauleskas with wife Szou and toddler Godo and hanger-on Carl Franzoni. "I'm concerned about the methedrine people are taking," Vito says. "It's obvious that the major drug companies are involved, and they are in charge of pushing the drugs that enervate the American people."

So much strangeness abounds. And Cohen's most ingenious decision comes in the frame he has chosen to place around all this specifically American nonconformity. The film opens with a sequence showing politician Thomas Dodd addressing the Christian Anti-Communist Crusade. "Students and activists are fighting against us," Dodd thunders. But what they don't realize is that "we are the revolutionaries—it will take all the patience and solidarity we have to fight back." The film concludes with one such revolutionary: actor Ronald Reagan and his beaming wife, pretty Nancy, recently installed, high above the clouds, in the California governor's mansion in Sacramento.

~

"High above the clouds live four or five magicians who spend their days casting wonderful spells," a narrator explains. "Come with me now to that wonderful place, where the eyes of men have never looked."[13]

The camera pans to George, Paul, and Ringo, working in a goofy laboratory. It looks like a set from a school play. Their roadie, Mal Evans, is there, too. Ringo wanders around, saying in a silly voice, "Where's the bus?" The four men are wearing strange red robes. This sequence doesn't make any logical sense; it's confusing even for a film—*Magical Mystery Tour*, released in December 1967—that most fans found impenetrable. Four, or *five*, magicians? I had thought there were only four Beatles. Does Mal count? Rewatch the film and you will see he's the only one not wearing a pointy hat. When John appears later, he wears a black robe. Is he the fifth Beatle? But that doesn't make sense.

"Meanwhile back on the bus, things are happening," the narrator continues, cameras cutting back to the Magical Mystery Tour, "and life waddles on."

~

Meanwhile back at the black bus, these errant sparks, the preternatural beings making up just one small part of a growing body of individuals the San Francisco *Oracle* had recently called a prophetic community, did not stay put.[14]

The group now numbered close to a dozen souls. The Spiral Staircase in Los Angeles had become their home base, but Charlie and the girls traveled often in the waning months of 1967. "Highly mobile at that time," Susan summarized, "we travelled all over Southern California in Charlie's school bus, which we had by that time painted black. We stayed in the bus, or with people we'd strike up friendships with, or in the woods, and we soon made our first trip out into the desert, Death Valley. Charlie seemed fascinated by it."[15]

At one point the group began a road trip to warmer climes, Florida, planning to travel cross-country by way of Patty's family home in Alabama.[16] Peculiar travel suggestions, the holy man teaches, may be dancing lessons from God. But a bad toothache stopped the bus in Texas. ("You can't pull them," Charlie told the doctor there. "I'm a singer—a performer—and I've got to have my teeth."[17]) Or maybe, as Lyn remembered, mechanical problems halted the journey.[18] And turning back, they passed through New Mexico before again breaking down in Winslow, Arizona.*

At this point, they hitch-hiked back to Los Angeles, a good eight-hour drive, where some people in the psychedelic underground had started referring to them as Crazy Charlie and his Girls.

"The whole black bus trip came to be called 'The Magical Mystery Tour,'" Ed Sanders reported in *The Family*, in agreement for once with the retrospective memories of commune members. "They were into such a trip of mystic transformation that the family evidently believed that there was an archetypal core personality in each human that could be discovered through acid-zap,

---

* Susan remembers arriving in New Mexico *after* Texas and staying "for several weeks, stopping off in a little college town and attracting considerable unpopularity" (p. 93). However, Lyn recalls "trekking barefoot through New Mexico's White Sands National Monument *before* Texas. The group had some trouble with the police for camping here. Specific incidents, memory experts say, often firm up our retrospective narratives. Here's one such incident. The group had hired someone to paint HOLLYWOOD PRODUCTIONS on the side of the black bus so that, if anyone stopped them, they could pretend to be a film crew. "We got her some white paint, and returned to see HOLIWOOD PRODUCTIONS in perfect six-inch block letters on both sides of the bus," Lyn writes. "Despite her French accent, none of us had thought to tell her how to spell it. Charlie said that we should add a number to the title, and chose the number 9 for no reason that I know of" (p. 191). (And nearly two years before the Beatles released "Revolution 9.") Now, a policeman knocked on the bus door. Roused from his deep sleep, Charlie, in the flowing white costume robes he customarily wore during this period, gestured to the sign and explained they were on a shoot. The cops let them off with a warning.

mind-moil, role-playing, bunch-punching, magic, blasting-past and communeism. This was the Magical Mystery Tour."[19]

~

As this Magical Mystery Tour commenced, another magus appears. Cupid apparently met the group at the Spiral Staircase in Los Angeles some months after filmmaker Kenneth Anger evicted him from the Westerfeld House, better known as "the Russian Embassy," in San Francisco.

In that cavernous, dilapidated home, Anger had been plotting his newest film, *Lucifer Rising*. Mick Jagger was later considered for the title role; so too was little Godo Paulekas, before the child's mysterious death. But the young man known as Cupid—Robert Beausoleil, or Bobby—had been Anger's first Lucifer. Born in Santa Barbara in 1947, Beausoleil had connections across the Los Angeles and San Francisco music scenes. People recognized him by his cherubic face (hence the nickname), his signature black top hat, and his traveling companions. Like Crazy Charlie, Bobby too seemed to be living with a harem of sorts.

Bobby allegedly auditioned for the Monkees, and played in an early incarnation of the band Love.[20] You can see him, briefly, in *Mondo Hollywood*; you can hear him on the final side of the first album released by Frank Zappa and the Mothers of Invention—he's one of the hungry freaks howling on "The Return of the Son of Monster Magnet (Unfinished Ballet in Two Tableaux)"— first movement, "Ritual Dance of the Child-Killer."

Lucifer Rising narrated the passing of the patriarchal age of the Father to one centered on the Child, as foretold by the Thelemic teachings of occultist Aleister Crowley. Asked to compose the soundtrack as well, Beausoleil now transformed his band, an experimental outfit called the Orkustra, into the Magick Powerhouse of Oz, the O encircling the Z on posters forming a kind of psychedelic sigil.[21] The group had marked the autumnal equinox with a fundraiser for the film on Thursday the twenty-first of September. "Everything was either related to magic or things that I liked," Anger told a journalist: the San Francisco Mime Troupe performed a short piece about Vietnam, and the Congress of Wonders did a sketch about superhero Flash Gordon.[22]

But then Lucifer allegedly absconded with the film—not a work print, but the original—that Anger had been projecting as Beausoleil and the Magick Powerhouse played. Eight thousand dollars and six months of work gone. And his Lucifer gone, too. Anger believed the theft to be "an inside job," perhaps "an act of personal vengeance," and fingered Cupid.[23] Bobby would say he just got sick of Anger, who hadn't actually filmed much of anything.

Cast out from the Russian Embassy, the guitarist found places here and there to crash, staying for a spell with a Buddhist and fellow musician. Cast out for madness, spells cast for love—stalking new gardens of earthly delights, it seems Bobby now found Charlie on the jungle paths of the Los Angeles underground.[24]

~

"The jungle is closing in on this little patch we've spent so long civilizing," Reagan had stumped during his 1966 campaign for governor of California. The actor helped pioneer this kind of political messaging, the dog whistle, stirring fears about Blacks in Watts, dropouts in San Francisco, and student activists in Berkeley (the "filthy speech" movement, as conservative revolutionaries put it).

Second cousin to the wolf whistle, the dog whistle invites listeners to examine the soft, hidden underside of speech, peeking beneath the apparent meaning of an address to uncover secrets hidden in plain view, an intensely satisfying emotional experience for the speaker's new intimates, hailed as superior to those too thick to understand the secret meaning (or worse, too honorable to admit to understanding). It's a form of political speech requiring acts of interpretation that make bystanders, whether they like it or not, complicit.

Using this device and others, Reagan could exhort without resorting to unseemly fulminating. "You and I are told we must choose between a left or a right," Reagan declaims in "A Time for Choosing" (1964). "But I suggest there is no such thing as a left or right. There is only an up or down." (Just who is telling us we have to choose? The passive construction obscures the agent.) "Up to man's age-old dream, the maximum of individual freedom consistent with law and order; or down, to the ant heap of totalitarianism." The mind goes high, the mind goes low: Reagan's concluding words seem to hold the weight of true prophecy. "You and I have a rendezvous with destiny. We'll preserve for our children this, the last best hope of man on earth, or we'll sentence them to take the last step into a thousand years of darkness."[25]

Delivered with Nancy's beatific, almost brainwashed smile beaming up at him, Reagan's apocalyptic warning almost sounds reasonable. (Once governor, Reagan launched the symbolic crackdown to stave off these endtimes, greenlighting a raid on City Lights Bookshop, for instance, purging its shelves of such smut as Lenore Kandel's *The Love Book* (1966). The chapbook initially sold only fifty copies; after the prosecution for obscenity, it would go on to sell over 20,000 in the Bay Area alone.[26]) Even so, brainwashed may not be entirely fair.

Or is it? "Nancy Reagan has an *interested* smile," as Joan Didion wrote in "Pretty Nancy" (1968), "the smile of a good wife, a good mother, a good hostess, the smile of someone who grew up in comfort and went to Smith College and has a father who is a distinguished neurosurgeon (her father's entry in the 1966–67 Who's Who runs nine lines longer than her husband's) and a husband who is the definition of Nice Guy, not to mention governor of California, the smile of a woman who seems to be playing out some middle-class American woman's daydream, circa 1948."[27]

~

Daydream believers loom large in the sequence concluding *Mondo Hollywood*. Cohen overlays the sound of a full-throated Reagan with the image of a bare-chested young seeker silhouetted against a great white Cross overlooking Los Angeles. "The time has come for us to forget about political campaigns," Reagan thunders, "and to think of this as a moral crusade, because *freedom itself* is at stake."

To understand this freedom, consider another sequence, an unabashedly voyeuristic one. A curvaceous sculptor, Valerie, lives with a real-life Guggenheim. "Everything bores me to death," Valerie says. "The only thing I find interesting is myself!" Her fifty-something patron gets turned on by playacting at being the maid. We watch wealthy Lady Guggenheim bathing and drying the thirty-something sculptor, kneeling to put her stockings on. The camera lingers on the younger women's soft cleavage before turning our gaze to the desirous look flashing from the craggy face of the "maid" dragging deeply from a cigarette. "Yes, I get very perverted at times," says Valerie, that sultry apple-head, in a voiceover. "I think most sophisticated people do."

And now a final sequence for consideration: a singing coven making the three-pointed Sign of the Pyramid, then a man calling himself King Solomon leading a group in astral projection, then a solemn Reagan speaking seriously about the drug problem, and about rock music, and now he's saying, "I might be against the Great Society, but I'm for the Creative Society," and then crafty Cohen inserts the following subtitle, framing our interpretation of the future president, and suggesting that things may not be quite what they seem:

Ronald Reagan
Elected Governor Of California—1966
On Astrologer's Advice Is Inaugurated At Midnight

~

At midnight during that aborted trip to Florida, Patty had a bad car crash. Three dogs appeared in the road out of nowhere. One seemed to look her right in the eye. Were they real? An apparition? Had Krenwinkel died, would others have lived?[28]

How much of our lives are predestined? The ego convinces us we are masters of our own fates, but everyone knows that's not really true. We have been condemned from childhood to live out the hang-ups of our parents. We live lives straitjacketed by our social class, skin color, gender. When we choose, we do so from among the strictly limited options available to us. Cultures, like poems, shape by restricting.[29]

~

And he became like Christ, egoless, in sharing possessions without restrictions. "If you're so laidback," someone said, "why don't you give away your bus?" And without hesitation, Charlie tossed him the keys. The person drove away, but then returned a few hours later. Easy come, easy go.[30] It often seemed that just as the group most needed something, they found it. The bus came into Manson's orbit in this way. A preacher named Dean Moorehouse had picked up Charlie hitchhiking in San Jose. He gifted Charlie a piano, which Charlie traded for the Volkswagen microbus, which Charlie next traded (with cash) for the school bus.[31]

Around this time, the commune met Bobby Beausoleil at a light show, possibly celebrating New Year's Eve. Cupid, "wearing a pointed beard and smoking a hand-carved skull pipe, arrived and found Charlie and the girls singing together."[32] At the time, Beausoleil must have been living with Gary Hinman, a thirty-something musician, sociology student, Buddhist, and chemist specializing in synthesizing hallucinogens.[33] Bobby would have crashed in the basement, which an altruistic Gary provided for the lost children running around Topanga Canyon to use.

~

Pleas from the many parents seeking to get in touch with their teenaged children ("runaways") make up a major portion of the back pages of underground newspapers from this period, so many passion plays in miniature printed at fifty cents per line (minimum charge, one dollar). Here's an especially cryptic one from the edition of the *Berkeley Barb* where Ken accused Bobby of stealing *Lucifer Rising*:

> STEPHEN JOHNSON we don't desire to try to force return. Are you OK? We can help Brad. Call BELLEVUE collect. MOM-DAD.[34]

~

Mom and dad, as we now know, they sure fuck you up.[35] At some point a murderous Dean Moorehouse, that man who gifted the piano that turned into a bus, came looking for his daughter, Ruth Ann. He put a gun on Charlie. But then, somehow, and dosed with sacramental LSD, the preacher left this encounter telling anyone who would listen that he was both Jesus Christ and the Devil—and so was Charlie. (Around this time, Manson had started telling people he was the Wizard, but not Christ.) Following the dictum that good stories must drive out true ones, perhaps we should narrate this tale in the next chapter, putting flesh to the bare bones of this encounter.[36]

At some point, Charlie did begin referring to himself as "Charles Willis Manson," modifying "Milles," his true middle name. Charles' Will Is Man's Son. And he seemed increasingly able to manifest supplies for the group, or, to invoke the Scientology term that the group used, postulating. Lodging, mechanical assistance, food: if properly exercised, the power of positive thinking could bring you these things. Ask, and you will receive. A spare room, or land to camp; a kindly mechanic, often blushing; a few sandwiches, or everyone's favorite, *zuzus*, the girls' childlike word for candy.

Knock, and a door will open. Just walk through. If that's what you *want* to do.

AFTER THAT FIRST ENCOUNTER, perhaps at the Spiral Staircase, Bobby and Charlie continued orbiting one another, establishing an easy rapport. Nearly all accounts follow Susan in describing Bobby as "an outstanding guitar player with an unusual ability to motivate young people, especially women."[37] He traveled at various times with several: Catherine Share, a sometimes actor; Kitty Lutesinger, who would later carry his child; and Leslie Van Houten, the homecoming queen from the supernice family who hanged at the Self Realization Fellowship.

A burned-out crash pad, nearly uninhabitable, and which Cupid had found on Horseshoe Drive in Topanga Canyon, fused the two groups at last. "This is Lucifer's place," Bobby told Lyn. He had just turned twenty years old, and Charlie, an auspicious thirty-three. As 1967 drew to a close, Bobby moved between this hovel on Horseshoe Drive and an apartment in town. "One afternoon he stopped by with this guitar, and a few words later," Lyn writes, "he and Charlie were playing what became a long musical conversation."

Allow her description of this flow-state assignation to stand in for all their future encounters: "Charlie's rhythms were fundamental, while Bobby's music soared above and around those rhythms. In visual terms, Bobby's music was ornate. His superior ability was obvious, but he was impatient to air it fully, taking off on his own and losing fusion, an Icarus-like lapse. There were meetings and partings. Their styles were different. Yet when the music rose above them and meshed, they looked like they were listening, like *they* were the instruments, and the music was playing them."

The day ended, and Bobby gifted Charlie his signature black top hat, "an obvious sign of respect."[38]

~

Signs and countersigns of all sorts, begging interpretation, flood *Magical Mystery Tour*. The conceit had been relatively straightforward: to create a freeform, experimental film chock-full of surrealistic moments and inspired, in part, by the trip that Ken Kesey, author of *One Flew Over the Cuckoo's Nest* (1962), and his band of Merry Pranksters had taken.

After Kesey invested proceeds from his Great American Novel into a sylvan retreat just south of San Francisco, the place became a commune of sorts, an experiment in finding a sensible way to live with friends. These friends boarded their technicolor school bus in 1964 for a psychedelic road trip that gonzo Tom Wolfe documented in *The Electric Kool-Aid Acid Test* (1968). After returning home, the group staged days-long retreats fueled by acid and rock music, funded by Kesey. *Cuckoo* money. Then on the sixth of October in 1966, the American government criminalized lysergic diethylamide-25. Ten-Six Six-Six. And that was that.

A playful, aestheticized *surreality*—not exactly *irrationality*—pervades the Beatles' film. Many critics panned these seemingly nonsensical sequences. Major McCartney in milit'ry garb at a desk bearing the slogan, *I you WAS*; a wild-eyed Lennon force-feeding someone spaghetti. The more successful moments, critics agreed, seemed to be the musical interludes, and the most successful of these had been the one featuring John's song, "I Am The Walrus." Lennon crafted the enigmatic text in part to defy the growing number of listeners who, since *Sgt. Pepper's*, had been seeking—and finding—deeper meanings in the group's work. Some had gone so far as to analyze Beatle lyrics as if they were poetry, as if the songs were art. So this lyric would be a bit of a shuck. "I was writing obscurely, *a la* Dylan," John later said, three months before someone shot him five times in the back.[39]

Watch the clip to see the four Beatles alternate between bright hippie drag and unsettling animal costumes: Walrus John, Rhinoceros Paul, Rabbit George, and Parrot Ringo. (Though, of course, you can't tell for sure who is actually underneath the rubber masks.) The clip intercuts quick-shot, surreal snippets. Four policemen, hand-in-hand, swaying on a wall. An airplane—maybe a bomber—flying overhead. John making love to a cello. At one point the person in the parrot mask drums dons round spectacles, though only for a few frames. But if that's John on the drum kit, then who is the Walrus?

John borrowed the image of the Walrus from Lewis Carroll's *Alice in Wonderland* (1865). "It never dawned on me that Lewis Carroll was commenting on the capitalist and social system," John later said. "I never went into that bit about what he really meant, like people are doing with the Beatles' work. Later, I went back and looked at it and realized that the walrus was the bad guy in the story and the carpenter was the good guy. I thought, *Oh, shit*, I picked the wrong guy. I should have said, 'I am the carpenter.' But that wouldn't have been the same, would it?"[40]

~

A similar problem of interpretation plagues any exegetical reading of the concluding seconds of "I Am the Walrus," where someone has interpolated a snatch from a BBC radio play of *King Lear*: "Villain, take my purse," Oswald says. "If ever thou wilt thrive, bury my body, and give the letters which thou find'st about me to Edmund Earl of Gloucester." If it matters, that's the full context. On the recording, you can really only make out one line: *bury my body.*[41]

~

Our bodies often betray us. At least, mine does. But not Truman Capote's. He had an ear for dialogue and a brain for absolute recall, two facts that, apparently, do not contradict one another.

"Everyone wants to know how I got together with Manson," Bobby Beausoleil told Truman in a jailhouse interview some years after his conviction for the July 1969 murder of Gary Hinman. "It was through our music. He plays some, too." (As he had with interviewees for *In Cold Blood*, Capote worked without making notes or using a tape recorder, thanks to that "absolute recall.")

"One night I was driving around with a bunch of my ladies," Bobby continued. "Well, we came to this old roadhouse, beer place, with a lot of cars outside. So we went inside, and there was Charlie with some of his ladies. We all got to talking, played some together; the next day Charlie came to see me in my van, and we all, his people and my people, ended up camping out together. Brothers and sisters. A family."[42]

~

The fraternal bonds linking the Fab Four had already begun fraying at this point, though like many families, they may not yet have realized this. In the sequence for "I Am The Walrus," Paul seemed his usual, irrepressible self, and Ringo looked cheerful, too. John appeared stoned, and George, bored (he had wanted to leave for a retreat with a new guru the group had met a few months earlier).

Elsewhere, *Playboy* magazine declared that 1967 had been the Year of Sharon Tate. *Valley of the Dolls* (1967) had recently earned her the first positive reviews of her career, though another film, a quick-hit horror parody, would prove even more consequential. Sharon met director Roman Polanski on the set of *The Fearless Vampire Killers* (1967) and quickly cut romantic ties with her longtime boyfriend, celebrity hairdresser Jay Sebring. Roman would later disavow the film; he and Sharon wed in London on the twentieth of January in 1968.

At that same moment, the Beach Boys began realizing just how badly father Murry had mismanaged their funds. Brian began increasingly relying on drugs to pacify his mind; he would soon spend time under psychiatric care.[43] What would the rest of the new year bring?

~

As the new year began, the Milky Way held its first rehearsal.[44] The following account comes from Ernie Knapp, a young guy who—after getting kicked out of college in San Diego for smoking marijuana—had started playing in bands around Los Angeles. Two guys had told Ernie that Crazy Charlie was looking for musicians. Setting up his gear in the house at Horseshoe Road, Ernie tuned up and launched into Cream's "Sunshine of Your Love," released a month earlier. He passed the audition.

The more experienced musicians intimidated Ernie, as did members of a local motorcycle gang he remembers hanging out. "Charlie said, 'Hey, the kid is nervous but give him a chance and he'll be fine,'" Ernie later recalled. "So I relaxed and then it was good."[45]

At their only rehearsal, the group learned eight songs: Charlie's originals (with "kind of old-fashioned jazz chords and real meandering progressions that didn't go really anywhere") and several covers ("a few standards—rock and blues songs that everybody knew"). Would the repertoire have included "Clang Clang?" "Your Home Is Where You're Happy?" "Sick City?" "Look At Your Game Girl?" Charlie had laid down these tracks two months earlier; memoirs frequently mention them circulating at the time. Did the girls hang out? The sorority had recently welcomed Brenda, "a witch-handed girl," as Lynette remembers her, "who had brought us to the art of colored threads."[46] Maybe they embroidered, idle hands keeping busy, as they sat and listened to the rehearsal.

The band allegedly failed their audition at the Topanga Corral the following Saturday afternoon. The Milky Way, with this lineup, wouldn't play again. It's strange that a poor showing at a half-filled bar arrested the group's momentum at this point. After all, Charlie seems to have been taking the advice of his contacts at Universal in getting the band together in the first place. And if he had been as musically ambitious as later accounts claim, why didn't the group give it another shot?

~

Of course, it may be pointless to ask why *anything* happens. One approach to history from this period, modeled by theorist Jim Garrison in his 1967 memorandum, "Time and Propinquity," suggests we abandon our search for logical, cause-and-effect relations. Instead, we should look for surface patterns, coincidences, instances where individuals or ideas approach one another in time and space.[47]

Propinquity means nearness, with all that word's connotations, rather than mere proximity. The analyst seeks moments of propinquity because, according to Garrison, they inevitably reveal the deeper, hidden structures of real power.[48] Because cranks and conspiracy theorists sometimes use this method, relying on it can be dangerous.

Garrison had been working as the district attorney in New Orleans when he began crafting this approach. It guided his investigation into the conspiracy to assassinate John F. Kennedy. While he did bring one alleged conspirator, Clay Shaw, to trial, a jury of Shaw's peers voted to acquit after deliberating for just one hour in March 1969.[49]

~

The humiliation of the Milky Way, if it had been a humiliation, coincided with Jann Wenner's humiliation of Brian Wilson in *Rolling Stone*. The Beach Boys hype machine, helmed by Derek Taylor—ex-publicist of the Beatles—had helped set Wilson up for this fall with a campaign to brand the troubled musician as a "pop genius."[50]

As live performers, Wenner wrote, the Beach Boys were "a totally disappointing group," but on record, an "excellent" one. But the songs on their new album, *Smiley Smile* (1967), ranged from "not very interesting" to "pleasant enough" to "pretty, well produced" to "pointless." The problem seemed to be that Brian Wilson had let the hype go to his head. And worse, the Beach Boys had "gotten hung up in trying to catch the Beatles. . . . It is a lesson a lot of groups are going to have to pay close attention to. To match the Beatles is impossible; instead of dropping what you do, develop it from within as far as it will go, and rock and roll, as the Beatles demonstrate time after time, can go a long way."

And how far might the Beatles go? They reinvent themselves with each record; each new release "totally outdates all the material which they had just finished updating. How they do it is anybody's guess, but I recall a conversation in the back of the Avalon Ballroom about what the Beatles might do after *Sgt. Pepper's*. Someone suggested they would set the Bible to music. 'Ah no,' was the reply. 'They'll write their own.'"[51]

AND THE GROUP CONTINUED GROWING, and evolving. A bearded man named Bruce had joined. So did a young woman named Stephanie, and one named Nancy, and another named Didi. "Look at her," Charlie said to Lyn one day, the two listening to the teenaged girl strum a guitar and sing. "She's ten times the actress her mother is without even trying."*⁵²

A teenager named Paul Watkins soon joined the group as well. Paul later testified for the prosecution, who called him Manson's "second-in-command." In his memoir, Paul described himself as "a fugitive flower child in search of enlightenment and truth." He had been student body president, had played the French horn in the school band. Then he simply walked away. "The world seemed utterly insane to me," he writes: friends were returning from Vietnam in coffins, riots blazed across American cities, the threat of nuclear war hung heavy over the carnage.

"But the roots went deeper," he continues. "I remember my parents on the day John Kennedy was shot and how that event devastated them and so many others. It seemed, in a way, that many never got over it, that afterward they just stuck their heads in the sand and decided to live without feelings, without seeing. They didn't recognize in the midst of all the violence, assassinations, profiteering, and suffering of the late sixties that there was a new spirit being born, something hopeful in the air."⁵³

In January 1968, Paul turned seventeen years old in a tent he had pitched amongst eucalyptus and oaks just a short hike from Topanga Canyon Boulevard. A marijuana bust, a brief trip back to his parents, another escape, more hanging out, and two months later, after making music with the birds in the trees surrounding his makeshift encampment, Paul packed up his horn and hiked down into the Canyon to see a friend. The teenaged boy's friend had moved, and the new inhabitants—"two naked, wispy-legged teenage girls"—greeted him.

"Is Jay around?" Paul asked, according to his memoir.

"Jay doesn't live here anymore," one replied. "I'm Snake and this is Brenda ... Would you like to come in?" He accepted, walking dazed into the welcoming smells of the roaring fireplace and bright-burning joints. About twelve people had assembled, mostly young women, around a low table in the living room headed by a shirtless man holding an acoustic guitar.

---

* Deirdre Shaw soon left the group and her parents, Angela Lansbury and Peter Shaw, relocated the family to Ireland. "Murder, she thwarted," glossed the *New York Post* (October 12, 2022). "There were factions up in the hills above Malibu that were dedicated to deadly pursuits," the actress told an interviewer decades later. Essays in this genre—close encounters with Charles Manson—continue to recur with some regularity even today. "Danny Trejo Talks Charles Manson Hypnosis in Prison," reports *Buzzfeed* (July 9, 2021). "Neil Young Once Compared Charles Manson to Bob Dylan," explained *Far Out Magazine* (January 12, 2022). "Bryan Cranston Shares Chilling Charles Manson Story: 'I Was Within His Grasp,'" reports *IndieWire* (November 20, 2017).

"I'm Charlie," said Manson. "Won't you stay and make music with us?"[54] Paul stayed.

~

As the Beatles arrived in Rishikesh, a film crew stood ready to document their stay at the Maharishi Mahesh Yogi's Academy of Meditation.[55] No documentary, it turned out, ended up being released.

George with Patty and John with Cyn had departed the United Kingdom for India in early February; Ringo with Maureen and Paul with Jane Asher followed a few days later. The English folk-rock songwriter Donovan joined, too, as did Beach Boy Mike Love along with actress Mia Farrow, recently liberated from an unhappy marriage with Frank Sinatra, and her sister. The group fell into a relaxed routine: meditating, swimming, making music, and attending seminars with the Maharishi.

A laughing, smiling sprite with a happy face, the Maharishi Maheshi Yogi, a forty-year-old man who had founded the philosophical system that would become Transcendental Meditation, could be many things. "He's a great guy," Donovan told *Rolling Stone* after spending several days with the guru in Los Angeles at the end of 1967, "and there's a lot of speculation about whether he's just another one [of those false prophets . . . but] I saw him and I knew that he was *what I instinctively knew* was a holy man. Basically, in me, without putting it through the process of thought even, I knew that this man was the one that was direct. [. . .] He doesn't let on but he knows that he came here for a purpose. He got the Beatles and sent them to India. *He's straightening everybody out.*"[56]

At the same time, the Maharishi's stance on some issues showed the holy man to be a more complex figure. The peaceful, selfless man seemed to support the US-led war in Vietnam; the simple guru had also hired an expensive public relations firm. At press conferences, he addressed how industry could increase worker productivity through meditation; he skirted questions about his Academy's profit margins. His philosophy itself had certain sharp, jagged edges that unbelievers began uncharitably pointing out. "People are in poverty because they lack intelligence and because of laziness," Maharishi told reporters in New York. "Christ," a journalist murmured. "It's Ayn Rand with a beard."[57]

In Rishikesh, cameras tailed the serene seminarians, capturing blissful Beatles with guitars in hand and group portraits of celebrity supplicants at the holy man's foot. Asked what he hoped to make of the experience, Ringo said, "peace and answers."

But the drummer cautioned: "It's not going to come in a week, you know."[58]

~

It's comforting to think that we can find answers by asking the right questions in the right way. Here's how Paul Watkins addressed the problem—and reassured his readers—in his memoir's short, prefatory "Author's Note."

"Nothing that has been written thus far has come close to explaining [the story of Charles Manson and the Family]," writes Watkins. "But it can be explained. I can explain it. It's taken a long time, I've paid my dues, and I want to tell it now, as it really was. I ask only that the reader recall the ambience of the late sixties—perhaps the most turbulent and chaotic time in American in the last thirty years."[59]

As required by conventional academic practice, these words have now been properly attributed to Paul Watkins, though not his ghostwriter, Guillermo Soledad, which—another note explains—"is the pen name of a member of the faculty of the University of California at Santa Barbara." With some digging, it might be possible to reveal the true identity of this person, and so possibly understand why they have chosen as their *nom de plume* something so evocative as "Billy Lonesome."

~

The Maharishi looks slightly sorrowful, though not necessarily lonesome, in advertisements for his record, *Maharishi Mahesh Yogi*, released in 1967 on World Pacific Records. It's the downcast eyes, framed by wavy hair reaching past his shoulders and the full beard, streaked with white. The copy pitching this record ("An Album To Experience!") reads:

> The Beatles' Spiritual Teacher Speaks To The Youth Of The World On
>   LOVE
>   And The Untapped Source of Power That Lies Within.

Mike Love tried to talk his bandmates into releasing another spoken-word album by the Maharishi on their new label, Brother Records. That plan came to naught. But Love did succeed in pitching a tour. After returning from India, the Beach Boys organized seventeen dates supporting the guru across the United States in May, to be followed by a Festival of Peace. The Maharishi had previously committed to a period of monastic silence following his recent high-profile seminars with American and British celebrities. But apparently, he now changed his mind.

"Have you seen *Life* this week?" the guru replied when a journalist asked. "They did a four-page color spread on me!"[60]

~

Learning to meditate through the Maharishi's seminars proved—as advertised—straightforward. "You go to several public lectures first, which are cheerful and encouraging," Kurt Vonnegut wrote in *Esquire*. "You are told lovingly that this thing is easy, never fails to make a person more blissful and virtuous and effective, if it is done correctly. The lecturer does not explain what meditation feels like because he cannot. It must be *experienced*, he says."

Vonnegut's wife attends seminars, though the author remains circumspect. "This new religion (which-is-not-a-religion-but-a-technique) offers tremendous pleasure, opposes no existing institutions or attitudes, demands no sacrifices or outward demonstrations of virtue, and is absolutely risk free. It will sweep the middle classes of the world as the planet dies—as the planet is surely dying—of poisoned air and water."[61]

So it goes.

Ringo and Maureen had lasted just over a week before bowing out and returning to England. The others lasted longer. Donovan taught John and Paul the fingerpicking style that would appear over several tracks on their next album; the Beatles wrote a stack of songs. Sometime around the fifteenth of March, a tape recorder captured the voices of John and Paul and maybe Donovan and Mike and perhaps George singing what's come to be known as "Spiritual Regeneration Song." We know because the Beatles-led Beach Boys pastiche broke down into a birthday song for Beach Boy Mike Love, born on the Ides of March.[62]

Paul and Jane left Rishikesh a day or so later; the Lennons and the Harrisons remained another few weeks. John thought the Maharishi had made untoward advances toward a woman at the retreat; the group later disavowed the guru.[63]

~

No true guru yet, Charlie remained utterly fallible in the first months of 1968. Elements of a philosophy might be discerned from firsthand accounts, but no true program as such. We have the music, of course. The group sex and acid, the white robes and now also water ceremonies, allegedly, and the postulating and manifesting. And the pseudo-mystical magpie rap, stitched together from bits and pieces found in diverse sources: the self-help shorthand, the psy-talk about actualization and ego, the loose Scientology (and Scientology-adjacent) doctrines, it all congealed into a general, hip argot infused with a fascination for the esoteric and the occult.

The word esoteric derives from the Greek *esōterikós*, or "belonging to an inner circle," while occult comes from the Latin *occultus*, meaning "hidden." Members of the commune certainly seem to have felt themselves to belong to the circle of the initiated; at sermon-like addresses, which former member Dianne has said the group soon referred to as "talk-tos," Charlie increasingly began revealing much that had been hidden, conjuring visions of a future world of brotherhood and love that would replace the present one of harassment, environmental degradation, and fear.[64]

~

That conjurers may become kings represents something like a human universal, at least according to James Frazer. "And while the distinction between the human and the divine is still imperfectly drawn," wrote Frazer in *The Golden Bough*, "it is often imagined that men may themselves attain to godhead, not merely after their death, but in their lifetime, through the temporary or permanent possession of their whole nature by a great and powerful spirit."[65]

So let us not dismiss, as if we could, that which has been hidden from us.

~

And from the inky black sky, dotted with galaxies and stars, dropped down a stick among the Joshua trees. Roman and Sharon muffled giggles as Peter's eyes grew wide as saucers. The couple had become fast friends with Sellers and his new girlfriend, Mia Farrow.

Mia had recently split from her husband, Frank Sinatra, who had sent divorce papers to the set of *Rosemary's Baby*. (The coward hadn't even telephoned her to break the news first; he hated the fashionably short haircut she'd gotten, and just *lost* it when Polanski's film ran over schedule, bumping her appearance on a pedestrian movie set to star Ol' Blue Eyes himself.) Peter would soon be working with Ringo Starr on *The Magic Christian* (1968), though his best film must surely be *The Mouse That Roared* (1959), a satire depicting the hostile takeover of the United States by a company of archers from the fictional European country of Grand Fenwick.

But now Mia and Peter, along with Sharon and Roman, frolicked stoned among the Joshua trees on that warm evening in 1968 as Roman slipped away, hurling a stick into the air, so it might appear to have been deposited by ghostly hands from the beyond, fly away, fly, fly away.

~

And now I can faintly hear the archers arching back their slings: And they let loose a new song before the throne, and before the four beasts, and the elders.[66]

~

And maybe that kindly elder with the smiling face hadn't really tried something with Mia's sister, Prudence. George Harrison never really believed John, and came to see the holy man as bringing about a turn essential for humanity, as rousing the peoples of the world, making them see what was actually going on.

People "seriously term this scene of waking up, going out to work, going home again, going to sleep, dreaming, waking up again and all that—reality! But in actual fact you're into illusion—it's nothing to do with reality because reality is God alone. Everything else is illusion." That's what George told *Rolling Stone* in February 1968.

"Those people in the Himalayas, the Yogi who are very advanced spiritually, and all the ones on other planets, well it's just a joke to them all this that we do and call reality; I mean it's even a joke if you just take yourself out of it and watch all the things going on. It's a joke. And the joke's on the people who take it seriously. There's so much more to it. You see every so often somebody comes to the earth, like Jesus did, and they've been coming every so often, these people, divine incarnation, like Buddha, Jesus, and all that. There's always these people coming and they are the truth, like God, this great force whatever it is, manifesting itself into a physical form.

"And there are *quite a few people walking around on earth this minute* who have attained that—all over the world, in the Himalayas, in America, everywhere—and they just look like funny little old men. I mean, like Maharishi, they look like that. People of course don't take much notice of them or put 'em down, when *all these people are doing is telling the truth*—they're always there. I read somewhere that the next fella like that, the next Messiah like, he'll come and he'll just be too much."

And here's the upshot of all that, which I've taken the liberty of slightly reformatting and italicizing for emphasis: "Anybody who doesn't believe that he's the one, [well] then *he'll just show 'em*, you know. He's just gonna come down and *zap them all.*"⁶⁷

~

Oo-ee-oo!

LIGHT-HEADED, BEGINNING TO FEEL DIZZY, Dianne lied down in the warm summer grass and closed her eyes. She and several of the girls had been fasting, consuming nothing but honey, water, and some lemon juice for over a week. Charlie had said that "eating food was a thought construct." The growing group may have been running low on supplies, too.

Opening her eyes, she began imagining what it would be like if she "were a snake, slithering between the blades of grass and the rocks under the beaming sun. I wasn't on acid or dehydrated—I was simply allowing my mind to wander."⁶⁸

And so Dianne Lake became Snake, assigned that totem animal whom Christians call cursed above every beast of the field.⁶⁹ Upon they belly shalt thy go, those Christians say, and dust shalt thou eat all the days of thy life. Only it wasn't exactly like that. The fourteen-year-old felt the name endowed her with new energies, almost providing a mask under which she might reinvent herself. She later said that, at the time, she had loved it.⁷⁰

Someone told Ed Sanders, and he duly reported in *The Family*, that the name had been bestowed "evidently in tribute to the transverse ophidian wiggles she made during intercourse."⁷¹ So this turned out to be untrue, too. Just something someone said.

~

And the LORD God said, It is not good that the man should be alone; I will make him an help meet for him.

And out of the ground the LORD God formed every beast of the field, and every fowl of the air; and brought them unto Adam to see what he would call them: and whatsoever Adam called every living creature, that was the name thereof.

And Adam gave names to all cattle, and to the fowl of the air, and to every beast of the field; but for Adam there was not found an help meet for him.

And the LORD God caused a deep sleep to fall upon Adam, and he slept: and he took one of his ribs, and closed up the flesh instead thereof;

And the rib, which the LORD God had taken from man, made he a woman, and brought her unto the man.

And Adam said, "This is now bone of my bones, and flesh of my flesh: she shall be called Woman, because she was taken out of Man."

Therefore shall a man leave his father and his mother, and shall cleave unto his wife: and they shall be one flesh.

And they were both naked, the man and his wife, and were not ashamed.⁷²

~

And why should any of us be ashamed? Back on Sunset Boulevard, sun-kissed Dennis Wilson had been going through changes, and he was not ashamed. His wife had filed for divorce, and he began, so to speak, sowing his wild oats (a euphemism men use to describe other men pursuing aggressively promiscuous sexual activity). He and two friends, Gregg Jakobson and Terry Melcher, even gave themselves a pathetic nickname, the Golden Penetrators, and set to seducing the daughters of the Hollywood elite.⁷³

With Dennis on the cusp of his rendezvous with "the Family," we might now examine a contemporary portrait of the star-crossed drummer by Beach Boy intimate David Anderle.* Anderle had worked at Brother Records in 1967 before leaving, freaked out by the psychological disintegration he witnessed there. In the early months of 1968, he provided some frank insights into the group in a wide-ranging interview with Paul Williams about the inner workings of the Beach Boys clan.

An unkind word from father Murry put Brian into a tailspin for days, Anderle said, while praise injected him with a sense of euphoria. Brian ranged from "raving lunatic" to "absolute saint." Mike Love figures in this account as the business-minded force seeking to keep the ship seaworthy; Carl Wilson provides a kind of spiritual ballast. And then there's Dennis.

"Dennis is the kind of person that will ask you to go shopping with him, and whatever he buys for himself he'll buy for you," Anderle told Williams. "That's Dennis. He will go out to get a motorcycle, and if you're with him, he'll buy

---

* You may recognize Anderle's name from an odd, oft-repeated story from this period. In 1966, David rendered brother Brian in oils. The painting captured Brian in an orange collarless shirt and blue jeans, perched on an ottoman, almost receding into a burnt-red background decorated with blue and red and orange flower-suns. On seeing the portrait, Brian stood stock-still for what seemed an eternity, counting the abstract images, slowly realizing their occult numerological significance. The canvas had, quite literally, Brian thought, captured his soul. You can find an early version of this account in the October 28, 1971, edition of *Rolling Stone*.

you a motorcycle. Incredibly ... always on edge, completely on edge, you never know with Dennis at any second whether he's gonna explode or not. No matter whether he's happy or sad. He is completely free, an animal, a free animal ... who is almost always controlled by his emotions, and very seldomly by his head. A beautiful younger brother, and one that Brian can relate to—a very easy brother relationship for Brian to relate to and also a source of incredible enjoyment for Brian."

And here's the most telling part, at least from my perspective: "All the fantasies Brian would get, Dennis would take even farther. In other words, Brian would come up with the ideas, but once he would lay them on Dennis' head, they were gone. I mean, Dennis would shoot, em *right to the extreme*."[74]

~

As we turn toward examining increasingly extreme behaviors, we should retain a measure of historical perspective. Consider, for instance, the Albigensians.

Condemned by the Church and then extirpated centuries ago, members of the group believed in the duality of a good God with a wicked Rex Mundi, the King of the Earth. Albigensians opposed killing animals, and practiced vegetarianism. They also practiced celibacy, as sexual intercourse brings into being pure souls trapped within base flesh. After receiving the Consolamentum, a kind of baptism, cleansing their souls of sin, the adult initiate would refuse all food and drink. Even water, as an element of the material world, they deemed corrupt. So starved, the supplicant soon died.

Efforts to convert these heretics helped establish the Dominican Order, founded by a fanatic who wanted to save Albigensian souls. Their slaughter helped bring into being the Inquisition, too. Some scholars today wonder if they ever really existed, or whether we should understand them as nothing more than the flickering apparition at the center of a medieval moral panic.

In some ways, the modern-day heresies of 1960s California prove no more or less strange in comparison to these historical ones. Travelers on the psychedelic underground drew from science fiction, for instance, with individuals such as David Crosby (under the name "Samuel E. Omar") writing songs based on Heinlein's *Stranger in a Strange Land* ("the mind goes high / the mind goes low / to find my brothers").[75] Some groups even adopted the book's water rituals as a bonding exercise. New religious practices such as those found in the works of L. Ron Hubbard spread far and wide, too. Hubbard's discoveries lay somewhere on the spectrum between therapy and revelation. He renamed the soul, *thetan*, arguing this precedes and outlives us (and taking inspiration from 1907 experiments weighing bodies directly before and after death, and showing a consistent drop of twenty-one grams in mass). He invented auditing, a personal inventory-taking that helped "clear" an individual of harmful "engrams," the traces of prior traumatic experiences. In liberating oneself from these emotional imprints, practitioners entered a new condition of existence, as "clears."

Human beings invent for themselves practices, whether baptism or the Consolamentum or water rituals or auditing, to ease their transition from one phase of life to another. Strip away the jargon from postwar practices, and you find an underlying theory about the radical powers of the individual's mind. We can improve ourselves, heal our hearts, attain new states of humanly wrought grace. We can even hack our minds, whether through meditation, yoga and other bodily practices, or even through the power of conscious autosuggestion. Try it now: Every day, in every way, I'm getting better and better.[76] Can you feel yourself changing? Say it again, and again. Every day, in every way...

What limits can be placed on an individual so freed through these powers of the self? The Maharishi taught that transcendental meditation could enable practitioners to levitate, and even fly. In *Dianetics*, L. Ron Hubbard proposed that once "clear," an individual could not merely improve his mood, but "by these increases in ability he is now brought up to a point where *he can control or handle his entire environment*."[77] Such an ability can be developed through the "awareness of awareness unit." Hubbard juxtaposes the "analytical mind" to this "unit" that, in making a person conscious of their own consciousness (that is, aware of their awareness), facilitates the emergence of powerful new functions: "It does not need eyes. It does not need a vehicle in which to travel. All it needs to do is to postulate its existence in a certain location and then look from that point of existence. In order to do this it has to be willing to be cause. It has to be willing to be an effect. But if it can do this it can go much further—*it can create and change space*."[78]

Hubbard's descriptions of these phenomena can be quite difficult to parse.* More reputable biographers often point out that Manson encountered these ideas while in prison, even joining a Scientology study group.[79] He also took a correspondence class based on Dale Carnegie's 1937 book *How to Win Friends and Influence People*. (Though it's unclear whether Carnegie's advice in chapters such as "Be a Leader: How to Change People Without Giving Offense or Arousing

---

* Better difficult than deadly, which the author's earlier science fiction books were. Eleven of the thirteen people who read Hubbard's first manuscript, *The Black Sword*, allegedly committed suicide. The most dramatic death came when a reader walked into a meeting between L. Ron Hubbard and his publisher and, without a word, went straight to the window, unclasped it, and leapt, plummeting to his death. Words matter, as this parable illustrates.

Resentment" would have been more influential than, say, Manson's experience as a pimp and small-time con man.)

More significant may have been the commune's encounters on the streets of San Francisco in 1967 with members of a heretical Scientology sect calling themselves the Process Church of the Final Judgment. Established in 1966 by two former Scientologists, Robert de Grimston and Mary Ann MacLean, the Process Church grew quickly, establishing small groups throughout North America.[80] Processeans believed in the incarnate existence of four deities, Jehovah, Lucifer, Satan, and Christ, internal to all human beings. Each individual comprises a blending of elements from these deities, though a single one typically predominates. The group became well known for their striking black robes, their swastika-like insignia, their massive companion hounds, and the bright fantastical magazines they sold on themes such as "Sex" or "Fear" or "Love" or "Death."[81] (A diagnostic test in one issue revealed me to be predominantly Luciferan, with a strong secondary streak of Jehovan, and my daughter, Juanita, to be almost entirely Satanic.)

There's conflicting evidence as to how closely Charlie engaged with Processeans prior to the August 1969 killings, though Paul McCartney and Mick Jagger, among others, did—at least in passing.[82] Quotes from these two musicians appear in the Church's issue on "Love." Following a jailhouse interview in 1970, Charlie would appear in the issue on "Death."

~

Here's the issue: When stories fold in and repeat, over and above and into one another, the observer must bring order, an ineluctably conservative practice, by selecting and discarding, by labeling certain accounts "false," and other ones, "truthful." Without slipping into rank apophany, can we avoid presenting the contradictions that inevitably arise among accounts as evidencing the falsity of one story or the truth of another?

Both Susan Atkins and Phil Kaufman, an ex-con who put Charlie in touch with Stromberg at Universal, for instance, tell a remarkably similar story of their first meetings with Manson. Each says they first encountered a small man, strumming a guitar, and singing "Shadow of Your Smile."[83] Mere coincidence? Or plagiarism? Kaufman first put a version of this story in print a decade after Atkins published her memoir. If he borrowed (or "stole") this detail, does that disqualify everything else he remembers?

Sometimes firsthand accounts fit together like two puzzle pieces, the one revealing insights into the other. In 1979, Paul Watkins described his first encounter with the Family, related a few pages ago, with two nude girls opening the door at the house on Horseshoe Road. In 2017, Dianne Lake—one of those two girls—claimed that Charlie instructed them to greet Paul. Manson wanted, Dianne suggests, to ensnare new followers. Together the two accounts make sense: each fosters a deeper understanding of the other.

In bringing order to the messy disorder of experiences, authors demand much of their readers: at least trust, if not also fealty, to say nothing of awe. With that in mind, consider how Bugliosi draws the snare around us in a remarkable passage in *Helter Skelter* on the true identity of Manson. The prosecutor begins by claiming that, from the July 1967 arrest connected with the runaway Ruth Ann Moorehouse, soon renamed Ouisch, Manson began rendering his full name Charles Willis Manson. Bugliosi next cites two interviewees who describe Charlie dragging out the words to sound as follows: "Charles' Will Is Man's Son."[84] Finally, Bugliosi pulls back to reveal the larger import of this shift.

"Manson claimed that the members of the Family were the original Christians, reincarnated, and that the Romans had returned as the establishment. It was now time, Manson told his closest followers, for the Romans to have their turn on the cross."[85]

~

After Charlie revealed this true identity, Dianne recalls, the commune ingested hallucinogens and experienced a group religious experience. She opened her eyes to see a vision of Charlie crucified, "a stigmata of color pulsating through his hands and on his ankles." She fell asleep, and awoke to hear singing and Charlie's guitar. "They were some of the same songs I'd heard on the bus," she writes, "*designed to make us feel a part of the whole he was creating.*"[86]

In his memoir, Paul recalls Charlie joking about his own crucifixion; the account by Susan contains several moments where she believed Charlie to be Christ (though noting that Manson never actually told her he was Jesus Christ incarnate).[87] But also recall the hippie we met in the last chapter, in New York City, a person who, as reported by that square English professor, Delbert Earisman, experienced his own psychedelics-inspired stigmata.

How do these stories square? What sense should we make of them? Should we bring order to these accounts? Is so, how? Must we collapse them into one?

~

We are one, we are one, we are one.
Always is always forever.
We are one, we are one, we are one.

ON OR AROUND THE FIFTH OF APRIL IN 1968, members of the commune gathered to assist Mother Mary. Brunner had fallen pregnant in the months preceding the move to the Spiral Staircase; the women of the group now attended her as she labored. The event entered the group's self-mythology almost immediately: Mary's quiet dignity and Charlie's calm; the sanitized razor blade used to effect a crude episiotomy for the breech presentation; the guitar string used to tie off the umbilical cord; the hawk that appeared overhead at the child's emergence to inspire one of his names.

Children were sacred, Charlie now instructed the group. They would raise the child collectively, with no one person imprinting their hang-ups on the child, as usually happens. They named him Michael Valentine, after Heinlein's protagonist in *Stranger in a Strange Land*. Despite Charlie's objections, the girls soon took to calling him Pooh Bear.

~

And members of the group acquired new names as well. At auspicious moments, name changes often signify initiation into a new phase of life. A baptismal name added; a slave name exchanged for X. What rite of passage did the group now mark?

The shared experience of Pooh Bear's birth cohered the group in a way sex, drugs, and music had not, making them more like a family. The new names, however, seem to have been largely utilitarian. Recent entanglements with the police had rendered the old ones hazardous; underage commune members also needed identification papers. So Dianne became Dianne Bluestein and gained six years in age, while adolescent Ruth Ann Moorehouse became Mrs. Rachel Susan Morse.

Others received more fantastical names. Susan Atkins became Sadie Mae Glutz, Pat Krenwinkel became Katie B. Everglad, Ella Jo Bailey became Ella Beth Cinder, and Charlie became Hymie Hobsnopper. A friend from Charlie's prison days provided forged documents.[88] Other aliases also began proliferating. Vincent Bugliosi presented these in a helpful glossary in *Helter Skelter* titled "Cast of Characters."[89] In the main text, Bugliosi distinguished an alias by writing *t/n* after its appearance, as in: "Sadie Mae Glutz, t/n Susan Atkins." This shorthand indicates "true name," and alerts the reader that someone may be trying to pull a fast one.

~

And soon these latter-day Albigensians moved onto a small horse ranch in Chatsworth, about an hour's hitchhiking from downtown Los Angeles. Rejecting the material world, like their predecessors, they demanded of themselves the perfection of poverty, albeit with two crucial differences. The commune continued to explore the sensual pleasures of the flesh. And this, alongside a new focus: on the ecstatic practice of communal music-making.

3

April 1968 to September 1968

or, A Group of Beatle Addicts

DENNIS WILSON CLIMBED, HAND OVER HAND, pulling himself and then Ella Jo followed by Katie (t/n Patricia Krenwinkel) up and into a treehouse on the verdant estate once owned by Oklahoma's Favorite Son.[1] Sunlight streamed through the leaves, dappling the drummer's fine golden hair. This retreat had fostered one of the erstwhile baron's first efforts at songwriting; he had playacted stoned amanuensis to an avian visitor.

Accounts vary as to the precise sequence of events that come next. And how could they not? But here's what may have happened: Dennis picked up the two hitchhikers and invited them back to the home he rented at 14400 Sunset Boulevard. They visited in the treehouse, as described above, and then the Beach Boy dropped them at their new haunt, the Spahn Movie Ranch, just off Santa Susana Pass outside Los Angeles. The drummer then went to a recording session, which stretched long into the early hours of the next morning.

On returning home, Wilson found the black Holiwood Productions bus in his driveway, a gaggle of girls in his living room, and Charlie. "A friendship developed," Ed Sanders summarized, "and Manson's group underwent a multimonth mooch on Wilson's resources that drained him of about $100,000 in '68 money."[2]

These are the bare facts. But what if we employ metonymy, using this device as a sort of literary witching rod? Can we divine a larger story lurking behind these bare facts? Here goes: Oklahoma-born multi-purpose song-and-dance man Will Rogers built the sprawling wood-paneled hunting lodge at 14400 Sunset Boulevard in 1923. The vaudeville actor's schtick, a plain-spoken, trick-roping, joke-rustling cowboy, had made him a wealthy man. He often opened his stage show with the line, "All I know is what I read in the papers."

Rogers then moved into Westerns. Americans at that time loved their no-nonsense stars. These men were men, even if they sometimes sang. Playacting "the conquest of the frontier," enacting the bloody rites by which a nation had been founded. And they enacted these rites over, and over again.[3]

~

The Santa Susana Pass homed several ranches where rugged, serious men with square jaws went to playact the conquest of the frontier in the 1950s and early 1960s. Someone had named the area after Susanna of Rome, daughter of Saint Gabinus, martyred under the Emperor Diocletian. The Romans cut off her head when she refused to marry a pagan; Catholics celebrated her feast day on the eleventh of August until 1969.[4]

What happened in 1969 that made them stop? Apparently, scholars began to think that accounts of the life of Susanna of Rome had been entirely made up.

~

Oo-ee-oo! In *The Family* (1971), Ed Sanders used this repeated interjection to note apophenic, quasi-supernatural occurrences of possibly hidden significance. Other American authors and their gonzo fellow travelers in this period often used this device, the refrain, to emphasize moments or themes, to point to something without coming out and saying it.

In *Slaughterhouse-Five* (1969), for instance, Kurt Vonnegut famously repeats the words "so it goes" whenever someone dies. Sanders seems less scrupulous in his usage; the refrain appears to be less substance, and more style. A six-letter trace, rendering the author's personal voice, signaling—if anything—a perhaps ironic detachment.

~

And I heard a voice from heaven, as the voice of many waters, and as the voice of a great thunder: and I heard the voice of harpers harping with their harps: And they sang as it were a new song before the throne, and before the four beasts, and the elders: *and no man could learn that song but the hundred* and *forty* and *four thousand, which were redeemed from the earth.*[5]

~

14400 Sunset Boulevard? The hundred *and* forty *and* four thousand of the Book of Revelation 14:2–3?

~

Oo-ee-oo!

"You know man, you got your father in you," Charlie told Dennis at their first meeting. "He took over your mind, and that's why you don't believe in your own music. You got to give up all that. That's nothing but a reflection in the wrong mirror."[6]

If you picture Dennis as the ruggedly bearded man on the cover of *Pacific Ocean Blue* (1977), then it may be difficult to recall that he had just turned twenty-three years old when he met Charlie. When the Beach Boys released "Surfin' Safari" (1962), Dennis had not yet "come of age." Soon world-wise through the group's constant touring (and his own whoring), the drummer's pleasure-seeking had streaks of idealism, his contemporaries often note, that slipped easily from naïveté into euphoria.

Dennis would give you the shirt off his back. He'd disappear for days. He'd sleep with your wife, though without malice aforethought. He wanted to write songs. He would not turn twenty-four until the following December.

~

On the fourth of December, believers celebrate Santa Barbara, betrayed by a pagan father.[7] The wealthy merchant, alarmed by the many suitors the girl had attracted, like moths to a flame, had shut young Barbara up in a tower on his sprawling estates. Years went by: darkness whitened the skin of the beautiful girl, and her thick blonde locks grew long. Her only contact with the outside world came via a basket, lowered for food.

Then one day the basket returned a Bible. Barbara devoured the holy object. She pledged herself to its mysteries. And as her passion for the book knew no limits, so did Barbara begin wasting away, foregoing all worldly things in order to better absorb its stories. Her loving father, the pagan, sent for a doctor. But unbeknownst to him, the doctor secretly practiced Christianity. The man baptized the girl.

Barbara grew stronger, and soon had workmen on her father's estate install a third window in her tower, these portals to the outside world now symbolizing the Father, the Son, and the Holy Spirit. Her angry father cast the girl out. The Romans tortured her, demanding she renounce her triune Godhead. But Barbara wouldn't. They stripped her and made her walk naked through the streets; a Holy mist developed that hid her nakedness. At last, her homicidal father decided to end her life.

But as each attempt failed, the girl grew ever more beautiful. The glary light of the Holy Spirit, later accounts claimed, illuminated her soul. Until at last the unfaithful father grasped her long locks and struck a blow to her neck with a knife, beheading the girl. Sparks and fire exploded from the trunk of the body. The heavens opened. A bolt of lightning struck and killed the father where he stood. That's why if you fear lightning, you can invoke Santa Barbara's name for protection. If you want to harness the power of lightning, you can invoke her name, too.

~

Ba-ba-*baa*, Ba-*baa*-bara Ann! Someone named Fred Fassert wrote the song with that frenzied, mindnumbing refrain, though the Beach Boys made it famous.

Dennis might not have drummed on that recording session; in the early days, they often had to replace his parts with unnamed session players. Did Dennis mind?

~

Dennis only later began writing his own songs. His earliest efforts have a weird, uncanny aura. With his first, "Little Bird," Dennis collaborated with poet Stephen Kalinich on the lyric. The two men had been looking up from the roughhewn floor of the treehouse on the Will Rogers estate when a songbird came and sang a song. The song, if you take its lyric literally, seems to be about this: "How *it* began."

The Beach Boys recorded "Little Bird" on the last day of February in 1968, which had been a leap year. The track appears on the album *Friends*, released just about the same time Dennis met Katie and Ella Jo in April. And it's a curious little song, quite strange and so also beautiful, with its off-kilter bass punctuations and sing-song *wah wah wah* harmonies and strangely asymmetric repetitions punctuating an almost through-composed form, nearly never repeating when you think it might.

What a day! What a day!

Much of the vocal harmonies had been reworked from "Child Is Father of the Man," one of Brian's failed experiments intended for the ill-starred SMiLE. "Child" takes the form of a stopping-starting kind of static round, with a frenetically repressed build-up (*the ch- ch- ch- chil'—is fa-ther-of-the-ma-a-a-*

a-n) that, try as hard as it might, just won't climax. I hear vestiges of that stutter in the bassline of "Little Bird." Maybe you can, too?

Oooh what a beautiful day *it is*!

And if I think about it too much, that subterranean scaffolding of "Child Is Father of the Man" begins to pervert and sour "Little Bird." What does that phrase from Brian's song even mean? Simply that our childhood experiences—good or bad, and instilling within us either security and safety, or traumas untold—inevitably shape our grown-up lives. You can find the line in an old poem by William Wordsworth, where he seems to frame it in a largely positive sense. If the appearance of a rainbow plucked at your heartstrings when you were a kid, Wordsworth says, it'll probably continue pluckin' at 'em until the day you die.

~

Growing up, I remember seeing my father cry on only two occasions; once was at the end of the documentary film *Imagine: John Lennon* (1988).

Eight years earlier, my father had learned of Lennon's death the way many Americans would, from broadcaster Howard Cosell during a break in the action on Monday Night Football. With three seconds remaining in the game, John Smith, the New England Patriots placekicker, stepped up to attempt a game-tying field goal. I cannot remember this; it happened two years before my birth. Cosell's partner vamped, "and I don't care what's on the line, Howard, you have got to say what we know in the booth."

"Yes, we have to say it: remember this is just a football game, no matter who wins or loses," Cosell told viewers. "An unspeakable tragedy, confirmed to us by ABC News in New York City. John Lennon, outside of his apartment building on the west side of New York City, the most famous, perhaps, of all of the Beatles, shot twice in the back, rushed to Roosevelt Hospital, dead on arrival. Hard to go back to the game after that newsflash."

A sick man named Mark David Chapman had shot Lennon. Chapman thought Lennon betrayed the world, that Lennon—like all adults—was a *phony*. Prior to the murder, and to help investigators understand the heinous act, Chapman left displayed an assortment of objects in his rented room at the YMCA. "So [the tableau] would say, 'Look, this is me,'" he later said. "'Probably, this is the real me.'" A passport, two photographs of himself, an album by Todd Rundgren, and a pocket Bible, opened to the Gospel of John, had been arranged to encircle a small poster of Dorothy and the Cowardly Lion from the *Wizard of Oz*.[8]

On his way to the Dakota Building where John lived, Chapman bought a copy of J. D. Salinger's *Catcher in the Rye*. He sometimes signed letters "Holden Caulfield," after its protagonist (though he had signed out from work for the final time a month earlier as "John Lennon"). Flipping through the novel's pages, Chapman's eyes rested on a line on page 197 of his paperback copy, reading, "It was Monday and all, and pretty near Christmas . . . ," which he took to be a sign to act. "History and time," Chapman later explained to a biographer. "Synchronicity."[9]

~

After the shooting, Chapman sat reading this paperback not far from the front gates of the Dakota Building we see in Roman Polanski's horrible *Rosemary's Baby*, released in early June 1968. You will recall the wrought-iron gates from the scene where Mia Farrow's character, Rosemary, returns home with her husband to find a police cordon.

The young woman in the apartment next door had plummeted to her death, apparently a tragic suicide. She had been living with a friendly older couple. The couple are active in their local magic circle, though we do not learn this until much later, when they begin grooming Rosemary to carry the child of Satan, played by the real-life high priest of the Church of Satan, Anton LaVey. (Or so he often claimed; this may not be true.)

Sharon Tate helped Roman plot out the ugliest scene of the film: when the witchy older couple drug Rosemary, enabling the Devil to inseminate her lifeless body. The two, Sharon and Roman, blocked out the sequence during an acid trip just after filming had gotten underway.[10]

~

In a gambit that Dianne Lake realized "was likely a script he had acted out many times before," Dennis brought three girls from the commune to a Beach Boys family getaway at Lake Havasu.[11] The family played their roles perfectly: the good wives winced at the lithe, too-young hippie chicks, while the men looked the other way.

Ella Jo, Nancy, and Dianne gorged on the plentiful food, and fell asleep on the sand by the lake in the warm California night. Over the following days they swam and boated, and came to an uneasy truce with the Wilson family members, even breaking bread with them. At some point soon after returning to Los Angeles, Dianne, Nancy, Lyn, and a new girl, Sandra Good, began nesting in Will Rogers' grand old log cabin at 14400 Sunset Boulevard. As spring turned into summer, everyone else remained at the Spahn Movie Ranch.

~

The preceding events must have happened sometime in late May or early June, after the Beach Boys had concluded their failed tour with the Maharishi Mahesh Yogi. The musicians had planned to play a set at each date, followed by an hour-long lecture. A two-tone red-and-black placard advertising the May 6 concert in Boston depicts the smiling, bearded yogi ("Man is born to enjoy!" script suggests him saying) with the black turtlenecked musicians inset ("One Night Only!").

The Boston Garden would have been the largest venue they played before heading west to the Hollywood Bowl. Most shows had been scheduled for more modest spaces, such as the Kiel Auditorium in St Louis or a hall on the campus of Nevada Southern University. But the Boston performance, and all subsequent dates, had to be canceled. Though *Life* had declared 1968 to be The Year of the Guru, lagging ticket sales and poor reviews could not be overcome.[12] The fifth and final appearance was in Hartford, Connecticut, at Bushnell Memorial Hall.

~

Erected in 1930, Bushnell Memorial Hall paid tribute to the Reverend Dr. Horace Bushnell, a long-dead Congregational pastor and prolific theologian. In *Moral Uses of Dark Things* (1868), Bushnell pondered "the darkest of all dark things in the catalogue of the world's suffering allotments," the "subject of insanity." By this he meant the condition we leave our minds and bodies by poisoning ourselves with too much drink or food, as well as with a punishing work ethic that leaves no time for reflection. The "wrongs men do against themselves are twentyfold, or possibly even a thousandfold greater in amount of damage than the wrongs they do against each other; and yet they very seldom think of them as being any wrong at all."[13]

The result can be catastrophic, a kind of psychopolitical dispossession where the individual loses control of their self. "*Society* possesses them, and so completely dominates in their habit," Bushnell continues, "that any coming short of its conventionalisms or fashions goads them to distraction; their own self-keeping force is so far taken away, that their judgments themselves are reduced to a kind of insanity." "They get possessed by other men in the same manner; one by some other that he thinks a hero or a genius; one by the name and successes of a great operator in the market; one by the fascinating airs and gayeties of a libertine; one by a charlatan or a quack; and another by a false prophet. Every soul in evil is under some kind of bad instigation or possession, that comes upon him as a gale of impulsion, swaying his objects and actions, and so far abating in him the sovereign keeping of his own right reason."[14]

~

With so many events piling up between April and June of 1968, our narrative thread has begun fraying. We have not noted that commune members found themselves in print for the first time, following an arrest for public vagrancy that yielded the infamous mugshot of Charlie that later appeared on the cover of *Life*. (To avoid possession charges, everyone swallowed the drugs they had on their persons.) The headline for that news article read, "Fourteen Hippies Arrested."

Nor have we noted a second appearance in print, following the relocation of Sadie Mae (t/n Susan) with Mary, Ella Jo, and Katie (t/n Patty) to Mendocino County in May. Newspapers in June reported the arrest of "the Witches of Mendocino" for allegedly dosing a handful of high schoolers*. The young women remained in county jail until the following August; Manson's ex-parole officer, now directing a government study into how methamphetamines might induce violence in human beings, fostered Mary's child.[15]

And most significantly, the main group moved into the Spahn Movie Ranch at 1200 Santa Susana Road, occupying the disused Outlaw Shacks at the back of the property in exchange for their labor. George Spahn, an elderly man with failing eyesight and a quick, filthy wit, had bought the property in 1953.

Just an hour from downtown Los Angeles, the Ranch had once provided filmmakers a convenient location for shooting the Westerns that dominated the 1950s. But while a few episodes of *Bonanza* had recently been filmed there, the Ranch's final films had been lowbrow, exploitation fare: a notoriously bad horror film, *The Creeping Terror*, in 1964, and two years later, a softcore film,

---

* In her memoir, Atkins claims they acted in self-defence during this curious episode, which has given rise to numerous theories. Had Charlie sent a group to recruit new members for what had become a cult? Were they scouting new locations? Other theories suggest the commune's first killings occurred during this period: the unsolved murders of Nancy Warren, her granddaughter Clyda Dulaney, and the pregnant Clyda's unborn child. No evidence, other than a few suggestive traces of propinquity, points to the commune's involvement.

The girls apparently settled in a house in Boonville, where they would have heard Boontling. A folk language invented in the late nineteenth century, Boontling mixes indigenous, Spanish, Gaelic, and Irish borrowings with locally significant inventions. "Zeese" means coffee, so named for a local coffee lover, for instance, while "oshtook," borrowed from Pomoan, means one-eyed man. A curious theory, aired increasingly frequently over the past decade or so by lay researchers, suggests that this esoteric argot inspired the commune to create their own secret language in the months that followed.

The Ramrodder, featuring Cupid (t/n Bobby) and Catherine Share, whom you might know as Gypsy. George kept the Ranch afloat by hiring horses out so visitors could ride the winding trails off Santa Susana Pass.

Commune members exploited Spahn's frailty and loneliness, one narrative explains, with Charlie instructing Lyn to keep him pliant with kindness and sex. That's how she acquired her new nickname: Squeaky, for the sound she made when George ran his fingers up her thigh. The main group skulked around the back of the lot, and George never quite knew how many were living there or what they were doing. That's one story. But maybe George cherished the group. Squeaky (t/n Lyn) later described the relationship as warm, and George's intentions as fatherly, if a bit gruff. The implication that Manson pimped her out to George? Absolutely false, Fromme has always argued, outright slander.

Interviewed in late 1969, George's longtime associate Ruby Pearl had this to say: "They were actually wonderful people. They were artists, and musicians, and they were singers, and they had wonderful personalities—each, and every one of them. And they never quarreled or caused any trouble, and they did everything we asked them to. They did the dishes and the cooking . . . and little chores all around the ranch."

According to Ruby, Charlie came to the ranch a bit later than the rest of the group. "Music, that was his sole interest," she recalled. "He'd sit on the rock, and play guitar. He'd get up and walk around, get some paper and go write some music, and everywhere he went, some of the girls kind of followed him, and laughed and talked and sang."[16]

~

And at the end of May, the four Beatles convened at George's estate to begin laughing and talking and singing and rehearsing the songs that would become *The Beatles*. This album would allegedly become Charlie's Bible, its sprawling four sides providing the grist their perverse exegetical readings milled into murder.

"You got a good road game here, Charlie," a visitor to the commune reportedly said around this time, using jailbird slang for a hustle. "Don't blow it."

"I haven't got a road game," Manson replied. And then advised: "You're too smart. You don't want to be around here."[17]

Phil Kaufman had done time with Charlie; he's actually the con who gave Manson the contact at Universal. Phil crashed with the group at the Horseshoe Road house for about two months in early 1968 before leaving to work as the driver for Marianne Faithfull and Mick Jagger, then in Los Angeles with his band, the Rolling Stones, to record *Beggars Banquet* from March to July.

Another reason that Phil left is because he thought Charlie was trying to brainwash him. But Phil saw through the mind games, even if the girls did not. "When I first met 'im when I got out, that wasn't the guy I knew in the [prison] yard, singing 'The Shadow of Your Smile,'" Kaufman later said. "Charlie went from Frankie Laine to kind of an acid music. He was using it, [the music] was a tool . . . These girls were lost, these children were lost. And peace and love, that was his bait."[18]

A GREAT PILE OF CLOTHES GREW, A PULSING TECHNICOLOR COLLECTION of scarves and costume jewelry and dresses and robes and shirts, rising from the floor of an Outlaw Shack on the Spahn Movie Ranch. And the commune members drew from this collective wardrobe, playacting themselves and others as the days grew long and hot off the Santa Susana Pass. "If you don't have any philosophy, you don't have any rules," Fromme later said. "I've made my own world. It may sound like an Alice-in-Wonderland world, but it makes sense."[19] This period came to be understood as a new stage in the group's MMT, or Magical Mystery Tour.

"So, nobody was anybody in particular," Charlie told an acolyte three decades later. "We was all playacting. It's an MMT. It's a joke. It's like, somebody makes a move and everybody turns into cowboys. And then somebody else makes a move and everybody goes back and puts their motorcycle gear on."[20]

Members of the group playacted cowboys and Indians just as children do; they even constructed crude tipis. Then they'd play taigey bikers, drinkin' and cussin' and carryin' on. Next they'd become movie stars: silk shirts, sourced from Hollywood friends, dark sunglasses, big fat cigars. Or maybe hillbillies. Or pistol-wielding toughs. "We were children at play," recalled a newcomer, nicknamed Tex by old George Spahn, "living the fantasies we made."[21]

~

A sprawling literature examines the fantasies we make, the positions we take within different social situations, positions that too often obligate those we love most to defend or attack or retreat. And for what? When it comes to sex and love, or happiness and contentment, or career and sense of purpose, why do we live our lives through roles not of our own making? Roles that keep us from authentic experiences? Why play such games?[22]

As a metaphor, "the game" feels intuitive to most Westerners. It conjures a common-sense perspective: a world inhabited by winners and losers, or protagonists and opponents, as well as rules and objectives and strategies. It reduces, purposefully (if not always usefully), the messiness of life into a series of transactions. The healthy analytical person, argued Eric Berne in the bestselling *Games People Play* (1964), may parse social life as nothing more than a discrete number of procedures, operations, rituals, and pastimes. He defines a game as "a recurring set of transactions, often repetitious, superficially plausible, *with a concealed motivation*; or more colloquially, a series of moves with a snare, or 'gimmick.'"[23]

So games are not necessarily fun, and in fact, often cause pain. And they obscure our hidden desires and drives. Surely you see the problem here. We believe ourselves to be fully conscious agents, but as soon as we insert ourselves into a social situation, we begin playacting roles—almost as if we were on stage—conditioned by deeply held psychological needs, healthy or otherwise.

Healing begins when we recognize these dynamics, these games. Berne helpfully provides a thesaurus of common ones. There's the "Schlemiel" (a Yiddish word for an oaf): the clumsy guest who spills wine on the hostess, and with his profuse, abject apologies checkmates the host into forgiving him. "Since I'm polite," this boils down to, "you have to be polite, too"—a manifestation of anal regression. There's "The Stocking Game": the woman who in a social setting bends over to remark on a run in her stocking, and in so doing titillates the men (and angers the women). With her next move she scolds the perverts, or pleads ignorance to the prudes who have taken umbrage. If you do not recognize yourself in those games, perhaps consider a few others: there's the "Look How Hard I Tried," the "Sweetheart," the "They'll Be Glad They Knew Me," the "Frigid Woman," among others.

How do you escape a situation, Berne asks, where "human life is mainly a process of filling in time until the arrival of death, or Santa Claus, with very little choice, if any, of what kind of business one is going to transact during the long wait?"[24] How do you transcend the reality of culture—of the species? Is it possible to experience a life unmediated?[25]

Assembled in a ritual circle, Charlie and friends began howling and screaming and yowling and screeching—"a kind of tension release," in Little Paul's interpretation, "a collective purging of the soul"—until the sounds subsided. Holding hands, the group rocked back and forth as one. As one they removed their clothes. As one, they made love.[26]

The commune played other games, too. Leslie Van Houten has described a less ritualized one where Charlie mirrored your movements. He'd place himself in front of you, reflecting your expression, then raising his right hand as you raised your left, now moving his left hand as you moved your right. The mirror game worked to break down conceptions of self and time, Leslie concluded years later. "The whole idea was to let time disappear, there was no time—we're all living in Now," she said. "Now is the only time. See at first, the Magical Mystery Tour was that we'd all be cowboys, or gypsies, pirates—every day it was to wear a different role so that we could get more *out* of ourselves."[27]

In communes throughout North America, members playacted similar games of their own devising as a means to reconnect with lives unmediated by the bonds of family and society. At the Hog Farm, where Dianne Lake's family lived, commune members held theme days for pretend play and fantasy; more serious settlements held workshops or seminars. Music-making and hallucinogen-taking threaded together people and their projects. Each seemed, in its own way, to reveal the hidden links among all living things.[28]

Many of the people now living at Spahn Movie Ranch had been attempting to escape the games we call "family" or "school" or "work" long before meeting Charlie. Steve Grogan, later renamed Clem, for instance, had been camping at the Spahn Movie Ranch when the group arrived. A talented singer and guitarist, he'd left home at fifteen years old. At a parole hearing in 1981, Clem recalled a pre-Manson life taking drugs and experimenting with Buddhism and meditation in order to elude the "plastic" life of his parents: "It was just go to work, you die and you're buried and that was it."

Before settling at Spahn, the teenager visited monasteries, as well as encounter therapy groups and other communes. "I'd learn what they had to say," Grogan recalled. "I was constantly programming myself to different teachings and things like that. Basic format of all those teachings is that you have to unlearn all that you have been programmed in the past so you become in contact with your true self."[29]

April 1968 to September 1968 83

~

"I don't think it's normal, it's normal to have a self," Manson would later say.³⁰ "If you don't have a self then you don't have any problems, but you become everything around you. In other words, if you're out in the woods or you're up in a cabin like that, somewhere like that, and you don't have no external self programming—like TV or radio or friends, or you know something like that— you just automatically pick up everything. You know where the dogs [are] at all time[s]. You know where the birds are. Everything becomes a part of you, man. When everything becomes a part of you, you become a part of everything. You really wake up the God that's inside of you."³¹

~

Around this time, a young man arrived who could murder that God inside himself, incarnating (or at least impersonating) ego death. Brooks Poston sometimes crashed at the Will Rogers house; he seems to have met Dennis before joining Charlie's group. (So did another young guy named Charles Watson, the one George nicknamed Tex, an ex-high school-football-player-turned-small-time-drugdealer from Denton, Texas who had been playing a game called "Middle-Class Drop-Out."³²)

Brooks played guitar well, and could put himself into a catatonic state, apparently at will. One day, the story goes, Charlie told him to die. And he did. (If it matters, this happened sometime in 1969, eight or so months on from the period under discussion here.) For four days and four nights, commune members cared for Brooks, cleaning and tending him. And on the fifth day, Charlie commanded him to rise*. And he did.³³

~

So many accounts of this summer suggest the stirrings of some occult admixture comprising a retreat into childhood and acid dreams, eastern philosophies and pop psychologies. Turn off your mind, so to speak, relax—float downstream. Come to the Now. Look at your game, girl, as Charlie's most well-known song instructs. Little Paul later referred to such moments as "group-therapy sessions."³⁴ And truly they seem to have been: reflections of a broader impulse to

---

* The story that Ed Sanders heard, and many other later reproduced, has an additional twist. At first, Brooks would not rise. So Charlie placed his personal vest underneath the slumbering twenty-year-old and Brooks, not wanting to soil the vest, awoke

travel beneath the surface of the psyche, to discover—and then work—the levers of the self.

Were the sessions at Spahn Move Ranch more extreme than elsewhere? Consider the following case study of a woman diagnosed with frigidity in the early 1960s. "Since girlhood, the patient had been frightened of sex and later had intercourse as a marital duty," wrote Thomas M. Ling and John Buckman in the *Psychedelic Review*, at the time of publication in 1964, still a relatively straitlaced academic journal. She was "fond" of her husband, and their relationship during the daylight hours had proved largely "harmonious." (And the husband? He of course remained "fully potent, successful in his profession, in love with his wife.") Sessions with a psychiatrist had not helped; a gynecologist had pronounced her "physically normal."

After a few false starts, a regimen of LSD (from fifty to eighty micrograms, injected intramuscularly) and Ritalin (from ten to twenty milligrams, injected intravenously) produced remarkable effects. Though initial injections induced depression and anxiety, a breakthrough soon arrived:

> After the next injection of Ritalin, I pictured my father as a young man who rejected me. I felt disappointed, bitter and resentful. I could not understand why he did not love me. Then I seemed to travel backwards in time to a point where I had idolized him and felt possessive. My conscious mind prompted me that sex came into this and, at the same time, I knew it was because he was a man that this love was so important, but adult sexuality was not involved.[35]

Over five subsequent sessions, the woman recalled deeply buried emotions and feelings, imagining her father's disapproval of her as an infant, remembering a confusing encounter with a beloved uncle, and rediscovering joy and excitement in her body, now beginning to thaw.

The so-called frigidity had been "fully relieved" following the sessions, with success (defined as experiencing "a full and completely satisfying vaginal orgasm on every occasion") attained. "Her husband reports that the patient is a much happier and more relaxed person," the authors gush, "and that their sexual life has been revolutionized so that the marriage is now outstandingly happy."

Do not take this example to be exculpatory, as a kind of crude whataboutism, suggesting that everyone was doing strange things at this time. Instead consider just how many disparate strands of thought had to have been knotted together for this case study to "make sense": the psychoanalytic diagnosis, which undergirds a pharmaceutical intervention, required by normative expectations around the position of "wife" within mid-century American society, held in tensegrity by a thoroughgoing misogyny masquerading as medical expertise.

To put things more plainly: to believe that a woman who doesn't like sex with her husband should be fixed with drugs may also require us to believe that much of our lives have been shaped by an unconscious desire to sleep with our parents. Of course, who's to say that isn't true?

~

In the backpages of the *Berkeley Barb* or the *LA Free Press*, we might imagine an advertisement placed in the early months of 1968 at fifty cents per line (minimum charge of one dollar):

DRUMMER AND SEEKER –
Creatively stifled, seeking
new father, for love—direction.
WILL ROGERS CABIN. D. W.

~

And if we cannot place advertisements in the paper seeking what we need, that's because our desires often remain hidden until the moment they reveal themselves. At least that seems to be the logic underpinning much of the twentieth century in the West.

In its archetypical form, we find that logic embedded within the psychoanalytic encounter between analyst and analysand. Like all such logics, this one presents itself as universal and timeless, as transcending culture. But how long had analysts been parsing our unhidden drives and unconscious motivations? As Charlie mirrored Leslie's movements, psychoanalysis only just passed its half-century mark—if this practice were a man, he would have been in the prime of his genital stage.

But once you begin looking, you find that logic everywhere, and not just in psychoanalysis. We find it expressed as simply a consequence of modern life, in the notion that real truths remain hidden deep underground, waiting far beneath the surface of reality to be parsed. We find that logic expressed as an impulse toward interpretation, toward "reading between the lines," the primary method by which we moderns force *what's-really-going-on* to stand stark naked in the bracing light of truth.

Consider the phenomenon of "hidden persuaders," to use Vance Packard's felicitous phrasing. Hidden persuaders use the mass media to instill in us unbidden desires and drives to buy, buy, buy! Packard peoples his America of the 1950s with manipulators employing "ingenious techniques" and "mass psychoanalysis." "These depth manipulators are, in their operations, beneath the surface of conscious life," Packard prefaced *The Hidden Persuaders* (1957), "starting to acquire a power of persuasion that is becoming a matter of justifiable public scrutiny and concern."[36] The cover to my paperback edition from 1970—the book's fortieth printing—depicts a fish hook baited with a bright red cherry.

Postwar Americans became increasingly aware that manipulators working on our unconscious drives do so in plain sight. Such people once worked under the cloak of darkness, their plots to usurp our sovereignty revealed only at the very moment when, for instance, the assassin's knife flashed in the public square.[37] Now their wickedness stares us in the face. And so this situation required new techniques for revealing the truth, for parsing the depths roiling beneath the placid surface, for reading between the lines.

Indeed, we must keep sharply honed our exegetical skills. Have a look at your copy of Bob Dylan's *Bringing It All Back Home* (1965). The cover, littered with carefully arranged artifacts (not unlike Chapman's tableau at the YMCA), begs to be interpreted and analyzed. Now retrieve your first pressing of Dylan's *John Wesley Harding* (1967). Look closely and you may find images hidden in the bark of a tree. "The most obvious group of faces becomes apparent when the cover is turned upside down; at the top of the tree, in the lighter area, are at least seven faces," reported *Rolling Stone*. "By turning the cover in other directions, faces can be spotted near elbows, bushes and in the lining of coats."

Among these seven, do you see four Beatles? Many people did. How could they not? Just like when people see in a slice of burnt toast the face of Jesus Christ, or in a water stain, the Virgin Mary. Or when you are lying in the grass, and the cumulus billowing of clouds takes the shape of a loved one. The term for this phenomenon is pareidolia, apparently a universal trait of the species. Human beings, Western psychologists say, seek patterns, naturally finding order where none exists.

The photographer would not confirm or deny the existence of the faces. "It's like Dylan," he said, "very mystical."[38]

~

Why play this game? Why hide pop stars in the trees?

The paranoiac realizes that, in the pop world, something more insidious might be going on. "Communism, Hypnotism and the Beatles" (1965), published by the Rev. David A Noebel and his Christian Crusade Publications, outlined one potential use of recordings. "The communists, through their scientists, educators and entertainers, have contrived an elaborate, calculating and scientific technique directed at rendering a generation of American youth useful through nerve-jamming, mental deterioration and retardation."[39]

Too often rock's apologists, in mocking the content of these evangelical interpretations, ignore the significance of their methods, their style of argumentation. Noebel erects his analysis on close textual readings of commercially sold songs, taking as scaffolding now-forgotten forms of cold war knowledge about "menticide" and the "health" of the body politic. Recordings for young children, especially folk music records, Noebel claims, prepare them for later "nerve-jamming": softening their awareness of hypnotic techniques, even seeding Pavlovian mechanisms in these little sleeper agents. Dr. William J. Bryan noted that such records are "breeding a tremendous race of people who are going to be mentally ill—it's terrible, really horrible, the scope of this thing is fantastic—this is for the age group 2 to 5."[40] Suitably softened by Folkways recordings, the teenager now encounters Beatles recordings (as well as other teenybopper fare). These "create in him mental illness through artificial neurosis and prepare him for riot and ultimately revolution in order to destroy our American form of government and the basic Christian principles governing our way of life."[41]

But all is not lost. And forewarned is forearmed, because "the devices used in these records are so subtle," as Noebel quoted another expert saying, "that they very well may pass inspection by a well-meaning committee of physicians untrained in hypnosis, brainwashing and other such fields."[42] If we begin subjecting pop music recordings to close and suspicious readings, we can reveal the messages hidden within—and in so doing, protect our society from the coming revolution.

~

On 30 May, the Beatles began working on "Revolution," the first song they would record for an album tentatively titled, *A Doll's House*. They devoted June to this song, as well as to Paul's ballad, "Blackbird" and John's musique concrète "Revolution 9." (Ringo's "Don't Pass Me By," though it doesn't quite fit into our book's narrative, figures somewhere in this first month as well.) Then from 16 to 19 July, a second auspicious run: the Beatles begin work on "Cry Baby Cry," "Sexy Sadie," and "Helter Skelter."[43]

In September, they recorded "I Will" for the album now titled *The Beatles*, its packaging to be designed by Richard Hamilton. "Your song will fill the air!" sings Paul. "Sing it loud, so I can hear you!"

The Beatles recorded "Honey Pie" two weeks before the sessions concluded in October. "Sail across the Atlantic," Paul implored. "And be where you belong!"

IN THE SUMMER OF 1968, Charlie taught Dennis to play guitar. And he taught him a dance, called The Inhibition. "You have to imagine you're a frozen man and the ice is thawing out," Dennis told journalist David Griffiths, describing the dance later that year. "Start with your fingertips, then all the rest of you, then you extend it to a feeling that the whole universe is thawing out [. . .]."[44]

Charlie played guitar with Dennis. Dennis introduced Charlie to his friends. A few girls lived in the big log cabin at 14400 Sunset Boulevard. The others came with Charlie to visit from time to time. Dennis came to view Charlie as his guru: "His mother was a hooker, his father was a gangster, he'd drifted into crime but when I met him I found he had great musical ideas," said Dennis in that same 1968 interview. "We're writing songs together now. He's dumb, in some ways, but I accept his approach and have learnt from him." Dennis called him the Wizard.[45]

Who visited Dennis's home during this period and became acquainted with Charlie and the girls? How far did Dennis integrate Charlie into the Hollywood scene? Actor Michael Caine remembers meeting Manson at singer Mama Cass's home, a popular party pad for the new rock elite and their hangers-on just down the road from Dennis.[46] That night celebrity hairdresser Jay Sebring had attended with his ex-paramour, Sharon Tate, though their entourage left before Manson's arrived. Neil Young met Manson a few times, too. Neil played guitar with him, accompanying Charlie's strange sing-song improvisations.*

Though for many of the visitors to the Will Rogers house that summer, music would not be the main draw. The majority of Dennis's guests saw the girls as "a novelty act, a singing family group led by Charlie who loved sex and drugs," as Dianne later recalled, "and whatever misgivings they may have had about Charlie didn't stop them from joining in too."[47]

---

* Neil Young's testimony is not entirely reliable. In his autobiography, the songwriter recalls meeting Linda Kasabian, who wouldn't join the group until July of the following year. Though if you remember the Sixties, you weren't there, right?

~

Sex and drugs, sometimes shorn of rock 'n' roll. As the party at Dennis's home went on, Roman Polanski promoted his new film. "*Rosemary's Baby* is really one of the most remarkable films of the year, I think," Hugh Hefner tells Polanski in an interview taped at the Playboy Club in London. "Do you think that this trend we see going on right now—toward more boldness in regards to sex—is going to continue?"[48]

Roman thinks so; after all, civilization develops in cycles. We are perhaps coming out of a particularly prudish period. He gestures toward Sharon, prompting a story that sounds exaggerated about an arrest in Italy over the length of a skirt. Tate, preternaturally languid, cigarette in hand, angular limbs and tabescent cheeks all honed to a knife's edge, tells the story. And she's fine with nudity in film, by the way, though "if it's contrived, then it becomes vulgar."

The conversation next turns to violence. "I don't think that violence [on film] can make any harm to anyone," Roman says. Those who claim simulated violence may lead to real violence don't understand what they are talking about: "I don't believe in, 'Monkey see, monkey do.'"

Sociologists are now saying that cinematic violence, Hugh prompts, may in fact serve as a form of catharsis for viewers. "I'm positive, I'm positive!" Roman agrees, gesturing with his hands, pretty Sharon gazing at him the entire time. "I tell you what is really dangerous, and what kind of violence can inspire violence, it's the sterilized, the Hollywood type of violence. In typical Hollywood Western, they excite you during an hour and a half—they *tease* you against this bad man who beats everybody—he's so *nasty*, and you cannot *stand* him anymore. And at the last moment, a good man with [a] white hat comes and draws and bumps him off—without any blood, it's [a] *clean job*—and somehow subconsciously it develops in your brain [the] idea that somebody bothers you, then you can take judgment upon him, and very easy you can get rid of him without any blood, or convulsions, without vomiting"—Sharon for a moment looks away, sips from her tumbler, then resumes her gaze as the soliloquizing continues—"I saw war, I saw violence, I saw all of the things, they didn't make *me* more violent."

Roman drones on. (He doesn't mind blood in film, it is just "paint.") Sharon keeps observing him. (The violent scenes in his films are, for him, "amusements.")

"Violence in our society has an old history, in any Catholic School you see a man nailed to the Cross, with blood dripping from His side and from His head"—now Roman is speaking of Jesus Christ, the Son of God—"the most popular book, especially in this country, is the Bible, and every second page you have unbelievable descriptions of violence—you know?—and so I do not believe that cinema can make a little bit more."

"And nudity," Sharon contributes.

At last Roman pauses to take a sip from his tumbler, and Hugh launches into a bland rap about how sex, and love, and nudity, and *sex*, are just about the most beautiful things in the world, man, just really beautiful. The Playboy Bunnies keep circulating, and the guests clink glasses, and the camera rolls on.

~

At 14400 Sunset Boulevard, the clinking of glasses inevitably gave way to soft embraces. In his memoir, Mike Love claimed he met Manson just once, going with fellow Beach Boy Bruce Johnston to check out the singer Dennis had been talking about signing to Brother Records. The girls cooked dinner with food scrounged from the bins behind a supermarket in Pacific Palisades; and then afterward, Manson convened the group in the large, wood-paneled den. Someone turned on a strobe light, illuminating girls supine, draped across the room, unclothed.

"He started passing out LSD tablets and orchestrating sex partners," Love wrote. "I love the female form, but this was too much even for me. The place was hot and claustrophobic, so I walked out to take a shower."

Squeaky appeared, the siren sent to coax Love back to the den. Then Manson walked in.

"You can't do that," he said.

"Excuse me?"

"You can't leave the group."

"I'm really sorry, Charlie," Love remembered saying. "But Bruce and I have to get back to the studio."[49]

Love also explains that Dennis brought Charlie into the Beach Boys offices and arranged a recording date at Brian's home studio in Bel Air. He also paid for dental work and other medical bills, among other things, spending nearly one-hundred-thousand dollars. At some point, Dennis brought one of Charlie's songs to the group, "Cease to Exist," too, which the Beach Boys rearranged and recorded. All this happened, more or less, though as we will see, Love may have confused parts of the timeline.*

---

* Love suggests Dennis had contact with the group until August 1968, and that the recording session at Brian's house occurred in July of that year. Dianne Lake's memoir places an incident with a knife

And the group's mythology continued to grow. Charlie had postulated an exciting, lavish life for the group seemingly out of thin air. The girls began taking Dennis's Rolls Royce out to scrounge food from supermarkets, a practice commemorated in a new song, "Garbage Dump." And they rubbed shoulders with real celebrities. Several girls had previous brushes with this crowd. Catherine Gillies, nicknamed Capistrano or Cappy, for instance, had previously crashed with the Buffalo Springfield. But now some people in the Hollywood scene thought members of the commune might actually become stars.

"They're space ladies," Dennis would tell that journalist, Griffiths. "And they'd make a great group. I'm thinking of launching them as the Family Gems."[50] The group grew to about thirty or so souls, with several bringing new musical skills. The young woman named Gypsy (t/n Catherine Share) played violin; the young man named Clem (t/n Steve Grogan) played guitar and sang. Neil Young apparently pitched Manson to his label. "I told Mo Ostin about him, [at] Warner Brothers—'This guy is unbelievable'—he makes up the songs as he goes along, and they're all good."[51]

Nothing came of that alleged conversation. But Young has long remained consistent in his assessment of Manson. "He's like one of the main movers and shakers of time—when you look back at Jesus and all these people, Charlie was like that," Young later said. "But he was kind of . . . skewed. You can tell by reading his words. He's real smart. He's very deceptive, though. Tricky. Confuses you."[52]

---

at Brian's house within this timeline as well. Beach Boys recording engineer Stephen Desper suggests the visit to Brian's home studio occurred either nine or twelve months later. Because the later 1969 date makes for a more dramatic narrative arc, we will wait until Chapter Five to hear the story of this incident.

More generally speaking, the sequence of events in this time period has given rise to confusion. In *Helter Skelter*, Vincent Bugliosi claims that Dennis had little or no contact with the group between August 1968 and August 1969, when Manson reappeared to threaten him and his family. Bugliosi also echoes the most common version of How The Beach Boy Met The Murderer, a story also found in accounts by Ed Sanders and Dianne Lake. Dennis picked up hitch-hiking Katie (t/n Pat) and Ella Jo in April. Hours later, Charlie appeared—and almost immediately, brought Dennis under his sway. (Bugliosi doesn't mention the trip to Lake Havasu, a detail found only in the Lake memoir.)

Yet this contradicts the story Dennis himself told the Record Mirror in December 1968, long before he had any reason to revise descriptions of his recent exploits: "I went up into the mountains with my houseboy to take an LSD trip. We met two girls hitch-hiking. One of them was pregnant. We gave them a lift, and a purse was left in the car. About a month later, near Malibu, I saw the pregnant girl again, only this time she'd had her baby. I was overjoyed for her and it was through her that I met all the other girls. I told them about our involvement with the Maharishi and they told me they too had a guru, a guy named Charlie who'd recently come out of jail after 12 years."

No other account includes the details about the purse, the houseboy, or the month-long pause—most suggest, as I have in the opening to this chapter, that Dennis came home to the ominous black bus the very night he met the girls. There's no documentary evidence that either girl was pregnant at this time. Mother Mary would give birth in early April, allegedly before Dennis met the group; Sexy Sadie would give birth in early October, well after.

It's difficult, getting a handle on what is fact, and what is fiction, especially when it comes to stories from this period. We must remember that these people were living through an age in which the ground was shifting and the foundations were shaking.[53] It seems likely that more people in the Los Angeles area knew Crazy Charlie and the girls than later let on. The music and film scenes had started converging. And for a brief moment, musicians—not film actors—became the real rock stars in New Hollywood.

This period has given rise to an alternate theory about the violence to come—that Charlie's rejection by the beautiful people spurred his murderous rage. We can call this the Rejection Hypothesis. Author Wenzell Brown gives this thesis supernatural contours in his pulpy *Possess and Conquer* (1975). Here's how Brown narrates what might have happened in a thinly veiled, wholly inaccurate, retelling.

A bearded, white-robed hippie leads his dastardly flock of brainwashed girls up to a palatial estate. Chuck Boleyn (a thinly disguised Charles Manson) alongside Flora (a Sadie character) and the other girls have just left Stallion City (Spahn Ranch) for the home of starlet Kitty Moore (Sharon Tate) and European *artiste* Wolf Vedder (Roman Polanski).

These self-important Hollywood elites have previously rejected Chuck and his group. Now the commune returns, seemingly to take their revenge.

"What do you want? Money? Jewels?" Kitty asks them, as the knife-wielding group rampages through the home.

"No, only the truth," Chuck replies.[54]

News of the massacre occupies front pages throughout the United States for weeks. But only one journalist, in Brown's sci-fi retelling of the story, catches on to the true meaning of the killings: "He wondered in print whether Boleyn was a man at all. Could he not be an extraterrestrial being from outer space, the forerunner of some destructive horde who would overrun and destroy the earth? People mocked at the idea and called it a comic-strip gimmick. Yet, even so, a cold wind of fear belied their laughter."[55]

All major acts of American violence, in Wenzell Brown's book, from the Tate-LaBianca killings, to the Texas State clocktower sniper, to the cruelty of sadistic bikers, can be traced to aliens who come back to earth with astronauts from the July 1969 Apollo moon landing. These shapeshifting extraterrestrials commit random acts of spectacular violence in order to induce widespread panic, to make Americans feel as if their society is coming apart at the seams. As the situation grows bleaker, a shadowy propaganda group begins broadcasting messages hypnotic in their perverse cheerfulness: "Do not resist. If you are marked for death, you will die. Your fate has already been established. Do not stand in the road of progress; do not seek to avoid the inevitable."

And then, as Brown narrates: "In the background, mingled with the clash of music, issued another message, which not all could hear: 'Destroy your neighbor. Kill—kill—kill.'"[56]

While we should not make too much of some lurid paperback, let us note that in attributing the violence of the 1960s to extraterrestrials—that is, to anything *but* the material conditions of our own world—this narration could not be more American. It's a history of violence that is, quite literally, not of this world. Chuck Boleyn (t/n Charles Manson) provides a mere vessel for an irrational sadism. But who can actually author such cruelty? No one, Brown suggested, produced by American society. No one of this earth.

~

Consider another narration, not of this earth, a strange piece of fanfiction more recently posted on a Beach Boys message board.[57] In 1966, Charlie leaves prison and almost immediately bumps into producer Terry Melcher. Come on down to Los Angeles, Terry tells him, make a demo—and meet the Beach Boys. That's how Charlie ended up at the sessions for "Good Vibrations." Good vibes, acid, religion, peace: the ex-con caught on quick, and then set to working on the psychologically fragile Brian.

Fanfic Charlie interpreted the Bible for Brian. The five angels in the ninth chapter of the Book of Revelation who become four? "That's the Beach Boys, man. When you quit touring, they became four!" The biblical "faces of men, but hair of women?" "That's the long hair of the Beach Boys!"

As Charlie enters the group's inner circle, Brian comes increasingly under his sway. When the group tours Europe in early 1966, Charlie and Brian stay in Los Angeles. A concept album soon begins taking shape. Here are the song titles: "Heroes & Villains & Hippies & Pigs" and "Illegitimate Child is the Father to the Charlie" and "Surf's Up, It's Charlie Time" and "Cease to Exist." Horrified by this new, experimental direction, the Beach Boys brain trust bans Charlie from Brian's home.

And so Charlie turns to Apple Records. Beatle Paul produces the diminutive American, recording a single, "Cease to Exist" b/w a cover of "Helter Skelter." But when new manager Allen Klein arrives, Charlie's singing career comes to an end. The recording remains in the vault. Only "a few test pressings of Charlie's single survive," the fanfic reimagining concludes, "and fetch very high prices at rock auctions."

~

"Charlie never had a musical bone in his body," Dennis Wilson allegedly told Vincent Bugliosi. The two would "sing and talk, Dennis said, while the girls cleaned house, cooked, and catered to their needs." And yet he pitched Charlie to his friends—and soon even set up a recording date.

"Looking back on his involvement with the Family," Bugliosi related in *Helter Skelter*, "Dennis told me: 'I'm the luckiest guy in the world, because I got off only losing my money.'"[58]

~

When you love, you don't count the cost.[59] At some point in August, Tex and Clem totaled Dennis's Ferrari 275 GTB. They walked away unscathed. But, some authors would suggest, this was the final straw for Dennis. The current location of the vehicle may be unknown.

~

Author Wenzell Brown dedicated *Possess and Conqueror* to Hans Stefan Santesson (1914–75), author, editor of fantasy and science fiction, and board member and one-time president of the Society for the Investigation of the Unexplained (SITU).

"It is our credo that 'Science is the pursuit of the Unknown,'" founder Ivan Sanderson wrote in the Society's Newsletter No. 1 (May 1967), "and it is, therefore, the frontiers and borderlands of both recorded facts and of novel inquiry that are of primary interest to us."[60]

ON THE EIGHTH OF AUGUST, Charlie and the girls arrived at Gold Star Studios for a recording date. Dennis's good friend Gregg Jakobson organized the session, intended to show the brothers Beach Boy what Charlie could do. The commune brought a number of new songs. The girls had started backing Charlie in loose, sing-song unison sometime during that first summer at the Spahn Movie Ranch.

Some of the new songs chronicled the commune's exploits. "Garbage Dump" described dumpster-diving for discarded food behind grocery stores, its loose repetitive verses, jokey interjections, and Charlie's faux twang suggesting an origin in Manson's half-improvised rap-singing. Other songs reflected a new philosophical turn. "Cease to Exist," like its older counterpart in the commune's repertoire, "Ego Is A Too Much Thing," critiqued how society, family, and media programs us to think and behave in particular ways.

Loosen the grip: let go. Like when Paul Watkins rejoined the group in July, after taking off for a few months to housesit up in the mountains. Stop running around looking for *something*, Charlie advised him. What do you *have* to do, man? The point is, there's nothing *to* do. Dig?[61]

For some reason, Watkins doesn't mention this August 1968 recording studio visit in his memoir. Then again, it can be difficult to keep track of all these different sessions; at some point someone needs to disentangle all the contradictory evidence about these recording dates.[62] In a paragraph or so we will read Lynette Fromme's description of the session that I'm placing at Gold Star Studio in August 1968. Squeaky remembers the session having been organized by "a record producer," as having been "the third or fourth time [Charlie] had been invited by different producers to do this," and as occurring when the group lived "at the ranch" as well as "a year before the desert music."

The "record producer" could be Gregg Jakobson, though would this have been the third or fourth recording date? (It would have only in the unlikely event that Manson recorded at Brian Wilson's house in July 1968.[63]) The larger group lived at Spahn Movie Ranch from May to October 1968, then from March to September 1969; the "desert songs" would be written between November 1968 and January 1969.[64] If this session happened a "a year before the desert music," where does that leave matters? It's unclear.

In any case, here's the recording date Squeaky describes, which may (or may not) have occurred in August 1968. On the night of the session, Charlie instructed the whole group—some two dozen people—to come along. "It was unreal": they filled the bus, all wearing colorful costumes and bearing musical instruments. Not everyone could perform as part of a group; they'd only just started singing together for fun a few months earlier. The black bus pulled up to the curb at 6252 Santa Monica Boulevard, and its occupants spilled out. Fromme invites us to imagine what the engineers—"two balding technicians"—thought.

They had prepared to record a single, scruffy guy and his guitar. "Charlie and the producer cajoled them while Bobby and Clem positioned extra microphones for a circle like we had at home."

And now Fromme provides the most vivid description on record of what Charlie and the commune must have sounded like in the summer of 1968—what Neil Young, Dennis Wilson, Terry Melcher, Mama Cass, and anyone else who may (or may not) have encountered them would have heard during the summer months of 1968. "Clem, Bobby, and Charlie played, as always, some good instrumentals. Mary's flute and Gypsy's violin were not half bad, and the elephant calls from Paul's french horn roamed a range between interesting and strange, but all that in combination with Snake on the potato flute and several of us on knives and spoons created a cacophonous conglomeration only barely related to music. The technicians blanched, but Charlie joked the whole time. On his suggestion that we kick back and relax, we took deep breaths, letting them out slowly and then with sound. Behind closed lids, we saw sound take shape and color, rise and weave, branch and open, then fall together in the best harmony of the evening."[65]

~

Sound's capacity to take shape and color, to rise and weave and branch and open, to enable us to fall *together* as one: isn't that the power of music? And the power of popular music in particular?

In its most extreme form, this capacity can be found in a hippie exploitation film, *Wild In The Streets* (1968), that depicted the unlikely political career of a young rock singer named Max Frost. We meet Frost campaigning for a Kennedy-esque politician running on a platform to lower the voting age to eighteen. This tanned faux Kennedy is no dummy: he realizes that by harnessing the music of young people, he can direct their power. But a power-hungry Frost and his group hijack the campaign with a song that calls for lowering the voting age to *fourteen*. Yellow-bellied politicians cave to their demands, and this newly empowered adolescent voting bloc supports Frost and his friends, allowing a commune of Hollywood hangers-on to infiltrate the United States government. Before long, Frost becomes president of the United States. (There's more to it: the new hippie politicians force Congress to lower the minimum age for the presidency, for instance, by dosing that august body with LSD.)

It's a remarkable morality tale about the Youth and a rock 'n' roll Pied Piper who, through carefully constructed songs, does not merely voice the desires of young people, but convenes them as a politically efficacious bloc. Just how unlikely was this dystopian state of affairs?

"Once you've experienced a concert by a group like the Beatles or the Doors, the fascist potential of pop music becomes inescapable," wrote film critic Roger Ebert, reviewing the film in the *Chicago Sun Times*. "There is a primitive force in these mass demonstrations that breaks down individualism and creates a joyous mob."[66]

~

No recordings of the full, joyous mob seem to exist. Or if they do, they haven't been released and probably never will. And even if they do exist, who knows how they would sound to our ears today?

Because I've left out the punchline to Fromme's story. Following the cacophonous conglomeration—after the collective exhale of the commune in full flow, after the subsiding of the last shudders of this musical orgasm—one of the square, middle-aged, balding engineers apparently said:

"Would you do that again? We didn't have a level."[67]

~

Didn't have a level. The punchline works by highlighting the gap between the music-makers and the technicians. Because doesn't the power of rock lie precisely in its capacity to stir our precognitive senses, to give shape to the linguistically inexpressible? Doesn't the music make intuitive sense? Which is not at all the same thing, of course, as making sense.

~

And what had the purpose of these recording sessions even been? In the most authoritative recent accounting of the Manson Family, true-crime author Jeff Guinn has suggested that Dennis and Greg, because they liked hanging out with the young women in the commune, enabled Manson's recording dreams. Jakobson organized the session to "keep Charlie happy, and to get some idea of how his songs might sound on tape," and "the results were listenable but not much more."[68] Manson had been very pleased with the sessions and, according to Guinn, "he offered the tapes to anyone willing to listen and help him get signed to a label. John Phillips of the Mamas and the Papas and mega-agent Rudi Altobelli, whose client list included popular folk singer Buffy Sainte-Marie, both heard the tapes and passed."[69]

And what had Manson felt about the session—and these alleged rejections? "Charlie's faith in himself remained unshaken," Guinn avers. "If people like Phillips and Altobelli turned him down, that reflected poorly on their judgment, not his music. He hung on to the tapes in case anyone else important might be persuaded to listen to them. More than ever, he was determined that Dennis Wilson had to come through for him with Brother Records. They were friends, so Wilson owed it to him."[70]

~

Wilson owed him. By insinuating a cause-and-effect relationship, this device—foreshadowing—prepares the reader for upcoming events and plot twists. The relationship between Charlie and Dennis, the reader now begins to realize, will soon cause problems for Wilson and his friends.

~

Because foreshadowing exercises a powerful effect on readers, authors must take care to use it properly. This device necessarily excises the static surrounding a moment or person or event, leaving an elemental core that leads readers step-by-step along a predetermined pathway prepared by their wily author. In this way foreshadowing strips away the messiness of human experience, as all writing—an exercise in translation from one medium (living our lives) to another (the written word)—must.*

---

* While the notion that the work of an ethnographer represents a form of translation became a major concern within anthropology two decades later, here note an especially intriguing instance of propinquity. At this very moment, and not far from the Spahn Movie Ranch, the University of California Press published undergraduate UCLA anthropology student Carlos Castaneda's ethnography of shamanism, *The Teachings of Don Juan: A Yaqui Way of Knowledge* (1968). As an epigraph, Castaneda invoked the sociologist Georg Simmel. "Nothing more can be attempted than to establish the beginning and the direction of an infinitely long road," Simmel had written in 1950. "The pretension of any systematic and definitive completeness would be, at least, a self-illusion. Perfection can here be obtained by the individual student only in the subjective sense that he communicates everything he has been able to see."

But more pertinent for our purposes is the foreword to *The Teachings of Don Juan* by professional anthropologist Walter Goldschmitt. "This book is both ethnography and allegory," Goldschmitt begins. We know that different orders of reality exist, that different peoples have different gods and different beliefs and different values and so on. But it goes deeper than that. Even "the worlds of different peoples have different shapes," and their "very metaphysical presuppositions differ: space does not conform to Euclidean geometry, time does not form a continuous unidirectional flow, causation does not conform to Aristotelian logic, man is not differentiated from non-man or life from death, as in our world." We cannot but fail in our attempts to understand other worlds, but Castaneda's book, Goldschmitt claims, succeeds in allowing us a glimpse of alternatives.

And that's key. "The central importance of entering into worlds other than our own—and hence of anthropology itself—lies in the fact that the experience leads us to understand that our own world is also a cultural construct," he writes. "By experiencing other worlds, then, we see our own

Here we can use this device to prepare ourselves for what soon will come, in fact, what soon must come, to pass. A week or so after the August recording session, the first full authorized biography of the Beatles appeared on bookstore shelves. Penned by Hunter S. Davies, an intimate of the group, the book went far beyond the usual teenybopper dross found in previous accounts.

Life magazine excerpted *The Beatles* (1968) across two issues. In a lengthy exerpt in the first issue, we learn about the musicians' home life: Cyn trying to give John a line, for instance, when he's looking for a rhyme with "time." We access their experimenting in the recording studio ("they know what they want, even if they can't explain it"). All that studio time comes at an enormous cost, but producer George Martin explains its necessity. "I once saw a film of Picasso at work," the producer tells Davies. "He starts with an idea, then overlays it with something else. Sometimes the original idea can get obliterated."[71]

The second issue of *Life* included a creative photo-essay, inspired by lyrics, from photographer Art Kane. "The voice of the Beatle has now been heard by almost all the young people in the land and it is easily recognized by any adult who harbors one," *Life* editor George P. Hunt noted in his customary introductory editorial. "Art Kane has been more exposed to it than most; he has a son. Anthony, 13, who is a serious student of Beatle lyrics, and Art himself has been a fan from the beginning." How did the veteran photographer prepare for this assignment? You should read the next line, with my added emphases, as an example of foreshadowing. "I took my stack of Beatle records," Art told the editor, "and *I played them steadily in my studio*, at home and beside the pool in the country until *all the lyrics were humming in my head*."[72]

~

Through focused concentration deeper meanings inevitably reveal themselves. Such meanings provide the exegete with material for further interpretation, and possibly even action. This seems to be what happened at the commune, at least according to psychologist Karlene Faith, who befriended Leslie Van Houten in prison and subsequently analyzed Leslie's experiences. The commune, a "tribe of disciples," provided an audience for Manson's circuitous raps and sing-song

---

for what it is and are thereby enabled also to see fleetingly what the real world, the one between our own cultural construct and those other worlds, must in fact be like. Hence the allegory, as well as the ethnography. . . . As in all proper allegory, what one sees lies with the beholder, and needs no exegesis here" (pp. 9–10).

riddles. "If you're looking you'll never find," Faith cites as an example, "don't try to keep up or you'll be left behind."[73]

"Over time his devotees became prepared to live for him, to die for him," the prison psychologist continues, "and if the cosmic forces required it of them, to kill for him, trusting that it would be for the good of humanity just as any good soldier must." And then Faith cites a couplet from this period:

> Thou shalt not kill, said my daddy
>   Mother agreed, as she served a meat patty

~

Read the texts, and take them seriously. That exegetical impulse can also be found across the rock press from this period, as in the following letter from a young person writing to express his gratitude to *Rolling Stone* for printing the lyrics to Beatle songs in a previous issue.

> Sirs:
>
> The excitement of receiving the official words to "I Am The Walrus" was hard to bear. The song is a condensation of the Beatles today, just as "Wear Your Love Like Heaven" is Donovan today. "Walrus" is the transmission of instantaneous awareness from J, P, G, & R to us. This is the state of the world, and the emotion we all feel consciously or unconsciously. Someone has to convey this emotion, and the Beatles do convey it. This, much more than a song or a poem, is a representation of everything that is today.
>
> The bombardment of the world on the individual is so perfectly expressed. I'm crying. [. . .]
>
> No matter how hard we try to remove reality, it is still all around us. If we don't like a song on the radio, we can change the station, but we learn soon that all music is really part of one.
>
> All reality is a reality of one. As in [sic] "A Day In the Life," we are reminded again that "I am he as you are he as you are me and we are all together." Oneness!
>
> [Name withheld]
> Pacifica, California[74]

Feel the letter writer's excitement. That these four British musicians *know* what's going on; that this new magazine, *Rolling Stone*, takes them seriously, printing the lyrics to "Walrus" in full; that his own efforts—to escape the pressures of the past, to efface an unreal reality, to live in the Now—find reflection and affirmation in the lyrics of the biggest musical group in the world.

ALL CHARGES AGAINST THE WITCHES OF MENDOCINO would be dropped on the sixteenth of August. A few weeks later, Sadie Mae gave birth to the group's second child, christened Zezozose Zadfrack. By then the group had returned to the Spahn Movie Ranch. Dennis had moved out of 14400 Sunset Boulevard.

"Someone at Brother Records checked Manson's background and discovered his criminal past," Mike Love later wrote, "and our accountants were raising flags about unexplained expenditures on Dennis's charge card."[75] The accountants had been giving each of the Beach Boys a set allowance at this time; despite selling millions of records, they were nearly completely broke. Though this explanation doesn't quite make sense. After all, Dennis had known about Charlie's criminal past; Manson's rapsheet was part of his appeal. Or maybe Charlie somehow scared Dennis, causing him to cut ties with the group? At least one account suggests that Manson began preaching a more apocalyptic vision at this point, though most authors place this turn later.[76] Perhaps the freaky lifestyle freaked out the Beach Boy, so he moved out of Will Rogers' old house and had a manager evict the group. Though how scared could Dennis have been? As we will see, he and his friends continued to visit the commune, and the Beach Boys spent four days that September recording one of Charlie's songs, "Cease to Exist," revised to "Never Learn Not To Love."[77]

And firsthand accounts from members of the commune suggest another set of motivations. "He was gonna just drop everything and come and be with us—whether it was living in a tent, or whatever," Sandra Good later remembered. "And his brothers basically said, 'You know, you're bound by contract, and if you renege we're gonna have you committed. We're gonna get psychiatric testimony that you've flipped your lid, and so you're a slave to this contract,' and that was that. Dennis loved Charlie. Actually, I don't think his brothers cared too much for us. Their wives were kind of threatened by us. We weren't out to steal anybody's boyfriend or husband, but they were threatened by our overall lifestyle. But we got along with everybody, actually."[78]

~

I'm crying.

1 Peace.

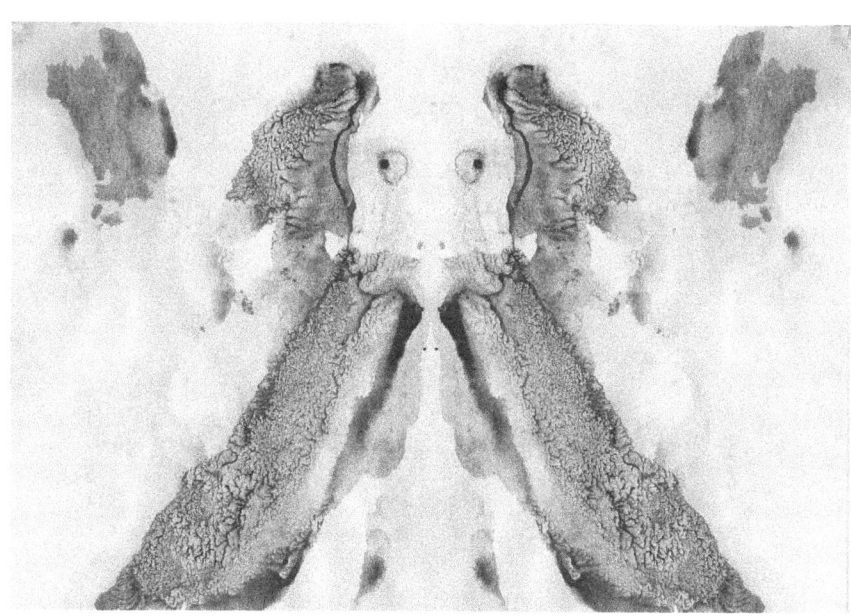

2 Inkblot.

3 "The Hanged Man."

4 Barker Ranch in Death Valley.

5 Exhibit 228.

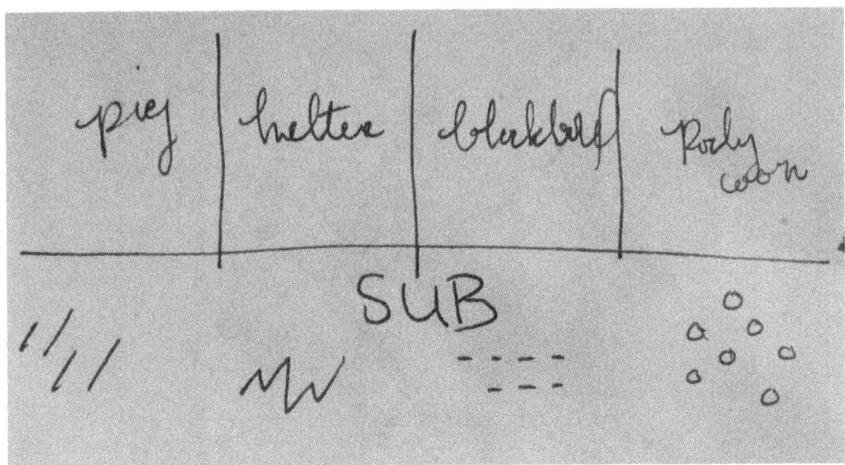

6 Manson analyzes the White Album.

In *Rolling Stone* (June 25, 1970, p. 36), Charlie "started drawing some lines on the back of a sheet of white paper, three vertical lines and one horizontal line. In the bottom area he writes the word SUB." He populated the columns with song titles: "Pig[gies]," "Helter [Skelter]," "Blackbird," and "Rocky [Rac]coon." He then made marks below: slashes, a zigzagged line, dashes, small circles.

"This bottom part is the subconscious," Charlie explains. "At the end of each song there is a little tag piece on it, a couple of notes. Or like in 'Piggies' there's 'oink, oink, oink.' Just these couple of sounds. And all these sounds are repeated in 'Revolution 9.' Like in 'Revolution 9,' all these pieces are fitted together and they predict the violent overthrow of the white man." Did the Beatles know not what they were doing? "I think it's a subconscious thing," Charlie answered. "I don't know whether they did or not. But it's there. It's an association in the subconscious. This music is bringing on the revolution, the unorganized overthrow of the Establishment. The Beatles know in the sense that the subconscious knows."

7 "Who Are These People?"

8 "Secret Pictures."

"Usually you are shown a landscape with trees, bushes, flowers and other bits of nature. The caption reads something like this: 'Concealed somewhere in this picture is a donkey pulling a cart with a boy in it. Can you find them?' Try as you might, usually you could not find the hidden picture until you turned a page farther back in the magazine which would reveal how cleverly the artist had hidden it from us. If we study the landscape we realize that the whole picture was painted in such a way as to conceal the real picture within, and once we see the 'real picture,' it stands out like the proverbial painful digit." Gary Allen, *None Dare Call It Conspiracy* (1971, p. 7).

4

October 1968 to July 1969

or, Rumor's Children

ON ALL HALLOW'S EVE Charlie and the group left the Spahn Movie Ranch. Capistrano, t/n Catherine Gillies, that young woman who used to hang with the Buffalo Springfield, knew a place in Death Valley where they could crash.

Manson had long planned this move to the desert, perhaps since that first trip through the California redwoods in the summer of 1967. The group needed space: for living, and for making music, and for Charlie to write new songs. Cappy's grandmother owned a few dwellings on a bit of land. So turning off the main road, Charlie bumped the black bus over unpaved roads as far as it could go before stopping at the foot of Goler Wash.

After a few hours' exertion in the warm autumn sun, the group reached Myers Ranch. If this were to become their permanent residence, they would need rugged vehicles for supply runs; the bus could access the encampments only via the high, northern pass from Nevada. Watching as the commune began exploring the land, Cappy grew uneasy. (She had told her grandmother she'd be staying with a few girlfriends.) So they hiked down to another, smaller site not far away. That's how Barker Ranch became their new home.

How isolated were they? Far from the polluting lights of the big smoke, whorls of green-blue-purple seemed poised to absorb all things living. The sky's silence threatened to swallow you whole. That might be a cliché, but it's the truth. Yet while the drive into Los Angeles took a good five or six hours, there was only one way in or out. And in places like this, the locals can spot a brightsider at a hundred yards. Still, the residents weren't the sort to get too involved in other people's business.

That suited Charlie fine. As he'd often tell the younger guys, "a man should never put his business in the street."[1]

~

And so as 1968 drew to a close, the commune really dropped out. What had they sought to escape? The same problems as everyone else. Journalist Paul O'Neill had summarized the situation in a year-end feature for *Life* magazine. "The vast, grunting majority of us led the soft life in 1968, that year of protest and lamentation," he wrote. "Air pollution hurt our eyes. Politics and new taxes tried our tempers. Still, they caused us little physical hardship and neither, to be blunt about it, did the Tet offensive, woe in Czechoslovakia, two hideous assassinations, the student revolution, the sexual revolution, hippies, yippies, Black Panthers or even, in most cases, the draft."

Yet even those living far from the frontlines of these battles for liberation, whether personal, sexual, political, or racial, had felt something shift. These events "scared us so much that we almost forgot The Bomb," O'Neill continued. "They made us uneasy about our own values and suspicious about those of our fellows. They clouded the future. And when we looked to the past for reassurance, like travelers in quicksand looking back at solid ground, we found it curiously distorted by the passage of time."[2]

~

Distortions of time and space at this point begin overwhelming accounts of the commune, as now individuals increasingly seem to lose control of their selves. In one such instance, Charlie took a girl to the ground, clasping her arms tightly, bringing their faces close, coaxing. Don't look away from your fear, he said, stare into the void. Her screams subsided and she melted into the acid trip.

That episode recalled to me a visit to a sharehouse peopled, it seemed, more by dogs than human beings.[3] A resident had pulled up its floorboards, revealing the dirt beneath. The front bedroom had been given over entirely to massive tanks filled with bulbous white and orange and black fishes, its former occupant relegated to a small unheated garage out back. The dogs ran wild snapping along the narrow hallways, pacified only when another great big black-bearded resident pulled one from the pack, placing the animal on its back and baring in its face his nicotine-stained teeth. I recall it being an unhappy place; at least, it was a very strange place. I'm not sure you could find it now.

~

Unhappy images, nightmares from Chicago, haunted the pages of mainstream magazines as the commune settled into Death Valley. *Life* readers gawked at a cop in riot gear as he pepper-sprayed a demonstrator, the placard in his arms reading, "End the WAR in Illinois / Send the COPS Home!"

A journalist watching through a large, plate-glass window reported how police cornered a group of demonstrators, leaving them no escape route. "Frightened men and women banged . . . against the window, that it might get knocked in. As I backed away a few feet I could see a smudge of blood on the glass outside." The window cracked, then shattered, the demonstrators forcing themselves through its jagged teeth, the police continuing to beat them as they bled.

A police radio made the following exchange at 1:29 a.m. early Tuesday:

"1814, get a wagon over at 1436. We've got an injured hippie."
"1436 North Wells?"
"North Wells."

In the background, crosstalk from other squad cars weighed in: "That's no emergency." "Let him take a bus." "Kick the fucker." "Knock his teeth out." "Throw him in a wastepaper basket."[4]

~

No emergency can be so disturbing that, with appropriate distance, the conscientious historian cannot disentangle and explain its constituent parts, making sense even where none before existed. At least, that's what we say.

Those who have experienced a true emergency know how the immediacy of trauma contorts time and memory. These contortions destabilize your sense of self, in part by disarticulating your lived experience from any seemingly rational, objective framing of "the real world," especially as scaffolded by clock- or calendar-time. A moment may feel like an hour; a month may pass in an instant. Perhaps this unsettles us because we in the West so often believe our selves to comprise an accumulation of experiences. We rarely acknowledge how "after the fact," to borrow a phrase, our seemingly empirical experiences exist only as stories, and that these stories form the building blocks of the narratives we use to make sense of our selves and our world. ("We're all nothing but bags of stories," as the discredited anthropologist Carlos Castaneda often said.[5])

That's not to denigrate storymaking. In Western societies, people often find making sense of insensible events to be therapeutic. Retrospectively placing moments and events in their proper sequence can salve even the deepest wounds, though in many cases, such reconstructions provide only a measure of comfort; we may never really make sense of every single trace of our past lives.

Such personal, individual acts of reconstruction seem to me not so different from the professional practice of writing history. Yet we too rarely admit that the credentialed historian is in the business of providing to his readers comfort. Or that his revising of the past is accomplished in the service of the future—and that it may be incomplete.

~

"Nothing stands between man and the fulfillment of his dream but facts, and facts are the creations of imagining," said Neville Goddard in "The Secret of Imagining" (1960). "If man changes his imagining he will change the facts. Man and his past are one continuous structure. This structure contains all of the facts which have been conserved and still operate below the threshold of his surface mind. For him, it is merely history. For him, it *seems* unalterable: a dead and firmly fixed past."

But as Goddard explains, this is not really true. The past lives: it affects our present. And so we "must go back in memory, seek for and destroy the causes of evil however far back they lie. This going into the past and replaying a scene of the past in imagination as it ought to have been played the first time, I call revision—and revision results in repeal. Changing our lives means changing the past."

To the Barbados-born ex-dancer and mystic, the power of imagining represents an expression of that God within us, as "[d]ivine imagining and human imagining are not two powers at all but one." In the 1950s, Goddard's radio and television broadcasts out of Los Angeles reached hundreds of thousands of listeners sympathetic to the notion that we hold within us a capacity to rewrite our pasts, and in so doing, to take control of our futures. How many of Goddard's listeners fully realized the radical implications of this idea—that the imaginations of a few might also dominate the many? "Human history, with its forms of governments, its revolutions, its wars, and in fact the rise and fall of nations, could be written in terms of the imaginal activities of men and women. All imaginative men and women are forever casting forth enchantments, and all passive men and women, who have no powerful imaginative lives, are continually *passing under the spell of their power*."[6]

Two weeks before the desert move, and to marshal their collective energies toward the exploration of new horizons, the commune staged a ritual at the Spahn Movie Ranch.

"We redecorated and rearranged the living room, placing couches all around the periphery, and mattresses on the floors," recalled Paul. "We covered the mattresses with a thick green satin carpet and scattered giant silk pillows everywhere. The girls made curtains out of satin and bought imported porcelain containers to hold *zuzus* [candy] and candles. They also purchased a filigreed waist-high hookah pipe, a Persian incense burner, and a golden hand-engraved goblet to hold our stash of hash and Colombian weed. After a week of 'tuning,' everyone was ready."[7]

Participants wore homemade clothes embroidered with vividly psychedelic scenes of animals and nature. They called these togs their "no-sense-makes-sense clothes: shirts that had pocket flaps where there were no pockets, buttonholes where there were no buttons. Clothing designed for comfort and beauty and to free the mind."[8] Charlie wore a brightly embroidered vest that the girls had for months been slaving over, so to speak, a garment embroidered with scenes depicting the group's time together.

From the start, nothing went right. A positive psychedelic experience, as Timothy Leary and others advised, demanded a carefully arranged setting and sensitive guide. But the acid proved far stronger than expected, and the howling wind outside created an unsettling backdrop. Breaking one of his cardinal rules, Charlie bailed. And then, the group disintegrated. Flailing limbs, darkness and wailing, commune members hurting themselves in the madness. One young heefus destroyed the carefully prepared ritual space. He soon after disappeared.

"I saw countless past lives," Paul reported, "an eternity of death scenes: people expiring—in fires, battles, countless wars. I saw limbs being lopped off, heads falling from the chopping block; I saw shootouts, drownings, collisions, all manner of death. For a time it seemed purely sadistic; watching such carnage was no different from seeing the wind rustle the leaves; it was almost pleasurable. I watched it and it was all right. I watched it through the eyes of a cosmic and tranquil indifference. Yet, I was watching myself: these people were me in past lives, or perhaps all men in all lifetimes."[9]

And this was true letting go. Real ego death.

~

Visions of a generation destroyed by madness, as the poet wrote, starving hysterical naked? As Allen Ginsberg's friend Bob Dylan began saying, allegedly, soon after persons unknown killed Jack Kennedy: I'm *through* with those finger-pointing songs, that's all in the past. Because people like Dylan, who speak truth to power? What's going to happen to them? "They're going to be *killed*."[10]

At a 1964 concert in Montreal, Ringo had hid himself behind upturned cymbals after the papers reported threats from French-Canadian separatists. On the group's final American tour, two years later, more credible death threats—a response to Beatle John's infamous comments—inspired some venues to post sharpshooters.

"I don't know which will go first—rock 'n' roll or Christianity," John had told journalist Maureen Cleave in March 1966. "Jesus was all right but his disciples were thick and ordinary. It's them twisting it that ruins it for me."[11]

It's a pity that infamous quote remains the primary trace from such a strange, wide-ranging profile. Because Cleave gives such a fascinating glimpse into Lennon's home life: the room filled with model race cars; the suit of armor, bought on a whim; a newly purchased gorilla suit; an emerging fascination with the Celts.

"I am on Boadicea's side—all those bloody blue-eyed blondes chopping people up," Lennon tells Cleave. "I have an awful feeling wishing I was there—not there with scabs and sores but there through reading about it. The books don't give you more than a paragraph about how they lived; I have to imagine that."

Over the next four weeks, Cleave profiled Ringo, Paul, and George, as well as Brian Epstein, for the *Evening Standard*. No controversial takes can be found in those bland public relations exercises. And yet if the people in power truly understood the potential of rock musicians, commentators such as critic Ralph Gleason soon claimed, they'd be terrified. The struggle indeed seemed to be at hand; the youthful hordes had reached the castle.

"The real question is whether or not the decayed, blind, reactionary forces of the dying civilization will be able to hold off the New Generation," Gleason wrote in *Rolling Stone*, "like Hitler's army in Russia behind hedgehog defenses, long enough to brainwash enough of its offspring to keep the freedom of art from expanding."

If you subscribe to this view, that rock provided a revolutionary mechanism for young people, then surely groups such as the Beatles would need to hide the true meaning of their work. Because as soon as the threat these revolutionary groups posed to the social order outweighed the profits accrued by their record companies, the violence of the state would begin to be exercised. For in a society that "fears its young people deeply and desperately," there can be no other reaction.[12] We can name this almost autonomic reaction, Gleason writes elsewhere, autolysis: the social body eating itself alive.[13]

~

For three long days the living body of a man named Krishna Venta hanged in simulated crucifixion, not far in space from the Spahn Movie Ranch, but distant in years. That miracle had not saved the holy man from his flock. Venta later died in the catacombs beneath his group's compound in Chatsworth, killed when two disgruntled former cult members, angry that the charismatic leader had taken their money and seduced their wives, ignited the explosives hidden beneath their coats.

Though Venta had departed this earthly plane, his apocalyptic group lived on, and workers at the Spahn Movie Ranch sometimes attended their services. Born Albert Pencovic, Krishna Venta, a Jewish immigrant from Romania, founded the group in the late 1940s. The Fountain of the World espoused WKFL, the four precepts of Wisdom-Knowledge-Faith-Love. To join, members had only to give up all their earthly possessions and submit.

Krishna Venta claimed to have been Christ Himself returned to Earth. He preached that Communists and Black Americans would soon overthrow the United States government. And he predicted an imminent nuclear war. The faithful would wait out this holocaust, Venta claimed, growing their number to the 144,000 true believers prophesied in the Book of Revelation, living in the tunnels that cult members began digging under the compound.

Charlie and members of his commune visited the Fountain of Life often over a period of two months, presumably around the time they split with Dennis Wilson. Mother Mary and Pooh Bear lived full-time at the cult for a short period; Katie worked in their kitchen.[14] Paul Watkins seems circumspect about Charlie's motivations in visiting the cult, and credulous about the philosophical similarities between the groups.[15] Ed Sanders thought Charlie stole ideas whole cloth from them: enacting his own simulated crucifixion sometime in late August, for instance, as well as interpolating the WKFL worldview into his rap.[16] Sanders thought this because of the similarities between the two groups. But he also thought this because, well, that's just the kind of thing a conman like Manson would do.

~

The confidence man makes you believe something that simply isn't true. He seeks to "gain your confidence," a term that comes to us from *confidere*, meaning to believe, to be sure of something, to trust. Nestled within that original term, we find another term: *fidēs*.

You would err in rendering this term "faith," as the Christians later mistranslated it. That's because the pagan Romans originally used *fidēs* to denote "an essential element in the character of a man of public affairs." This virtue connoted "'reliability,' a sense of trust between two parties if a relationship between them was to exist."

Mutual trust, and reciprocity. A collection of responsibilities. The bond linking friends, or father and family, or master and slave.[17] Can we add to this list: singer and listener? (Or even, author and reader?)

~

In the relative calm of the desert, Charlie and Paul went to Indian Springs, a sweaty hike and short drive south from the commune's proposed encampment.

Here's how Charlie allegedly described meeting elderly Mrs. Barker, owner of the dilapidated ranch: "We found her, like old George, sitting on the front porch half asleep. Paul and I walked to the porch and introduced ourselves. I wasn't laying out any bull—I told her *truthfully* a group of us would like to stay at her ranch while we were putting together some arrangements for musical recordings. I also mentioned I did some song writing for the Beach Boys and, to add *credibility*, I gave her one of the gold records that had been presented to Dennis. She didn't object to our living there if we took care of the place."[18]

"Wow, ain't this great Charlie?" said Paul. "Goddamn, I'm glad we found this place! The 'man' (the police) ain't around to be fucking with us. Ain't no neighbors tryin' to get you to conform to their ideas."[19]

Here's how Paul related the same meeting: "We found her easily enough in a small, weather-tight cabin surrounded by a flaccid chain-link fence. She lived alone most of the time and that morning was seated on her front porch dozing with a newspaper in her lap. Charlie wasted no time in laying his rap on the gray-haired, grizzled old gal. 'It's like Paul and me are musicians . . . you know; we done some music with the Beach Boys—and now we need solitude to do our music, get our own gig together. Up there on that mountain at your ranch . . . well, it's about as pretty a place to compose music as I've ever seen

... right, Paul? And if we get lucky and sell some stuff, who knows, we might all get rich.'"

She nodded, taking it all in, sharp as a tack. The group could stay, provided they "fixed what needed fixin.'" Charlie handed her a Beach Boys gold record, Paul's account concurs, and the two stopped in Ballarat for soda on their way back to the commune's new desert home.[20]

~

In "What Kind of People Does a Religious Cult Attract" (October 1957), sociologist William R. Catton reported the results from questionnaires distributed to audience members at a series of six lectures Krishna Venta gave in Seattle, Washington, over the first two months of 1952.

In the first lecture, Venta presented his mission ("gathering of the elect"). Hecklers and protesters interrupted the second. The third lecture "dealt with prophecy"; the fourth, with hypnotism and telepathy. In the fifth lecture, Venta distinguished Jesus (the man) from Christ (God's co-Creator, as well as Venta himself). At the sixth lecture, Venta addressed press reports about his criminal record for passing bad checks. "Krishna was fond of the Book of Revelation," Catton reported in a footnote, "which attributes to Christ the following words: '... I will come like a thief, and you will not know at what hour I will come upon you.' Rev. 3:3."[21]

And so, to wit: what kind of people does a religious cult attract? Catton found curious observers, as well as a group he called "seekers," comprising those persons "cult-prone (institutionally alienated but religiously intense)." The overrepresentation of individuals who had previously experimented with Dianetics, he added, suggested the existence of a kind of "generalized cult-proneness."

"There are seekers, apparently, who move from cult to cult in a neverending quest."[22]

~

In December, two groups left Barker Ranch for supplies. Charlie took Tex and Sadie, along with a few of the girls and an ex-Vietnam vet named T. J. Wallerman, to Sacramento. Little Paul, along with Snake and Gypsy, went to Los Angeles. They dropped Gypsy off at the Spahn Movie Ranch to spell another new member who had been caring for George.

The Los Angeles group went to see the new Beatles film, *Yellow Submarine*. They hung out in Topanga Canyon, where they heard the new Beatles double album, *The Beatles*, released a few weeks earlier.[23] Charlie stopped by and heard it, too. "After that," Little Paul muses, "things were never the same." His group reached Barker Ranch first; Charlie followed after in the black bus, which he had taken over the high mountain pass on the Nevada side. The bus arrived in a wreck on New Year's Eve. A palpable excitement could be felt in the air.

"That night we all hiked up to the Meyers place and built a roaring fire," wrote Paul. "Everyone was back. We had a full supply of food, candy, beverages, and enough wood to keep the fire stoked and blazing. Charlie was completely energized; his mood charged everyone. It was like a ritual gathering of some desert tribe to make New Year's resolutions. A ceremony before the fire. The flames reflected in Charlie's eyes as he spoke:

"'Are you hep to what the Beatles are saying? . . . Dig it, they're telling it like it is. They put the revolution to music . . . it's "Helter Skelter." Helter-Skelter is coming down. Hey, their album is getting the young love ready, man, building up steam. Our album is going to *pop the cork right out of the bottle*.'"[24]

NEW SONGS BEGAN TAKING FORM in the hot dry air at Barker Ranch. "Before the desert, 'our' music had been, for the most part, a deep breathing exercise toward relaxation and release," Lyn later recalled. "We released words, but never wrote them down. What for? Suddenly they were writing down chords and words, employing Leslie, the business school graduate, to take shorthand. Suddenly, they had a message to send, and the message mattered."[25]

A musical collective took shape. Several of the men played guitar: Clem and Paul, and Bobby, and of course, Charlie. Gypsy played violin, Mary, flute, and Paul, flute and French horn. No longer did the young women sing simply, in unison: they now trained their voices in parts, their arrangements prefiguring a kind of utopian praxis of love and community. Or at least, emulating the current pop stuff you might have heard on the radio.

The men crafted these songs diligently, with Charlie taking the lead. "They tripped and came to a lot of thoughts based upon their awareness, their knowledge, and an old Hopi Indian who didn't even talk—he just smiled," Lyn claimed. "The songs explain it better than I could. I believe they had tuned into

'Now,' the endless space of what was, what is, and what could be. They read the trails."

These works would come to be called their desert songs. No recordings captured Manson singing them with the group, or at least, none have been made available to people like me and you. "I've often wished we had recorded some of the sessions we did at the Barker ranch at the base of the mountains," Paul harped in his memoir. "We worked hard; hours and hours. And it showed. As a professional musician, I can say without reservation that what we were doing was as good as, and in most cases better than, some of the top-selling recordings of the day. Though Charlie had spoken to us of violence—the violence of the revolution—there was never any talk of *us* doing anything but music."[26]

~

"Revolution" had been the first song recorded for what became *The Beatles*, a generous four sides' worth of sound released into the world just as the desert songs began materializing. Producer George Martin later said he wished the Beatles had exerted more editorial control, and released a stronger, more polished follow-up to their revelatory 1967 album *Sgt. Pepper's Lonely Hearts Club Band*. I wonder what songs they might have culled.

Many of the thirty tracks had been conceived in Rishikesh; the recordings took shape as Charlie bonded with Dennis during the summer months of 1968. People called it the White Album because artist Richard Hamilton had designed a plain white cover bearing only the embossed name of the group and a serial number. (The album had been released in a limited edition of five million.)[27] Full lyrics could be found on the reverse side of a collage insert crafted by Hamilton, presumably so listeners could know precisely what the Beatles had to say.

The White Album garnered positive reviews, a welcome return after the critical debacle of *Magical Mystery Tour*. Noting that rock represented "the first successful art form of the McLuhan age," Jann Wenner claimed the Beatles on this album "are so good that they not only expand the idiom, but they are also able to penetrate it and take it further."[28] "Many of the songs in this album," Al Aronowitz noted, "were written of, by and for children."[29] But no reviewer proved as enthusiastic as Allen Ginsberg. In *Rolling Stone*, Ginsberg filled two full pages in expounding on the virtues and meanings of the sprawling album.

In Paul's "Mother Nature's Son," the poet heard the truth that "we are only children and have the minds of children." John's "Yer Blues" expresses for him that "4am depression energy raw consciousness of disaster." In the end, Ginsberg wept, because so many moments articulated as no other medium could the underlying substance of human *being* itself: "the orphic wonder, experience for art's sake, the unsocializing of the animal." Ginsberg acknowledged that the first Beatles albums had been powerful. He referred to a short statement he made on the cusp of an anti-war protest three years earlier titled "Demonstration or Spectacle as Example, as Communication—or, How to Make a March/Spectacle." Organizers had then worried about potential violence at the March. Ginsberg had offered this solution: "At first sign of disturbance, public address systems swing into vast sound to loud Beatles 'I Wanna Hold Your Hand' and marchers instructed to dance."[30] The song, Ginsberg proposed, would exercise a pacifying effect on the crowds. Not soporific, of course, but able to transmute potential violence into pure joy.

All that had changed now. "Whew, boy!" he wrote in praise of "Revolution 9." "You can *hear* the boots a'marching."

~

Here's how commune member Sandra Good thought music-making figured into the life of the commune back in Death Valley: "We sang more than we talked. In Manson's words, 'It's our god, our religion.'"[31]

~

We sang more than we talked. You can hear the sounds of revolution. Should we understand such statements as hyperbole? Or something else? That's the problem. Figurative language compels us to read between the lines, and because the authors we have so far been drawing on in this book—and here, I'm referring to rock critics, as well as mid-century American novelists, New Journalism essayists, memoirists, and even post-1966 rock lyricists—made their bones in the space between fact and metaphor, it can be difficult to know where literal meaning begins or ends.

Drawing on sources that make such promiscuous use of the figurative highlights just how contested the line marking fact from fiction came to be during this period. Contestation over that line provided a kind of engine driving the production of knowledge in the postwar United States. That's why Walter Goldschmidt could praise Carlos Castaneda's first book, *The Teachings of Don Juan: A Yaqui Way of Knowledge* (1968), as "both ethnography and allegory." (For the more comprehensive examination of this revelation, refer back to pages 98-9.) Or else consider John Updike's discussion of Josiah Thompson's

Six Seconds in Dallas (1967). As its title suggests, Thompson's book performs a painstakingly moment-by-moment analysis of the seconds elapsed between the first and final gunshots that felled John F. Kennedy. It's a remarkable work, especially for a period when so many words had from loose using lost their edge; so careful, so meticulous. If you read it now, you will find only surface, an author merely describing evidence, refusing to make any conclusions at all, nevermind interpretations.

There is, for instance, the appearance of the so-called Umbrella Man. Just before the final shot strikes Kennedy, as the presidential motorcade approached, someone opened an umbrella. Who was this person? Josiah Thompson doesn't know, and neither do we. No rain had fallen since the very early hours of that warm Tuesday morning in November. So why did the man hold an umbrella? The black umbrella might have signaled hidden assassins; it might have hidden a mechanism for delivering a paralyzing agent; it might have been nothing, just one of those fluke things.

"We wonder whether a genuine mystery is being concealed here or whether any similar scrutiny of a minute section of time and space would yield similar strangenesses—gaps, inconsistencies, warps, and bubbles in the surface of circumstance," Updike wrote. "Perhaps, as with the elements of matter, investigation passes a threshold of common sense and enters a sub-atomic realm where laws are mocked, where persons have the life-span of beta particles and the transparency of neutrinos, and where a rough kind of averaging out must substitute for absolute truth. The truth about those seconds in Dallas is especially elusive; the search for it seems to demonstrate how perilously empiricism verges on magic."[32]

~

A rough kind of averaging out, of course, ignores the particularities that make stories worth telling, at least within the conventional generic forms of the postwar West. Taken as a whole, these particularities sometimes conjure insoluble questions, and perhaps reveal—if you are inclined to think in this way—untruths, or even misdirections.

Many accounts of the commune do not mention that Dennis Wilson, Gregg Jakobson, and possibly even Terry Melcher had remained in close contact with the commune during their early period in the desert. Paul doesn't say so in his otherwise thickly detailed account of the final two months of 1968. Vincent Bugliosi doesn't really, either.

Bugliosi's *Helter Skelter* requires Jakobson, as the key trial witness articulating Manson to the Helter Skelter prophecy, Terry Melcher, and Cielo Drive, to be an insider to the commune. But to maintain a measure of distance between Manson, Wilson, and Melcher, the character Jakobson cannot get too close. So Bugliosi notes that Jakobson "had over a hundred long talks with Charlie" during a relationship that lasted eighteen months.[33] But he also implies that these conversations happened in and around the Spahn Movie Ranch and Los Angeles.

Only once does Bugliosi hint in passing at a more robust engagement in Death Valley: "Yet once, *in the desert*, Jakobson had run over a tarantula, and Manson had angrily berated him for it. He had denounced others for killing rattlesnakes, picking flowers, even stepping on a blade of grass." The author may have intended this evidence of ecological concern to heighten the reader's horror at the next sentence: "To Manson *it was not wrong to kill a human being*, but it was wrong to kill an animal or plant. Yet he also said that nothing was wrong, *everything that happened was right*."[34] (Note that Bugliosi, slipping like a thief in the night into the mode of omniscient narrator, failed to place these words, this dangerous anti-anthropocentrism, in the mouth of any one individual.)

Yet Ed Sanders reported in 1971 that Dennis and Gregg both traveled back and forth quite regularly between Los Angeles and Death Valley. On November 24, 1968, Jakobson and Wilson went up to retrieve a jeep they'd loaned the group. (Or it may have been early December—that's the date Jakobson himself gave in a more recent interview.) The jeep had broken down somewhere in Goler Wash, so Dennis, Gregg, and Charlie hiked into the scrublands to find it. They had the vehicle towed to the town of Trona for repairs, and two weeks later, Jakobson returned on a motorcycle. Now the bike broke down, but the jeep was up and running. So he "threw his motorcycle in the back and went back to Los Angeles."[35]

The group seemed to be anything but isolated: coming and going on supply runs, entertaining old friends, even trekking into Nevada to crash with new friends. That's where, in *The Family*, you will find one of the strangest rumors that Ed Sanders reported. A wealthy woman named Charlene Cafritz, née Lawley, allegedly entertained Manson and a few of the commune members at her home in Reno for two weeks in December. She bought Charlie supplies and a Cadillac. He quickly gave away the car, and several of her thoroughbred horses. (To whom?) She also "took numerous motion pictures of Manson the and the family in Reno which no one seems to want to discuss. Mrs. Cafritz was a friend of Sharon Tate and Terry Melcher and many others associated with the oncoming tragedy."[36] No one has ever found those home films.

Cafritz apparently dated Dennis Wilson, too. And she allegedly remained in contact with commune members well after the murders, speaking by telephone to Gypsy at the Spahn Movie Ranch as late as August 1970. According to conspiracy-minded lay researchers, the wealthy woman offered to bankroll the commune's defense. Less than a month later, Cafritz was found dead from an overdose of Nembutal, a barbiturate that in high doses can cause respiratory arrest.[37]

The American government has often used this compound to execute those convicted of capital offenses. Note also that Cafritz's in-laws included powerfully connected political families in Washington D.C., and that, years later, her niece would marry the leader of NXIVM, a more recent so-called "sex cult." And that curiously, citizen-researchers have surfaced only a handful of confirmed photographs of the mysterious Mrs. Cafritz.[38]

~

A mystery can be solved, but a conspiracy must be proven. These are not their only differences. The former asks you to delay gratification until the big reveal at the end, while the latter provides the languid pleasure of soaking and wallowing in conjecture. Ultimately there's no gratification, only the ongoing ache, an approach that never comes. And yet it's the former that makes you feel cheap, used by mere tricks; the latter at least simulates what might pass for real magic in this, our modern age of disenchantment.[39]

Now here consider a note to listeners, from the back cover of *The Manson Family Sings the Songs of Charles Manson* (1987), a collection recorded in 1970 with Clem on vocals as Manson languished in prison: "The materials contained herein are not presented to provide you with cheap vicarious thrills. Beyond MANSON—the media circus, the creepy-crawly mega-monster—there remains the man and his family. For these end times they have a message, be it good or evil—or, perhaps beyond this—WHO REALLY IS IN PRISON, AND WHO IS FREE?"

None of this means, of course, that the truth does not exist. Consider the text found on the label to Side B from the same album: "Truthful I call him who goes into godless deserts, having broken his revering heart. In the yellow sands, burned by the sun, he squints thirstily at the islands abounding in wells, where living things rest under dark trees. Yet his thirst does not persuade him to become like these, dwelling in comfort; for where there are oases there are also idols.

"Hungry, violent, lonely, godless: thus the lion-will wants itself. Free from the happiness of slaves, redeemed from gods and adorations, fearless and fear-inspiring, great and lonely: such is the will of the truthful.

"Thus spoke Zarathustra."[40]

~

The Western philosopher Friedrich Nietzsche, in using the figure of Zarathustra as a mere literary device, of course misrepresented him. A dialectic of order and disorder, the real historical Zoroaster taught, maps onto a broader cluster of binaries that includes creation and uncreation, truth and untruth. How about empiricism and magic?

If the relationship between empiricism and magic can be described, then surely the essence of that relationship lies in its manner of parsing. A resolutely apophenic logic does not merely connect moments-images-sounds-texts; this surface-level logic actually constitutes the truth of their connections. We should put this more simply. What I mean to say is that quite often the truth is hiding in plain sight.[41]

In the postwar world, that truth may smoke your eyelids, obligating you to engage in exegetical readings. Not that this necessarily asked much of Americans. Anyone who bought an album could find, for instance, Dylan's secret messages: you just needed to interpret the words to his songs, or stare at the cover of *John Wesley Harding* until faces began appearing on the surface of the trees. And sometimes the messages couldn't be more obvious. The Beatles didn't even try to hide occultist Aleister Crowley's face in the crowd on the cover of *Sgt. Pepper's*; the Buffalo Springfield, of course, just came out and said it: *There's something happening here.*

On a television program in 1968, the media theorist Marshall McLuhan explained how the exegetical impulse can be understood as a consequence of the modern age, citing a report commissioned by IBM about "information overload."[42] In the postwar world, information bombards us: newspapers, radios, televisions, advertisements, all barking out numbers and text and images and sounds. "When you give people too much information, they instantly resort to pattern recognition," McLuhan lectured. "In other words, structuring experience." Confronted by too many signs at once, the normal human being seeks patterns. What does this mean for the substance and quality of our experience-in-the-world? Has our evolution from storytelling animals to pattern-seeking ones already begun? And most importantly, how do we know that the patterns we discern are the right ones?

Addressing this final point, McLuhan came to a perverse conclusion: an argument for the importance of Art. "The absolute indispensability of the contemporary artist is that he alone can give the pattern recognition—he alone has the sensory awareness to tell us what our world is made of." That is to say, only an artist can discover, and then transmit to us, from amongst the maddening proliferation of signs, the true meaning of our modern world.

~

Again, but now in earnest: Oo-ee-oo!

ON THE SECOND DAY OF JANUARY, THE YEAR NOW NINETEEN-SIXTY-NINE, Charlie and T. J. left chilly Barker Ranch high up in Death Valley for Los Angeles, where the two had a meeting with Dennis Wilson and Greg Jakobson.[43]

A week later, T. J. returned to the remote ranch with instructions. It was time to move back, "closer to the action." The talks had gone well, and Dennis had not merely seemed receptive, T. J. implied, but had started setting the wheels in motion for an album. "Hey, the shit is really coming down," T. J. told them. "Charlie says he's got a deal lined up with some guy named Melcher."[44]

~

Son of Doris Day and friend to dissolute Dennis, record producer Terry Melcher had lived at the Cielo Drive residence in 1968 with his girlfriend, actress Candice Bergen. Some say he met Charlie and his followers during that period, maybe several times.*[45]

---

* On Monday, August 23, 1971, Dean Martin's daughter, Deana, testified at the trial of Tex Watson as to the relationship among Wilson, Melcher, and the Manson commune. She recalls attending a party at Wilson's house in "July or October [1968]," and remembered seeing Tex at Melcher's house after the party moved there. On cross-examination, Deana then suggested that the date had been late September or early October. This would have been before the commune shifted to the desert, and after some sources claim Dennis had broken ties with the commune. "I believe it was October, because I was on my way to South Africa to make a movie October 12th, '68," Deana said, "and the party was a week or two before that." Melcher would deny knowing Manson during this period, suggesting he only met the group twice in May-June 1969; though apparently untrue, I have to this point decided to respect his version of events within my book's narrative.

By most accounts, Melcher was not necessarily a particularly gifted producer. Yet he had ties to the Hollywood elite through his mother, "America's sweetheart," and through his work with groups such as Paul Revere and the Raiders and the Byrds, garnering a certain cache in the rock and freak scenes. The implosion of that latter group helped give rise to what *Life* magazine called "the New Rock." It was "music that hooked the whole vibrating world," a glossy cover featuring Grace Slick and her hirsute bandmates in Jefferson Airplane. While the groups varied widely in their sound and expressive capacities, each "share a compassion for people and they're reaching out directly with their music," editor George P. Hunt explained. Grace Slick "has a way of commenting on society, using metaphor and allusion," while Country Joe and the Fish "have a kind of county fair burlesque way of attacking the system directly." And it's not just for fun: "they demand a lot from us."[46]

Illustrated with portraits by Art Kane ranging from intimate to surreal, Robin Richman's text cannot help but veer quickly into the figurative. Alongside photographer Kane capturing the Jefferson Airplane's members isolated in upright plastic caskets in the desert, Richman explained the group's import:

> The craft moves happily along over society's filler: a wastebasket lost in a sea of empty cans. A stop sign pointing to a greasy heart. Jefferson Airplane lands on an empty lot and its six-member crew become soloists. In their Plexiglas boxes, each has a different stance, each a different mood. Together they form a structure of thrust and counterthrust. Ballads of chance encounters in a stream of consciousness. Passenger, be free and easy. *Go along with allegory.*[47]

The upshot: "Fly Jefferson Airplane and it will be the first day of the rest of your life."

Next critic Richard Goldstein provided a short expository piece on the development of rock lyrics. (The old, dumb *doo-doo-dah-doo* stuff is just *fine*, Goldstein explains, because "the primary purpose of a lyric was to convey mood not meaning." He then analyzes the development of imagery in Beatles lyrics.) Now Frank Zappa explained how "rock has the answers to what your parents won't tell you." For Zappa, rock has serious social significance in freeing us from repression. Think about how much *energy* we used to expend in worrying about the sexual organs of ourselves and others! Think about the sex-crazed chaperone patrolling school dances with a ruler, keeping sweaty, grunting adolescents a prim eighteen inches apart. Look around today, and you will see just how much has changed. "Our present state of sociosexual enlightenment is, to a certain extent," Zappa proposed, "attributable to the evolution of rock and vice versa."[48]

The power of young people to shape society seemed unprecedented. But even the most sympathetic observers often sounded a note of caution. We should in some way respond to young people's demands, the anthropologist Margaret Mead would write, but we must also recognize the fuller context of such calls for change. Because while we have always had youthful dissenters, today their platform has changed in ways we have not yet fully comprehended. "The mass media write prescriptions for youthful behavior like cookbooks and circulate them all over the country," Mead said. "The behavior of a few enterprising young rebels becomes a model to many young people who don't belong but get swept into it. [. . .] This is the first generation who have been brought up by the mass media instead of parents."[49]

Here's what one advocate for the parents, the Head Psychologist for the Santa Barbara School District in California, someone working at the coalface, to turn a phrase, wrote in a Letter to the Editor about "the New Rock": "I feel rock music groups are adversely affecting the lives of our teen-agers. Their weird clothes, hair styles and bizarre living habits are widely copied. One isn't sure whether they are a reflection of a sick world or an encouragement to young people to plunge into a sick way of life."[50]

~

I'm just one of those restless people,
    that can never be satisfied—
with livin' in this sick old, sick old, sick-sick-sick city.

~

How to cure the sickness? At the tail end of 1968, an elite cabal of "antiseptic technocratic majority intellectuals" had gathered at Princeton to place American society on the analyst's couch, to diagnose what ailed their patient. One bemoaned the "complete collapse of liberal values." Another worried over a "terrifying wilderness of drugs, pornography and political hysteria." A sociologist pointed to the rise of a "juvenocracy," and the fall of traditional authorities. "The WASPs have abdicated and what has taken their place?" he asked. "Ants, fleas!"

These intellectuals, a journalist wrote, seemed to suffer from "what might be characterized as 'the Lolita complex'—the tendency to stare in fascination at youthful protest and to fantasize unnatural ideological intercourse with its irrationality."

And that's the one thing participants could agree on: the death of reason, now superseded by irony, absurdity, play, the surreal—"that rugged individualism may be giving way to ragged irrationalism in American life." The United States, they argued, had become "prophetic of the tensions of the modern age." And sooner or later, all of us must "answer for it."[51]

~

I'll never say never to always! I'll never say always to none!
To seem is to dream a dream aloud, 'cause one is one is one—

~

And answer, it seemed, we just might. Had you consulted the papers held by the Association for Research and Enlightenment in Virginia Beach during this period, you would have found predictions by Edgar Cayce—the early twentieth century's most prominent mystic, the so-called "sleeping prophet"—about the coming "earth changes" that would result in California falling into the sea sometime in early 1969.[52]

Author Curt Gentry, at the time working up a true-crime book with prosecutor Vincent Bugliosi, developed this conceit into a full speculative history titled *The Last Days of the Late, Great State of California* (1969). The state's destruction, as Gentry speculated, would result in the reorganization of American political life; it would end the American century. And it would signal the death of certain hopes. Might a California-born engineer of the future have solved problems of transportation, hunger, even war? Would a future California city have provided a model of interracial harmony?

"One of the saddest things in life—and the California story—is what might have been."[53]

~

Who fucked up Gabriel's horn, the horn from the Book of Revelation that signaled Christ's return? That's what poet Lenore Kandel wanted to know. Was it an inside job?[54]

~

What might have been had the Wilson-Manson collaboration continued? In February, the Beach Boys released one of Charlie's songs, "Never Learn Not To Love." Originally titled "Cease to Exist," the group had lightly revised certain lyrics and subjected the music to their dulcet harmonies. It's one of the more successful tracks on *20/20* (1969). (To hear for yourself the potential of Manson's songs as they continued to develop during this period, listen to this cover alongside the folksy demo released on the March 1970 album, *LIE*.) But to really judge the evolution of Charlie's songs, and to understand how the desert changed the sound of the commune, we can compare the two extant recordings of "Never Say Never To Always." On the version from 1967, you'll hear a few young women sing-songing this lilting waltz about ego death in nursery-rhyme unison; on the other, recorded in 1970 with Clem on lead vocals, you'll find the commune in full sail.

The girls sound simply *girlish* on the 1967 demo. There's really no other way to describe the voices aflutter, the crosstalk, the giggling. We hear the new arrangement commune members must have worked out in the desert on the 1970 demo, preserved for posterity as Charlie sat in prison. On this recording, Clem plays guitar and sings lead, with vocals by Gypsy, Cappy, Brenda, Ouisch, Squeaky, and Sandy soaring over and above and all around him. So much rehearsal must have gone into this carefully constructed arrangement. A kind of hippie hymn, its lyric demands interpretation. The final iteration of the verse has a beautifully lilting countermelody, a childlike fantasia that puts to shame nearly all the Beach Boys' post-*Pet Sounds* paint-by-numbers arrangements.

~

Look inside yourself for your father, all is none, all is none, none is one.
    It's time to call time from behind you, the illusion has been just a dream.
Valley of death and I'll find you, now is when on a sunshine beam.
So bring only your perfection, for there love shall surely be—
    No cold, pain, fear or hunger. You can see, you can see, you can see.

~

With an agreement apparently in place to begin recording these songs, most of the commune moved back to Los Angeles, to a large house at 21019 Gresham Street in Canoga Park that they called the Yellow Submarine (for its canary-yellow clapboard siding). There they continued to rehearse.

    Old George hadn't wanted them to return to the Spahn Movie Ranch, though the two sides would soon patch things up. Dianne, Brooks, and the improbably named Juanita Wildebush stayed on at Barker Ranch to maintain the remote outpost. But bored and feeling isolated, Dianne hitched a ride with a visiting Bobby Beausoleil back into town.

At the Yellow Submarine, she found a strange scene with Charlie, Tex, Leslie, Mary, Ouisch, Little Paul, Nancy, Sandy, Gypsy, and maybe Squeaky. "Charlie's demeanor seemed very different," she later wrote. "In his hand was a Bible, and nearby a record player was plugged in."[55] Over the previous few months, the group had fallen into a somewhat regular routine where, after the commune members had finished their communal meal, Charlie would get up and rap, sometimes for an hour or two without stopping. But now as he began to speak, something seemed different.

"For someone who'd showed us a thousand faces," Lake recalled, "this was one he must have kept to himself until now." Charlie was Jesus Christ, the Son of God. He had been crucified and died. And He had done it for the commune.

"I fought for as long as I could," Charlie told the group. "Then I shouted out in agony: 'God, why hast though forsaken me?' Then it all became clear. I had to give up. To live, I had to give everything up and simply surrender to death. And that is what I did. I died for you all."[56]

~

The sermons integrated elements from the apocalyptic Book of Revelation with repeated listenings to the Beatles White Album.* The exegetical readings of these texts emerged at once, as fully formed prophecy. Or perhaps, the commune's interpretations evolved over time. The talk-tos confirmed what some group members had started believing. Or the revelations came out of

---

* Dianne Lake places the White Album revelations at the Yellow Submarine house in late January 1969, just days after the Christ sermon described above (pp. 290-4). Ed Sanders agrees, claiming this "cultural instruction" followed earlier ones from the Beatles, suggesting the group had already been taking its lead from Beatle lyrics (p. 136). Lynette Fromme also supports this timeline, but with the key caveat that the group knew the Beatles were not directly communicating with them (p. 351).

In contrast, Vincent Bugliosi, working from interviews with commune member Brooks Poston, places the revelation on New Year's Eve, December 31, 1968, after Charlie heard the album on a trip into Los Angeles earlier that month (p. 244). Sadie notes that Charlie acquired the album in "late 1968," and soon became "convinced that he had some sort of apocalyptic connection with the Beatles"—though she "never really understood it" (p. 112). Her timeline, though, seems confused: she seems to suggest the group traveled back and forth from Los Angeles to Death Valley when Manson received the revelation, only acquiring Barker Ranch sometime later.

Tex Watson provides what must surely be an incorrect chronology of this period (pp. 96-104). He suggests the group moved to Barker Ranch much earlier, but then the majority of the commune left for an unspecified number of "aimless weeks" in Sacramento before returning to Spahn Ranch "sometime in the third week of November." He had to report to the draft board on December 2, where he failed the physical; he then left the group until March 1969. On his return, Charlie had already begun preaching both the Bible and the White Album. (Note that if we trust Watson, then Lake must be mistaken about seeing him in late January. Is she?).

nowhere, shocking them. Everyone took the Christ stuff seriously. But some, maybe, approached Charlie's eschatological musings as another kind of playacting.

Squeaky Fromme and several other commune members have always maintained that claims the group invested the music of the Beatles with apocalyptic meaning had been overblown. "The new Beatles *White Album* was as appealing as their others, but also different, with specific sounds between songs, and the same sounds gathered in the piece called 'Revolution 9,'" she writes. "Most interesting were the sounds of gunfire, the grunts of pigs, the screams and moans of people dying, of people making love, a baby's babble, a black man yelling 'Rise!' The album was timely. We believed that the song 'Blackbird' was written for the Black race. We chuckled on hearing 'Sexy Sadie' [because that was Susan's nickname], and wept with George Harrison's guitar. We acknowledged the genius that had created the album, *but we did not believe that the Beatles were talking to us, unless you included us in the soul of the world*. The album was just interesting."[57]

~

What songs might have appeared on the album Manson might have recorded during this period? Some people say the album comprised ten songs, most with full arrangements by top session musicians. The album, if it ever existed, has never appeared. But later demos of the desert songs do reveal apocalyptic themes. There's "Ra-Hide Away," discussed in some detail just below. Several songs seem quite explicit. There's "Die to be One": When the eagle flies, we will lie under the sun / When the eagle flies, we will die, die to be one. There's the eerie "No Wrong": Can you hear the fires roar? Standing outside the devil's door / No wrong, no wrong—come along! Others require much more interpretation, and of course, the knowledge of events yet to come. There's "Love's Death." And "Give Your Love (To Be Free)." Did these songs brainwash commune members? Conceal secret messages the group planned to unleash on an unsuspecting public? Or something else?

~

Subjecting an album to a mere surface "reading" demands we abjure exegesis, closing our ears to metaphor, allegory, symbolism. But what kind of a philistine takes anything so literally? As a form of human expression, even the most banal song requires at least a measure of interpretation, or so critics from the mid-1960s onward (not to mention cultural historians) would have us believe.

And this goes far beyond popular music. Our interpretations do not simply make us human, contemporary thinkers claimed—the interpretive act itself generates the worlds we inhabit. In *The Social Construction of Reality* (1966), for instance, Peter Berger and Thomas Luckmann parsed how human beings make life real through complex encounters with language and each other. From these encounters, Berger and Luckmann argued, we actively construct reality.[58] We co-create what seems to be an objective experience of the world, as one historian explains, though this seemingly objective experience remains "dependent on institutions and cultural frameworks that pre-exist and shape the individual, symbolically organizing the world through shared and enforced patterns of perception, signification, and conceptual organization."[59]

Efforts to understand that play between subjective and objective forces fueled postwar intellectual inquiry in the West. How should we understand the predicament of the modern subject, a subject who remains always-already a subject in two senses—at once the *subject of* experience, but simultaneously *subjected to* the whims and disciplining forces of language, culture, history, society? There's the rub.

Postwar psychoanalysis worked from the premise that such an individual had an interiority to be discovered or revealed. Unconscious urges drive this interiority, an interiority that can be accessed through the therapeutic encounter, but also liberated from the civilizing bonds of society *if only we do the work on ourselves*.[60] Small wonder the foremost proponent of this new form of psychoanalytic knowledge in the United States, Herbert Marcuse, became a darling of the counterculture.[61] Rock critic Richard Goldstein drew on *Eros and Civilization* (1955), for instance, to make sense of performances by Jim Morrison, analyzing performances and recordings by the Doors as articulating a kind of social criticism insofar as they made visible—and audible—the interiority of the musicians.[62]

We encounter a distinct but related set of pathways charted in the antipsychiatry philosophy of thinkers such as Thomas Szasz and R. D. Laing. In *The Divided Self: An Existential Study in Sanity and Madness* (1960), Laing contrasted the "ontologically secure" subject with the disintegrating subject, that so-called mad subject who refuses to "take the realness, aliveness, autonomy and identity of himself and others for granted."[63] What if we refuse to take the realness of our world for granted, too? And dig this: What if that which appears to be madness actually represents a rational response to a mad world—a world of violence and war, of conspiracies, a world of technocratic antihumanism?

The Politics of Experience and the Bird of Paradise (1967) deployed this antipsychiatry critique as method. In the first half of the book, Laing used the more-or-less expected academic apparatus. But in the second half, the psychiatrist employed a stream-of-conscious literary-experimental style, all fragmentation, allusion, and unreliability. Showing, not telling, allowing an argument to emerge from beneath the surface of the words on the page. This method, we should note, risks breaking the sacred trust binding author to reader. Without that trust—cultivated through careful citations, a seriousness of expression, concrete (rather than figurative) language—the author risks appearing unfaithful to his readers.

~

The appearance of good faith now requires me to admit to paraphrasing without proper referencing a few lines earlier in this book on page 5, a passage that, to me, encapsulated a key shift in American thought from the late 1960s into the 1970s. This passage, from Steve Martin's 1978 album, *A Wild and Crazy Guy*, has been my only flirtation with such unfaithfulness.

Here's the original passage: "You know, it's so hard to believe in *anything* anymore," the comedian quipped. "Like, religion is so mythological . . . And science, on the other hand, is just pure empiricism, which by virtue of its method excludes metaphysics. And I guess I wouldn't believe in anything if it wasn't for my lucky astrology mood watch."

~

A joke, and now a confession: Allen Ginsberg did not write the review that appeared earlier in this chapter. He did appear—briefly—in the January 1969 issue of *Rolling Stone*. "I'm feeling as well as you'd expect," he told editor Jann Wenner from his hospital bed. "It was worse at first; I didn't shit for a week—couldn't—and that included Thanksgiving dinner."

Ginsberg and Peter Orlovsky had just dropped off Lawrence Ferlinghetti at the airport in Albany when their car hit a patch of black ice, putting the poet in the hospital. Ginsberg liked how the *Stone* allowed musicians to wax lyrical on "metaphysics and politics and matters social." And in fact, he had actually agreed to review the White Album before the car smash scuppered those plans. That much is true.

Perhaps that false review should have had a footnote revealing the device. The note would have said that *this did not happen—but it could have*. It would have explained that some of the words in the false review had been taken verbatim from actual, real sources.[64] But that the overall approach and meaning and *thrust* of the thing, of course, had been an invention, a shuck.

IN MARCH THE COMMUNE MOVED back to the Spahn Movie Ranch. Dune buggies and car parts, as well as (in most accounts) guns, knives, and other weapons, began piling up out behind the Outlaw Shacks. Bikers and other unsavory characters, to use a euphemism, began visiting. Some stayed, like Donkey Dan DeCarlo, so nicknamed for an impressive physical attribute. Danny worked on bikes and cars, and provided a connection to a local gang, the Straight Satans. A few of his biker brothers visited, too: sometimes to buy drugs, other times to hang, and for a few weeks in March, to visit the Helter Skelter Club.[65]

The idea for the club came from someone visiting the ranch on legitimate business. After hiring a horse for the day, the woman mentioned she'd need to go home to freshen up before heading out to the Sunset Strip. Why not integrate a club into the ranch? A few commune members pitched the idea to old George, who agreed—for a cut. (George always seemed short of money; before the group moved out to the desert, Charlie had even paid a substantial outstanding tax bill using a new group member's savings.)

The group worked quickly to convert the old saloon, knocking down a wall and slapping on some paint. "The stage walls were blacked, overlapped with day-glo freeform, and lit by black lights," according to Squeaky, "and the dance floor had several moods of lighting, including the flashing strobes that appeared to fragment moving bodies."[66] Charlie, Bobby, and Clem jammed almost every night, resurrecting their band, The Milky Way. When they paused, Fromme recalls, patrons played "45 records we'd paid to stock in George's antique Wurlitzer jukebox."[67]

At this point Tex Watson, after a few months' dealing drugs with old friends, returned to the fold. He remembered the dance floor, the couches, the black lights strung from wall to wall, the song lyrics daubed in fluorescent paint. And he remembered a jar for donations standing in the corner: "so we can buy things to get ready for Helter Skelter," someone explained to him, "when it comes down."

He remembers the jukebox playing the White Album almost ceaselessly, its spinning pausing only for Charlie to sing his new songs.* The new songs, Tex writes, "seemed to borrow a lot of phrases and ideas from the White Album; they were all about Helter Skelter and being time for someone to rise and somebody else to flee to the desert." He recalls the girls singing a refrain in unison—the line, "better get your dune buggy ready"—but as no extant songs bear that line, he might be misremembering the track that would later be released as "Ride Away" (usually rendered "Ra-Hide Away").

"Everyone, who is The One, is out looking for the last door," the narrator opens. The girls sometimes punctuate his pleas with an interjection: "Ra-hide away!" Or else in unison, they repeat his points for emphasis ("don't look back, just go! go!," for instance, and "just follow the music! just follow the sounds!"). And as Tex suggests, this song does interleave other sources. The Beatles feature (a tagline, "it's comin' down quick!," evokes "Helter Skelter"), as does the Bible:

Yea though you walk through the Valley of Death
   I'll be be*side* you—
Ra-hide! Away!

Everyone knew these new songs, Tex wrote, and they all danced and sang and partied together: "Susan-Sadie in the middle of things doing her go-go number, while Charlie and the others sang at the top of their lungs and the psychedelic posters throbbed with their sickly colors in the black light."[68]

And over the scene loomed a mural, painted by a friend from San Francisco, and covering the wall above the couches lining the dance floor, though Tex forgets to mention it. So back to Squeaky for a description of the painting: "a city in flames as people on motorcycles fled to a clean land in the desert."[69]

~

On first reading that description, a feeling of *déjà vu*—a phenomenon that correlates positively with my cryptomnesia—unsettled me, so I was relieved to

---

* Could the "ancient Wurlitzer" play LPs? Surely he meant the regular stereo. This error might be an artifact of revision, a ghostwriter trying to fit too much information into too little space in *Will You Die For Me?*, which bears the note, "as told to Chaplain Ray." Chaplain Ray arranged the following plot points in a single chapter describing Tex's return to the commune: listening to the Beatles, the Helter Skelter prophecy, the group's growing violence, as well as Watson's own brainwashing. It's a dense section; in my own narrative, I have distributed these elements differently for purposes of pacing, if not also historical accuracy.

find the source of this memory in Nathanael West's novel, *The Day of the Locust* (1939). The hero of the novel, Tod Hackett, has come to Los Angeles to work in the film industry. Author West matriculated him at Yale University's School of Fine Arts; he then forced poor Tod to encounter a real murderer's row of losers, weirdos, freaks, and hustlers, all chewed up and spit out by the American dream. It's a horrible book. Tod falls in love with starlet Faye, who lures him into a morass of immorality. She does not love him; he fantasizes about taking her by force. Tod befriends a salt-of-the-earth, ingenuous man named Homer, who later clubs to death a child.

Oppressed by the wickedness and superficiality of his surroundings, Tod dreams of painting his magnum opus, a large-scale mural populated by all the "people who come to California to die," people hellbent on destroying Hollywood before fanning out to raze the rest of the United States. Had he painted this mural, he would have called it, "The Burning of Los Angeles."

~

An allegorical work, not to be taken literally.

~

And the fifth angel sounded, and I saw a star fall from heaven unto the earth: and to him was given the key of the bottomless pit.

And he opened the bottomless pit; and there arose a smoke out of the pit, as the smoke of a great furnace; and the sun and the air were darkened by reason of the smoke of the pit.

And there came out of the smoke *locusts* upon the earth: and unto them was given power, as the scorpions of the earth have power.[70]

~

Crawling across the circus floor, the scorpion holds its prey with forward pincers before striking with venomous tail. It does this only when absolutely necessary; the production of venom requires a serious metabolic investment. Protein-rich venom strangles the blood vessels, causing the creature's blood pressure to plummet, often resulting in death. So with smaller prey, the scorpion injects a form of prevenom, which works by blocking the proper functioning of nerve cells, in effect paralyzing its victim.[71]

All sorts of effects can be achieved by mucking around with a creature's nervous system. LSD works to modify the serotonin receptors on the surface of brain cells, for instance, changing how the central nervous system manages sensory input. In contrast, amphetamines rapidly increase the speed at which the central nervous system processes messages traveling between the brain and the body. As young people began experimenting with purposefully short-circuiting their nervous systems, often to induce states of pleasure and euphoria, or transcendence and even awareness, the government increasingly became interested in their recreational drug use. That's why Charlie's old parole officer Jubal (t/n Roger Smith), in a curious career move, had turned to exploring the effects of speed on formerly normal individuals.

Based in California, the Amphetamine Research Project wanted to learn how the Flower Children of 'Sixty-Seven had become the Speed Freaks of 'Sixty-Eight. Smith specifically wanted to learn about the effects of speed on violence within groups, including whether violence could be induced or facilitated by these drugs. Journalists have now collated a fascinating collection of apophenic moments suggesting that "the Manson Family" itself might have resulted from government programs seeking to understand and influence group dynamics—and to discredit the counterculture.[72] Yet we have returned to Roger Smith not to insinuate any sort of conspiracy, but rather to foreshadow a particular interpretation of events to come.

"The street level dealer is almost always a compulsive user of speed, struggling to maintain himself day to day," Smith wrote in the *Journal of Psychedelic Drugs*. "Rarely is he able to buy speed on consignment because he is regarded as untrustworthy. Because he generally deals openly on the street, he is frequently arrested or 'ripped off' by fellow users. Because he often shoots up his supply of speed before selling it, he is forced to heavily adulterate the drug or to sell another substance which resembles speed, a practice known as 'burning.'"[73]

~

But if we were to posit a conspiracy, there's much evidence showing that the American government funded some pretty far-out schemes between the 1950s and the 1970s. Certain schemes seem silly, farcical. CIA agents made plans to cause Fidel Castro's beard to fall out, for instance, rendering him a wimp or a sissy in the eyes of his fellow revolutionaries. But government-sponsored programs also sprayed domestic populations with anthrax, and dosed an untold number of civilians with mind-altering drugs. With operation Midnight Climax, agents in San Francisco tested the effects of sex and drugs on interrogations, training sex workers to lure johns to a CIA test center. Operation Artichoke allegedly used hypnosis and drugs to create violent sleeper agents, though of course these political assassins never succeeded.[74]

Certain programs defy belief. Dr. Donald Ewen Cameron, who evaluated Nazi Rudolf Hess at Nuremberg, served as president of both the American Psychiatric Association and the American Psychopathological Association.[75] He also received funding from MKUltra, a secret program to study mind control. These funds supported research into what he termed "psychic driving." Cameron recruited individuals with minor problems for studies where he sought to "depattern" them, stripping away their personality, before attempting to alter their behaviors and beliefs through repeated exposure to messages looped on bits of magnetic tape. Cameron isolated his subjects and injected them with drugs. Then headphones playing pre-recorded mantras pounded them with repetitive messaging. He did not use nonsense words, like "om" or "nosensemakessense." He used more insidious phrases. Your mother doesn't love you. Everyone hates you.[76]

Did such experiments work? That's hard to say. They succeeded in breaking people down, splitting formerly more-or-less healthy individuals into a heap of non-functioning parts. But there's little direct evidence that, after turning someone into a blank slate, the doctor or anyone else could implant new memories, or plans of action.

~

These real-world experiments would only be revealed in 1975 by the Church Committee, two years after the CIA director Richard Helms had ordered all documents related to mind-control programs be destroyed.

But similarly fantastical rumors permeated the counterculture in the late 1960s. The United States had organized a system of concentration camps, into which agents would place members of the counterculture.[77] The government planned to use drugs to pacify political dissidents. (Some believed that these dissidents might put LSD into the water supply to control their political opponents, or at least open them up to the possibility of enlightenment.[78]) The commune lived in this world of rumor and the fantastical, of course, a time and place where *anything* might seemingly be true.

Another drug rumor, invented in the sixties, remained circulating during my adolescence. Here's how I remember it. A young person crossing a state border comes to a police checkpoint. He's holding a few sheets of blotter paper, thin, absorbent, covered in printed smiley faces, impregnated with lysergic diethylamide-25. To avoid detection, the young man hides the sheets under his clothing. But nervous sweat causes the chemicals to absorb into his bloodstream. Hundreds of doses hit him simultaneously. This young person would spend the rest of his natural life in a hospital, believing himself to have turned into an orange, and scared to death that someone might come along and peel him.[79] I remember hearing this story from a friend in the early nineties.

~

Around this time, we tried ingesting *Musa sapientum Bananadine*, a compound allegedly found inside bananas. To prepare this hallucinogen, you first scrape and dry out the stringy parts clinging to the inside of the banana peel. You then roll them like a joint, and smoke them.

The *Berkeley Barb* printed instructions for preparing banana joints in early 1967; Donovan's song "Mellow Yellow," some people believe, referenced this. That recipe would be reprinted in *The Anarchist's Cookbook*, published by William Powell in 1971, where teenagers like me and my friends would find it, stripped of any countercultural winks and seemingly sincere, to the consternation of suburban parents for decades.

Some of us tried to smoke the insides of peanut shells, too, which also doesn't work. None of us saw through the thin veil separating our world from the next. None of us experienced anything other than sore throats.

~

Cameron had another strange idea: that psychological conditions could be contagious. Sick individuals represented an infection that, in certain cases, might lay low the body politic. All sorts of things could sicken individuals, and by extension, society. Nazi Germany obviously demonstrated mass psychosis. One of Cameron's colleagues, William Sargant, suggested that rock 'n' roll could destabilize American society by similarly infecting groups of people, enervating dancers and substituting anxious, repetitive motion for normal, healthy vitality.[80]

But then again, the deleterious effects of popular music represented just one among many disorienting factors of life in the modern world. "Twentieth century living, like tenth century living and living in the dawn-days when social security was a matter of a fast-moving pair of legs, is a business which keeps most of us guessing, mostly wrong, most of the time," Cameron wrote in *Life is for Living* (1948).

"Our days, and half our nights, are a wavering *chiaroscuro* of people growing up, getting middle-aged and old and changing so that you hardly know how to talk when you see them again; people jumping off bridges and under trains;

people leading lives dull and dreary and routine as dumbwaiters; people blazing with ecstasy, dying for ideals, dying from their own stupidities or living to bore others to death."[81]

~

Pressure mounted on the commune members living at the Spahn Movie Ranch over the spring months. Accounts largely agree that the group began converting dune buggies and other vehicles for travel into the desert; some other accounts suggest that at this time, or perhaps a bit later, members began training with small weapons. Charlie had always tailored messages to his audience. Now an influx of younger people helped push Manson's rap toward more revolutionary topics.[82] Sadie and Tex began taking amphetamines, too, even though Manson, some say, forbade it. Other individuals began manufacturing hallucinogens from belladonna, a dangerous plant with psychoactive compounds. At one point, Tex overdosed on the weed, turning himself into a zombie for days.[83]

Members of the motorcycle club the Straight Satans seem to have become more closely integrated with the commune during this period. The club's president gifted Charlie a sword at one point; biker Danny DeCarlo, going through a messy divorce, crashed with the group most nights. Did the presence of these one-percenters arouse any anticipation about violence?

~

"Hells Angels will be in London within the next week, on the way to straighten out Czechoslovakia," Beatle George wrote in a memo later that year. "They may look as though they are going to do you in but are very straight and do good things, so don't fear them or up-tight them. Try to assist them without neglecting your Apple business and without letting them take control of Savile Row."[84] The visit did not go well.

In *Hells Angels: A Strange and Terrible Saga* (1967), gonzo journalist Hunter S. Thompson portrayed bikers as rebels manifesting a deeply *American* alienation, not unlike that of student radicals or other seekers. They too emerged from the noxious miasma of the consumer society, mass media, and individualism. "Far from being freaks," Thompson wrote, "the Hells Angels are a logical product of the culture that now claims to be shocked at their existence."[85] The biker was "like Genghis Khan on an iron horse, a monster steed with a fiery anus," Thompson wrote, "flat out through the eye of a beer can and up your daughter's leg with no quarter asked and none given; show the squares some class, give em a whiff of those kicks they'll never know."[86]

Some people later claimed Charlie intended the Straight Satans to act as bodyguards for the commune when the race war he now called Helter Skelter started coming down. Later in 1969, the Rolling Stones invited a few Hells Angels to provide security at their free concert in Los Angeles. In retrospect, this decision also turned out to have been a mistake.

~

There's a danger in seeming too flippant, in using a tone that seems unserious, especially when writing within a genre that purports to be objective. That's because certain devices make no sense in certain contexts. We expect novels to use symbolism, for instance, and we valorize rock lyrics that can be "read" on multiple levels at once. But you would feel hoodwinked if the author of a nonfiction book planted subterranean messages beneath the surface of its text.[87]

Imagine that unfaithful author instructing you to dig down to find his book's real meanings. Or what if he said nothing, but in reading the work, you came to discover certain codes? Imagine counting words in each section, and finding that one passage had been carefully rendered to contain 777 words (a significant number in Western esotericism, signifying the Thirty-Two Paths of Wisdom in the Qabalah) or 33 words (a key number in Western Christianity, representing Elohim, uttered thirty-three times in the Creation Story, or King David, thirty-third in the line of descent between Adam and Christ, and so on). Or maybe you find 1111, or 13, or some other auspicious number. Would you lose faith in the author? Or yourself?

That's why we need genres, especially insofar as they provide the rules by which an author renders the messiness of human experience into stories that *make sense* in very particular ways. Memoirs align experiences with an accounting of one's self to mount truth claims: *I was there and I am me,* says Tex (or Sadie or Squeaky or Snake), *and this is what really went down.* In contrast, the genre of true crime relies on facticity and objectivity, usually in the service of a cult of expertise, whether forensic, criminological, or psychological, to make truth claims: *These facts explain the story beyond a reasonable doubt,* Bugliosi says, *and there can be no room for further speculation.* There are other genres, too. Gonzo journalism, for instance, mounts truth claims on the foundation of rich resonances among firsthand observation and visceral experience and plain old vibes: *This story is true,* Hunter S. Thompson says, *because a Hells Angel kicked the shit out of me.*

~

We shouldn't beat up on an author simply because we do not like the rules they have chosen to play by. So many have leveled criticisms at authors like Truman Capote, who allegedly "made up" elements of his true-crime masterpiece, *In Cold Blood* (1966). (Bobby Beausoleil said Truman invented most of the interview he published in *Music for Chameleons*, too.[88]) But don't we all stretch the truth here and there in offering an account of our selves and our worlds?

~

A musician like Bob Dylan had many selves, and we accept that as evidence of his genius. Dylan learned to switch between faces, almost like a performance, one biographer claims, from his hero Woody Guthrie.

"There ain't no one little certain self that is you," Guthrie wrote in an autobiography filled with exaggerations and even outright untruths. "I'm not some certain self. I'm a lot of selfs. A lot of minds and changes of minds. Moods by the wagon load."[89] (Eighty words.)

~

In early June, two men showed up at Spahn Movie Ranch to do some preliminary shooting for a documentary film (a deceitful genre, and a deceitful medium). Mike Deasy usually worked as a session musician, playing guitar with the vaunted Wrecking Crew. He had a mobile recording unit and, so the story goes, had been planning to record Native American groups.[90] "I said to Terry, '[Manson] should be captured on film,'" Gregg Jakobson recalled decades later. "'You're never going to capture this guy on [audio] tape. It'd be like having footage of Castro while he was still in the mountains or something. This guy was a real rebel. It had to be movie footage.'"[91] So Terry Melcher thought to invite Deasy along to record the commune.

According to official accounts, Melcher auditioned the commune in May, but had come away unimpressed. "Unfortunately, the music was below-average nothing," Melcher would later write, "and as far as I was concerned, Manson was like every other starving, hippie songwriter who was then jamming Sunset Boulevard, a hundred thousand every day, who looked, dressed, talked, and sang exactly like Charles Manson, sang about the same topics of peace and revolution, about the themes that were in the Beatles' albums."*

Melcher agreed with Jakobson that the commune might make an interesting subject for a television special, so the story goes. But everything went wrong. Someone dosed Deasy with LSD. There was some kind of violence, too; Charlie might have beat up Randy Starr, a one-armed stuntman known for a trick where he got dragged by the neck behind a horse, who worked at the ranch. Or maybe Tex and a few other people beat up Deasy. Or maybe the commune stole their equipment.

~

Though if Charlie really had been so keen for a recording contract, why wouldn't he have behaved in ways that helped him get one? Instead, he attacks people, threatens them, and commits all sorts of heinous acts.

Can we say, perhaps, that savagery breeds savagery?[92]

~

Eighty words. Eight-zero. Eight—oh. A cosmic number, eight, preceded by the number representing balance between the material and the spiritual worlds. A number referencing the planet Saturn, namesake of the Titan who, fearing the parricidal prophecy of Gaia, devoured each of his children in turn.

ON THE FIRST DAY OF JULY, Charlie shot a black man named Bernard Crowe. This event without question accelerated the disintegration of the commune and its trajectory toward increased violence.

The phone rang at the Spahn Movie Ranch, with Crowe looking for "Charles." On this point, all accounts agree. Charles "Tex" Watson had worked out a deal to

---

* This quote appears on page 245 of A. E. Hotchner's 1976 Doris Day biography, *Doris Day: Her Own Story*. Here Melcher placed the audition in "the summer of 1968," though other evidence seems to suggest this actually occurred much later. Given that the audition most likely occurred in April or May 1969, Melcher's ingenuousness at the scene—his friend Gregg Jakobson just happened upon the group, and "thought the setup was interesting on a cultural level as well as musical and that it might make a television special"—seems suspicious. In his authoritative biography, *Manson*, author Jeff Guinn accidentally cites Melcher's statement as appearing on pages 291–2 of Hotchner's book. You can find Melcher's words reproduced in *Manson* on page 222—an auspicious number, perhaps evoking the conspiracy to murder Christ as related in Luke 22:2: "And the chief priests and scribes sought how they might kill him; for they feared the people."

burn Lotsapoppa for about twenty-five hundred dollars in a scheme so baroque there's no way it could have worked. Tex's ex-girlfriend, Luella, knew Crowe, who would put up the money; Tex would take the money to the supplier, who would sell twenty-five kilos at a discount, with Tex keeping three kilos and Luella a couple hundred bucks. Only there was no supplier: Tex planned to just take the money and run.

Of course, things didn't quite work out that way. Crowe's partner held Luella as collateral, and when Tex took off, threatened to kill her. The scheme sure makes Tex look like some backdated-chuck. That's when Charlie—Charles Willis Manson—came into the picture, appearing at Crowe's apartment with T. J. Wallerman to liberate Luella (t/n Rosina Kruger). It doesn't quite matter what actually happened: T. J. and Charlie showed up with a gun, and T. J. didn't shoot; maybe Charlie gave it to Crowe and told him to "take a life, a life for a life."[93] They then might've struggled, and the gun went off. Or maybe Charlie just shot him. Then perhaps the next day, with residents at the Spahn Movie Ranch on high alert, someone saw on the news that a Black Panther had been killed.

~

Narratives about what the "killing" of Lotsapoppa (who was not a Black Panther) initiated here diverge. Perhaps the altercation heightened paranoia at the Ranch, pushing everyone to begin committing even more dangerous and risky acts. Tex had done the burn to raise money for the group, he would claim, on Charlie's direct orders. How quickly did the violence now spiral?

But then again, maybe Tex wasn't as integrated into the commune as investigators later claimed. After all, he had been outside the group, dealing drugs in Hollywood during the period in which Charlie allegedly began laying his heavy Helter Skelter trip on the group. Tex later represented himself as having briefly escaped Charlie's clutches, only to have been drawn back, seemingly not of his own free will. But maybe Charlie had lost control of the group? Or never really had control?

~

"We are all rumor's children," journalist C. Robert Jennings wrote in a short editorial published the day before the Los Angeles police department announced they had solved the Tate-LaBianca murders. "But new leisure, old caprice and the nakedness of Freudian insight have conspired to change even Webster's latest definition of rumor: 'an unconfirmed piece of information or explanation disseminated among the public by other than formal news agencies or sources.'

"Some recent horrors in American life suggest that informal sources no longer have a corner on the rumor market. Moreover, even the most royal of sources tend recklessly to feed on the fiction of the commonalty and eternalize it as fact. But ours is the age of the voyeur, and disclosure must be total (and totalitarian), even if it is tasteless, even if it is totally false. And often it is both."[94]

~

When a black family came to ride horses at the Spahn Movie Ranch a day or so later, that sealed it: Charlie had shot a Black Panther, and the riders had been conducting surveillance. The Black Panthers' comrades would soon descend on the old movie set at Chatsworth. Charlie allegedly stationed commune members on lookout duty. They strung field phones between dugouts. They kept constant vigil. Everyone armed themselves.

Now it was happening. Really happening.

Coming down.

Coming down fast.

5

July 1969 to December 1969

or, The Love and Terror Cult

CHARLIE SKIMMED THE SWITCHBLADE ACROSS HIS NAILS. But not much fazed Stephen Desper. Like when Dennis brought a woman to a recording session, requesting the engineer close-mic the muffled sounds of their lovemaking, sounds that allegedly can be found deep in the mix for "All I Want to Do" from *20/20* (1969). You might say Desper had become accustomed to outré antics in the studio at Brian's home.

Wilson family members lounged by the pool in Bel Air, according to one account, while Brian Wilson remained safely ensconced in his bedroom. A recalcitrant Charlie seemed incapable of taking direction. The young women he brought along seemed absolutely zonked. In an oft-cited quip, Brian's wife, Marilyn, wondered if she should disinfect the bathrooms after they left. According to one Beach Boy, she did.[1]

How many songs did Manson track? At least a handful, possibly an album's worth. Maybe "close to a hundred hours of Charlie's music," according to manager Nick Grillo, "[were recorded] at Brian's studio."[2] But Charlie wouldn't listen to Desper. Charlie wouldn't stay put in front of the microphone. Maybe Charlie placed a handgun on the engineer's console. Charlie definitely tried to intimidate him with the switchblade routine; everyone remembers that.

"I took the tapes to the office," Desper later recalled. "They asked me how it went, and I said, 'He won't take direction—and I don't think he's going to be produceable. But his songs are fairly good, I like the lyrics and so forth, so take a listen.'"[3]

~

By now this posture—pointing out inconsistencies and inscrutabilities in different accounts—must surely be wearing thin, whether it's essential to the nonfiction genre or not.

For instance, the timeline for the recording session doesn't quite make sense. Some secondary sources place the session sometime in 1968 or in March 1969, though Desper has elsewhere referred to the August murders as occurring "a couple weeks" after the session.[4] Over four pages in his unreliably self-serving autobiography, Mike Love suggested the following sequence of events: a recording session at Brian's home, a background check by Brother Records, the group's dawning realization about Manson's con, and the killing of a Black man at the Spahn Movie Ranch.[5] Cross-referencing these four pages with other accounts, we can note that the recording session probably happened in either March or July 1969, the police check in August 1968, the realization as early as July 1968. The killing—a grisly affair with an automatic weapon, that Love claimed Dennis had witnessed—does not seem to have ever happened.

"There's a metric ton of misinformation when it comes to the conventional wisdom surrounding Dennis & Charlie's relationship throughout '68–'69," wrote one contributor to the Beach Boys Everlasting Summer forum, "that I tried to address in an article I was solicited to write for one of the classic rock monthlies—before backing out halfway through when I realized that there's no way anybody's ever going to really get to the bottom of it. But I can bang on about my theories if anyone is interested."[6]

~

The passage of time inevitably smooths the rough and ragged edges of phenomena in the round, leaving only two-dimensional representations. With regards to the Tate-LaBianca killings, three primary narratives, and many more variants, remain. Like the wire armature of the sculptor, such scaffoldings precede and give shape to subsequent imaginings of the case. And in providing a framework for organizing our visions, these narrative scaffolds can be said to make the worlds we inhabit.

In this sense, narratives do not distill the past into its essential, true form as much as they conjure new possibilities. As a sort of alembic, the author's pen mediates between so-called source material (or more polemically, "evidence") and the published page.[7] Or so many commentators, as we have seen, had come to believe during this period.

~

We now arrive at the moment when radically divergent theories about what happened next begin to enter the public record, so to speak. Because most narrations of the commune begin and end here, the basic contours of these events bear repeating.

Recall that in early July, Tex burned a Black man named Lotsapoppa, t/n Bernard Crowe, which means he tried to cheat and steal from him. Manson, along with commune member T. J. Wallerman, then shot Crowe. Believing the drug dealer to be dead (he was not), and possibly also believing him to be a member of the Black Panthers (again, he was not), Charlie placed everyone at the Spahn Movie Ranch on high alert. At some point in the preceding months, they had armed themselves. Against police harassment, or in preparation for a race war. Or was their paranoia the expression of an emergent group psychosis?

At the end of July came a second possible drug burn, or perhaps simple armed robbery. Bobby Beausoleil had connected Straight Satans at the Ranch with Gary Hinman, a thirty-something graduate student who synthesized mescaline in his home lab. The bikers received a bum batch, and middleman Bobby, along with Mary and Sadie, went to retrieve their money. Or else Charlie heard that Gary had come into an inheritance, and sent the trio to shake him down. Over a chaotic three days, someone shot Hinman, and then Manson almost completely severed his ear with a sword. Beausoleil stabbed him to death, and someone painted messages on the walls in blood ("POLITICAL PIGGY" and a paw print) to suggest Black Panthers committed the grisly crime.

Now came the madness of those two infamous nights in August. After the police picked up Bobby Beausoleil, who had been driving the dead man's car, Manson ordered commune members to commit copycat murders to help exonerate his brother.[8] Or Charlie, enraged by Dennis Wilson's rejection, ordered the killings as a kind of psychotic revenge on "straight" society. Or several of the victims had been involved in selling drugs and just got burned. On the first night, Tex drove Sadie, Patty, and a young woman named Linda Kasabian, a new commune member who stayed in the car; Manson drove the second night, along with those four plus Katie and Clem, but left with Linda and Clem before the killings. These murders—five people at 10050 Cielo Drive, including the actress Sharon Tate, celebrity hairdresser Jay Sebring, coffee heiress Abigail Folger, sometimes drug dealer (and Roman Polanski hanger-on) Wojtek Frykowski, and a young guy named Steven Parent (who just happened to be in the wrong place at the wrong time), as well as two people at 3301 Waverly Drive, a well-off couple named Leno and Rosemary LaBianca—later came to be known as the Tate-LaBianca murders.

~

All storytellers, whether conscious of them or not, have motivations. Nevermind that the genres within which we work have their own, motivating logics, logics demanding particular kinds of evidence and approaches to argumentation. You see the problem. Can histories even be true?[9]

One thing is for sure. Over the coming months and years, events and details from this period came to be fixed in such a way that a jury, speaking on behalf of the People of the State of California, would decide to put a handful of commune members to death. And yet the larger constellation of stories that prosecutors, law enforcement, and journalists began presenting to the American public at the same time somehow remained unfixed, providing raw materials for everyone else—from lay researchers, to filmmakers and artists and musicians, to true-crime hacks, to legitimate authors like me—to combine and recombine, to use in exploring such diverse topics as drugs, popular music, the generation gap, free will, the rot at the heart of American society, or even (as here) the emergence and consolidation of a post-truth order.

~

So it goes.

ON THE MORNING OF THE SIXTEENTH OF AUGUST, less than a week after the Tate-LaBianca murders, scores of law enforcement officers descended on the Spahn Movie Ranch.

"Personally appeared before me on this 13th day of August, 1969," begins the affidavit supporting the search warrant, "the affiant, William C. Gleason, a peace officer, who, *on oath*, makes complaint, and deposes and says that he has and there is probable and reasonable cause to believe, *and that he does believe, that there is now on the premises located at and also described as* 12000 Santa Susana Road, Chatsworth, commonly known as Spahn Movie Ranch, consisting of approximately 200 acres of open ranch land, including all building, storage rooms, vehicles, garages and outbuildings of any kind located thereon. And on the person(s) of Charles Milles Manson, aka Charles Milles Summers, 5-7 in height, weighing 140 pounds, brown hair, brown eyes, DOB 11-11-34, with a tattoo of a woman's head on each arm, and a one-inch scar over his left eye. The following personal property, to wit: stolen automobile parts, including but not limited to VW frames, engines, transmissions, and carts thereof, and rifles, automatic pistols and rifles."

This affidavit collated a range of evidence and hearsay: materials that might "give one cause to believe," to make sure he *does* believe, that "the person(s)" of Charles Milles Manson committed a range of property crimes. It lists prior law enforcement visits to Chatsworth, establishing a pattern of suspicious activity and describing the ranch and its inhabitants in austere detail. At one such visit, officers tripped a field alarm system; "the only persons found were those who were asleep and didn't wake up with the alarm."

Those officers observed what appeared to be the group's primary residence: "The house was empty of furniture, but there was evidence that someone had been there just prior to [the officer's] arrival. On the floor was approximately 8 bed rolls. Around the door, stuck in the wall, were about 6 or 8 bayonets, and on the floor near the door was a box (200 rounds) of .32 caliber bullets. Also in this house was a military-type crank field phone, the same as those observed in the main building and house trailer just north of the main building.

On 15 July, the affidavit notes, law enforcement had surveilled the site by helicopter. At this point, the credulous reader may believe, and will have reasonable cause to believe, that something nefarious must have been going on. Officers also spoke to informants within the commune. On the first day of August, a "possible member of 'Satan Slaves' name of Summers" said "that his group anticipated an attack by the 'Black Panthers.'" ("Charles Summers, M/35" was one of Charlie's aliases.) But the affidavit's most detailed information concerning the group's mindset comes from a mysterious person who stayed with the commune for ten days in July. On the tenth of August, the affiant did aver, "said confidential reliable informant did speak with personal knowledge when imparting the information herein set forth, unless and except where specifically stated to be otherwise."

Here's the gist of what that said confidential reliable informant—the snitch—told law enforcement: that people in the Chatworth compound all had handguns and rifles, and many slept with them; that everyone seemed on edge, and Manson threatened them; that the singer "appears to be the leader of the group of 20–25 persons staying at the Spahn Movie Ranch."[10]

~

In London, the so-called King of the Witches, Alex Saunders, began telling everyone he had initiated Sharon Tate as a witch during the filming of her finest film, *Eye of the Devil* (1966). He claimed to have photographs showing a robe-bedecked Sharon participating in magick rituals. (The photographs he showed people were probably publicity shots from the film.)[11] In Los Angeles, gossip columnist Joe Hyams told readers that Sharon studied voodoo; another journalist claimed he attended a Black Mass at Jay Sebring's home alongside Sharon and other Hollywood elites, all clad in white robes.[12]

Anyone who was anyone told everyone else that Sharon had invited them to her home on Cielo Drive *that night*. There, but for the grace of God: Jacqueline Susann, Cass Elliott, Steve McQueen, Waylon Jennings, Richard Burton, Quincy Jones, Sergio Leone, Terry O'Neill, Ava Roosevelt . . . [13] Gossip rags reported all sorts of innuendo about the sex habits of the rich and famous victims: Jay Sebring's penchant for tying up young women with silken scarves, or whipping them, or making them tie him up, or whip him; the alleged orgies; Roman's short films of these depraved acts.

"You wouldn't believe how weird these people were," one detective told Barry Farrell at *Life* magazine. "If you live like that, what do you expect?"[14] Manson authors of all stripes inevitably invoke the detective's next, more quotable, observation, found on page four of the September 1969 issue of *Life* (the one with the cover depicting a very much alive Paul McCartney and family on his farm in Scotland): "live freaky, die freaky."

~

While *Helter Skelter* suggests that Manson had little contact with Wilson and Melcher from this point, more recent research has revealed that investigators turned up evidence to the contrary. One informant saw Melcher tripping, on his knees, begging Manson to forgive him. For what? The Beach Boys tour manager has more recently claimed that Melcher recorded a session with Manson while the group was "on a fairly long tour." (Would that have been in April 1969? Or June 1969?). He also recalled that FBI agents visited the group's office in August.[15] If you believe that, however, you'd have to start thinking there was some kind of cover-up going on.

~

To his credit, journalist Barry Farrell presented a more measured case, inviting us to understand Hollywood's paranoid reactions as a kind of Rorschach test that revealed people's deepest fears. "Everyone sees the murders in his own light," Farrell wrote. "Every story casts an interchangeable demon into the same blank scenario. Speed freaks or fags or Mafia contract men or black terrorists or witchcraft nuts or vigilante rednecks enter the house, do the job, slip away."

The most repeated rumor, eroticizing these crimes as an act of psychosexual revenge by persons unknown, had been debunked by the coroner's report. But the journalist claimed that we should take even debunked theories seriously—as an instrument for interpreting hidden social anxieties. "The rumors read like a graph of community paranoia," as Farrell continued. "Every story promotes the murders into assassinations, crimes of logical consequence in which some vision of the victims' way of living makes them accomplices in their own deaths. It is as if no one is satisfied with the crime until it can be perceived as a political act—the murder of a life style." And working backwards from the speculations, we can discern "an entire social attitude."

"Those with positive knowledge that the blacks did it are those who feel most threatened by the blacks. Those who identify most closely with the victims' way of life tend to see the hand of fascist America, snuffing out its young. Each new rumor works within its own vortex of fear, swirling around in uncollected fragments until it finally winds up proving, one way or another, that *the jig is up for us all.*"[16]

~

The jig may be up here too, as a wave of primary sources—such a disorienting tonal shift—now threatens to overwhelm our accounting of this story. As our narrative bears down on its conclusion, I begin feeling as if I have not read *anything*, and certainly not enough. At times I feel like an anatomist who, having excised from his specimen a single organ, slices with his trusty microtome ever more paper-thin segments to analyze. But has he lost sight of the whole? Or maybe like a film editor who, cutting together reels and reels of raw footage, crafting a plot, developing characters, even at times intimating moral consequences for their actions, worries—now that the time for concluding has come—that his account may not convince. That is, after all, the aim of any work worth its salt (though any reader might be forgiven for not taking too seriously the professions of a hopeless aporetic).

~

Concluding that essay in *Life*, Barry Farrell related a sick exchange that allegedly happened in a Hollywood club. Someone had seated themselves at his table: "I saw that the face hanging in the smoke across the table was moving its lips my way. I cupped my hand against the music and leaned close to hear. 'Let's hope Roman has enough sense to sell the rights to somebody good,' the face was shouting. I searched the face for some sign that it was joking. But no. The face was serious, sincere."[17]

~

Serious, sincere? Detached? Even "academic?" As the underlying aim has been to understand how stories about the musical lives of Charles Manson could have been told in their time and after, and because that time period questioned the very notion of authorship itself, what sort of authorial voice, I wondered in beginning to write this book, could capture these stories? One conscious of the impossibility of a truly omniscient narration? But too naïve to suspect such a voice may also prove unreliable?

Imagine the voice of The Fool in the Tarot, eyes cast heavenward, a figure who may be placed either at the beginning or the end of the cards comprising the Major Arcana. He plays a key role in a novel by Italo Calvino published just twelve months after California abolished the death penalty. A group of travelers meet by a tavern in a forest. They have been rendered mute, for reasons unknown. How will they tell their stories? A tarot deck is produced. And drawing its cards, each traveler begins making an account of themselves.

Do you know how the Tarot works? In the usual game, one person places cards from the deck in a predetermined pattern, "reading" these cards to explain past, present, or future fortunes. But in Calvino's tavern, each mute guest aims to tell their truth using the same pattern of cards as everyone else, cards that "are read and reread with different meanings," and as "each new card placed on the table explains or corrects the meaning of the previous card," a disordered profusion of narrations proliferates, as these "stories constantly risk stumbling over each other."[18]

"The tavern's customers jostle one another around the table, which has become covered with cards, or they labor to extract their stories from the melee of the tarots, and the more the stories become confused and disjointed, the more the scattered cards find their place in an orderly mosaic," the narrator says. "Is this pattern only the result of chance, or is one of us patiently putting it together?"[19]

~

Though it cannot be possible, an underlying pattern of violence seems to have provided the template for events that happened both after and before the August 1969 murders.

In February 1970, a twenty-six-year-old Army doctor—clean-cut, Princeton graduate, father of two—claimed four hippies murdered his wife and children. "Kill the pigs!" he heard them say before slipping into unconsciousness, at least according to his account. (Jeffrey MacDonald would himself later be convicted of the murders.)[20] The doctor must have taken this story from the news, must have thought that, given the media frenzy around the Manson Family, such a story would prove compelling to his audience.

But how to explain events preceding the August 1969 killings? In July 1969, Kurt Vonnegut examined the deaths of four Cape Cod women between late 1968 and early 1969. A local hippie named Tony Costa, one of the freaks who peopled the artistic communities far out on the tip of the peninsula, had been charged; the dismembered bodies were found near a small marijuana patch he tended, and sometimes invited girls out to see.

In this gonzo retelling, we learn that Vonnegut's daughter, Edith, actually knew the alleged killer, Tony; that the author's friend, Evelyn, whom local resident Norman Mailer put in touch with his publisher, has been writing a book about the case. An architect friend tells Vonnegut a black joke making the rounds. "Tony Costa, with his mustache and long sideburns and granny glasses and dark turtleneck, walked into the Everett H. Corson Cadillac agency in Hyannis, and priced an El Dorado. 'It'll cost you an arm and a leg,' said the salesman. And Tony said, 'It's a deal.'"[21]

The publication of *Slaughterhouse-Five* in March 1969 had catapulted Vonnegut to new heights of celebrity. But the novelist had gotten into the habit of writing these quick-hit magazine pieces to keep, so to speak, body and soul together.* He brings to these essays the same sharp ear for dialogue, the same sense for the singular telling detail, that propels his longer, fictional works.

"Is this going to be bad for the freaks?" one freak worried. Yes, seemed so: the district attorney, in a ghastly press conference, insinuated that signs of cannibalism had been found at the murder scene; writer Evelyn, in a local newspaper, claimed that the patch where the bodies were found had once been the site of witches' Sabbaths. The brother-in-law of a guard at the jail where Costa awaits trial might be able to get Vonnegut a look at the autopsy photos, he tells the author, and maybe more.

---

* *Slaughterhouse-Five* can be read as "a fiction of witness," as critic Wilfrid Sheed proposed, arguing that the work represented not a novel, but a parable, and that "Vonnegut does not theorize outside his parable." Sheed seems to have meant this as a criticism, but it nevertheless encapsulates something important about storymaking at this moment in time. For the fuller context of this discussion, see "Requiem to Billy Pilgrim's Progress," *Life* magazine (March 21, 1969), p. 9.

"I might even be able to buy a piece of the rope," Vonnegut writes, "*after* the trial. Business is business, after all, and always has been. There is money to be made on the fringes of famous murders. For instance: *I* am being paid."[22]

~

Apply tightly to your heart a tourniquet, advises the crime journalist Edna Buchanan, for most people who meet their maker, in some sense, deserved it.[23] This dictum applies especially to the kinds of people who find themselves dead through such sordid circumstances as drug use, or involvement with organized crime or gang violence.

Weep for the innocents slain at the hands of such persons. ("Perhaps it is not fair," as Ellery Queen writes, "but beauty desecrated arouses outrage not awakened by ordinary murder."[24]) And empathize with the upright men and women tasked with bringing criminals to justice, for restoring order. That's the hidden, conservative compact at the heart of the true-crime genre.

~

The authorities held members of the commune for only forty-eight hours. A misdated search warrant (or some other such minor bureaucratic problem) allegedly allowed the group to go free. In short order, Charlie and a few of the men took Shorty Shea (t/n Donald), a ranch hand, to an area just outside the Ranch and executed him. They thought he had snitched. He probably had.

People throughout Los Angeles now purchased firearms and home security systems; the price of German shepherds skyrocketed. Jerry Lewis, of all people, apparently had the city's most advanced private home security system installed at his home.[25] Lt. Col. Paul Tate, Sharon's father and an army intelligence officer, grew a beard and went undercover in the California underground. Ed Sanders arrived a few months later to begin trawling crash pads and chasing down leads, filling notebooks to overflowing with information and mysteries and stories.

~

The whole situation made the commune's relocation to the desert even more urgent. But a return to Barker Ranch would not be easy. Little Paul had moved back a few months earlier, missing the events of July and August. There he had found a new guru, a prospector named Paul Crockett. And Crockett had erected a psychic barrier around the perimeter of Goler Wash.

FOR THREE DAYS AND FOR THREE NIGHTS, the inhabitants of the Barker Ranch—Juanita Wildebush, Brooks Poston, Paul Watkins, and their new mentor, Paul Crockett—heard the distant roar, something like a motor. It sounded like "a low, ominous vibration, a kind of psychic rumbling," a harbinger of something or someone.[26] What could it be?

"Your friend Charlie," Crockett told Watkins. "I lifted the gate. Wish I wouldn't have. Listen to it . . . sure ain't the sounds of harmony, is it?"[27]

A scouting group arrived first, Brenda, Tex, and Bruce driving up the wash in a dusty yellow dune buggy. Charlie and the main group stayed back. Manson wanted Crockett's "agreement" before he'd come up. Crockett assented. Bruce went to get Charlie and the rest of the group, and an hour later, everyone sat around the ranch getting to know one another. Crockett played solitaire, laying the playing cards down in neat, patterned rows. Manson launched into his Helter Skelter rap. It was coming down now, he said, coming down fast. The move to the desert had begun. Ready or not, soon everyone would be going through some serious changes.

"Dig it? I am you, and you are me," Charlie rapped.

"No," Crockett said, looking up. "That ain't true. We are both spirits . . . that's true, both capable of postulating and perceiving that which we postulate. In that sense we are the same . . . but we have lived different lives and had different experiences, therefore I am not you and you are not me."[28] Could John have been wrong? (Maybe not, if the Walrus was Paul.)

~

Across the Atlantic, John told Paul and Ringo he was done. Lennon had just played the Toronto Peace Festival with the Plastic Ono Band; a week later, he quit the Beatles, though with two albums and a film yet to be released, the group kept this news tightly under wraps.

The group had been disintegrating for some time. The final album they recorded, their penultimate release, would be *Abbey Road* (1969). In another apophany, the foursome had shot its famous cover a day before the horrors at Cielo Drive unfolded.

~

The commune now resettled at Barker Ranch. The aerial photographs soon to be published worldwide would make the site look like the cratered surface of the moon. Meanwhile, press about the unsolved killings continued churning back in Los Angeles.

The most striking image from this period can be found in a pictorial within the pages of the August 29 edition of *Life* magazine. Under the headline, "A Tragic Trip to the House on the Hill," beside a glossy headshot of summery Sharon, Roman Polanski sits by the front door at 10050 Cielo Drive. He wears a white shirt over black slacks, clenching a hand, without expression. You can make out faded brown marks on the front door, the word PIG, daubed in blood—the caption reminds readers—by persons unknown.

Look at "the world-famous orgy house," Roman sardonically remarks to the journalist, Thomas Thompson. The director has heard all the sordid rumors. (A polygraph test ruled him out as a suspect.) You the reader gawk at photographs of the home's interior, alongside Thompson's descriptive text, highlighting certain details: the zebra rug where Sebring fell, as well as the spot where "Sharon Tate, stabbed a dozen times, slashed so brutally that murder became atrocity, collapsed and died in a jumble of oddities—a yellow candle stub, a teach-yourself-Japanese instruction kit, a mauve bedroom slipper, a book on natural childbirth."

What might that assemblage of items mean? (When has murder ever not also been an atrocity? Isn't part of the atrocity our leering at this scene?) Roman is not in the photograph. You the reader see another man, helpfully captioned "clairvoyant Peter Hurkos, who worked on the Boston Strangler case." The director had invited the medium to help find the killer (or killers).

The article presents a thumbnail sketch of Roman's life. The Warsaw upbringing, and its effect on his art. ("What is horror to you, may not be horror to me.") His "European attitude toward sex." And the journalist describes Roman and Sharon's cosmopolitan circle, which included such luminaries as the Beatles and Artur Rubinstein, but also "young and sometimes troubled newcomers, the rock singers, the friends of friends whom Roman often found at his table in a nightclub and rarely sent away."[29]

~

"There are the facts as I remember them," Paul Watkins writes in the Author's Note to his autobiography, *My Life With Charles Manson*, a statement that presumably applies to his tale about Paul Crockett, too. In any event, we need to rely on the Watkins account as the only one outlining Crockett's relationship to the commune in any detail.

Grizzled Paul Crockett enters most Manson Family narratives as the person who "deprogrammed" Watkins and Brooks Poston. He arrived prospecting at Goler Wash in March 1969, and moved into Barker Ranch in Death Valley just as Helter Skelter began coming down in Los Angeles. During the long hot days he taught Paul and Brooks to pan for gold; at night, they played mind games, with Crockett teaching the young men to channel the flow of energies around them. Sometimes, Paul thought, he sounded a bit like Manson.

Here's an example: "The rhythm of life can be understood in terms of cosmic octaves . . . in laws of seven . . . the scale," Crockett rapped. "All life is conditioned in action. It's no accident, ya know, that the word *do* is the same word as the first note of the musical scale, do. The scale begins with do and ends with do, and that, ya see, is the very pulse of life. Like they say, 'the beat just goes on.' When you play music 'consciously' with this kind of awareness, ya realize what power it really has. It's like them walls of Jericho . . . music brought them right to the ground. Music can bring down a lot of walls. It's the harmony ya make when ya mine ore out of the mountains . . . that clear precision of sound that lets ya inside the mystery. Ya hit that pick just right, and the sound takes ya right up the musical scale to the jackpot."[30]

Before prospecting, Crockett had lived full-time as a seeker, sampling theosophy, the odd Eastern religion, and Scientology. His mentor had been a practitioner of alternative medicine based in Carlsbad, New Mexico, and a devotee of inventor Dr. Ruth Drown.[31] Crockett seems to have suffered from an undiagnosable chronic condition affecting his limbs. A Drown-branded device had, after nine years of pain, cured him.[32] (Drown's devices helped regulate an imbalance of electrons in certain glands, or sometimes the marrow of your bones; over time, she claimed, patients could learn to better manage their body's magnetic field.)[33]

At some point Crockett began developing conceptology, a homegrown philosophical system that explained how power worked in the world through interpersonal relationships, or "agreements." We too often, Crockett taught, enter tacit, unconscious agreements without considering how they might shape our reality over time. Here's an example.

"Aren't you a little rascal!" says Grandma.

"We accept it for that day," Crockett told an interviewer in 1975, "but it becomes an impulse in our life. *We have to become a rascal* in order to keep this line of force going which was put there for us."

What happens when tensions arise among the different agreements we have entered? Our sense of reality breaks down. "Our agreements are literally circuits we build in our worlds," Crockett continued. "When they begin to cross one with the other, our worlds are so interlaced with contradictions that we begin to blow circuits. Pretty soon we can't *do* anything because we're crossing agreements that we've made since early childhood."[34]

Luckily, there's a solution: you can identify, and then change, these debilitating mental constructs.

~

"One of the troubles with society is that its direction was to adjust people to the norm," poet Lenore Kandel told interviewer Leonard Wolf in *Voices from the Love Generation* (1968). "The norm is sick. I don't think any of the people I'm involved with care to be adjusted to the sick."

In such circumstances, what should we then do?

"It isn't just telling the truth; it's living the truth. There's no exception to the rule. You just stay in the truth. And you live it, because it doesn't mean a thing if you [just] say it."

And what does that look like?

"The only way I could really give you an example is by living it."[35]

~

That medium Polanski hired, Peter Hurkos, turned out to be untrustworthy. He sold Polaroids of the House on the Hill, taken to help solve the crime, to a tabloid.

A day or so before Hurkos betrayed Roman, Truman Capote outlined what he described as his personal "fantasy" about what might have happened. The killer had been "a very young, enraged paranoid" known to the victims. He had probably been at the house earlier. Something must have triggered an attack of paranoia. He left to retrieve a gun and knife, returning well after the residents had gone to sleep. The act, Capote surmised, would have provided the paranoid with a measure of sexual release.[36]

~

The complete lack of release in "Maxwell's Silver Hammer"—a "ghastly miscalculation" by Paul, as one commentator correctly notes, "by far his worst lapse of taste under the auspices of the Beatles"—contributes to the song's stunning failure.[37] Could the track have been salvaged had John been allowed to recast the main character, a serial killer, as driven to homicide through psychosexual manias?

Sometime in March or April, stories had circulated that this song would appear on an album recorded in the months following the release of the White

Album. *Hot As Sun* would also include "Don't Let Me Down" (which ultimately appeared on *Let It Be*) and an eponymous track, "Hot As Sun" (which ended up on *McCartney*). ("Maxwell's Silver Hammer," of course, can be heard on *Abbey Road*.)

For decades, Beatle fans have played a parlor game where they create a "final" Beatles album from the cast-offs, B-sides, and solo album warm-ups recorded as the group began disintegrating. *Hot As Sun* belongs to this genre of imaginary releases. Writers Bruce and Steve Harris, who broke the "story" in *Rolling Stone* in September, even created a cloak-and-daggers backstory for this "lost" album. The plot begins at the Newport Folk Festival in 1968, where "a young student from the University of Miami with thick brown hair who is taken to smoking long Italian cigars met for the first time with a thin, dark man with a troubled face, a student at Penn State, and with a third young man, believed also to be a college student but of whom no description is available."

The three men had befriended a young woman, a secretary at Apple Records ("a good girl," but of course "not bright"). Over the course of a friendly evening, she had overshared: only three master tapes of *Hot As Sun* existed, and the Beatles hadn't taken copies home, as had previously been normal practice. Armed with this knowledge, the young men took separate cars to George Martin's home office, Apple Records, and EMI's studios on Abbey Road. By midnight, the thieves had reconvened in Paris with the purloined masters.

"It worked perfectly," the leader rasped. "Not a hitch. Smooth, just like I said."

"The coup of the century," another replied. "I mean, just imagine it."

"Yeah," the other said. "Just imagine."

"It was a crazy idea, all right," the leader continued. "The craziest. But it worked, and we're here, and we've got the tapes, they're there, and they don't. And it's gonna cost [the Beatles and George Martin] one hundred thousand dollars to get them back. $100,000. Not a bad take for a day's work."

George Martin paid the ransom. What else could he have done? But the master tapes would take a circuitous route back to the Fifth Beatle, from Paris to Algiers to London. And when they arrived, they were blank. Had the three Americans double-crossed the Beatles camp? No. There had been "a bomb scare, a political threat" during the flight to Algiers. Authorities had secretly x-rayed the men's luggage as a precaution, and "when a tape is subjected to X-ray it is erased. Completely. *Hot As Sun* has been X-rayed out of existence!" And that's the story of "The Beatles Album That No One Will Ever Hear."[38]

~

A couple years later, Paul and Brooks formed Desert Sun, a band you probably never have heard. Crockett managed them. Watkins and Poston, Crockett believed, needed to break down the "circuitry of agreements" Manson had constructed. And to truly break free, the young men needed new goals.

"If you live in the world of Charlie, it's in the past," Crockett said. "If you live in 'right now' all the time, you aren't gonna *do* anything because nothing exists in just now. You have to have something to do, someplace to go, something that is out of *now* into the future."[39]

~

Looking back from our vantage point, you may now see darkness falling over the last few months of the Sixties. Behold, a pale horse. Have we drawn that card bearing the death's-head, that armored atomy astride his white mount? If you interpret too literally this thirteenth card of the Major Arcana, labeled Death, you misread it: ignoring the golden crown lying on the Field of Life, failing to see the sun rising between two towers. Or setting? It's just like the night to play tricks. Isn't it?

And keeping your eyes open doesn't mean that you necessarily see. Remember the story of that heroine of the counterculture, the one who forgot to grow up? Recall the scene where Alice finds herself face-to-face with a "large mushroom growing near her, about the same height as herself, and when she had looked under it, and on both sides of it, and behind it, it occurred to her that she might as well look and see what was on the top of it."

So she did. And what did Alice find? That laconic Caterpillar. And remember what he asked?

~

We can only speculate as to when the idea for a book about "the Manson murders" first occurred to prosecutor Vincent Bugliosi. But we know that *Helter Skelter* tried to answer precisely that question: Who are these people? Who *is* Charles Manson?

In answering this question, *Helter Skelter* adopted the form of a parable: about bringing order to disorder, about making sense of events that in some essential sense seemed resistant to comprehension. As both overarching aim and plot device, *making sense* drives narrative in the true-crime genre. We may gawp at the victims, but we also wonder. Why did they get into the car? Why did they trust that person? How did they not *know*? (That's also why true-crime stories usually feature beautiful young white innocents. We "know" why sex workers, drug users, the working poor, and other marginalized people die. But why must the Sharon Tates of the world?)

An urge to understand the world in order to avoid the dangers that have befallen others, some observers claim, propels true-crime fandom.[40] This fandom in turn compels you to cultivate a suspicious, exegetical stance toward the world. Expert commentators model how to "read" these crimes, to recognize apophanies, to forge connections among disparate phenomena. One media critic, writing about her own real-life attack by a knife-wielding man, wonders what the true-crime community might have done had she died.

"Would my story have been the kind that was featured on a podcast, two bantering hosts dissecting my life and my book choices in between plugging ads for affordable furniture?" she asks. "I think I would rather get stabbed again than have TikTok users descend like vultures on my social media, zooming in on pictures of my messy bedroom to analyze the tedious minutiae of my deeply average life. Looking for warning signs, trying to find a way to convince yourself you'd survive is normal, a natural response to the paranoia and anxiety these stories inspire."

Where does that need for certainty come from? After all, we tolerate insecurity in so many aspects of our lives. Why should we feel paranoid about the vanishingly small probability of meeting death by violence? "Human beings have a remarkable capacity for self-delusion," the author posits, "it's hard wired into us, the only way we can function with the knowledge of our own mortality."[41]

~

As the commune moved back to the desert, murmurings about Paul McCartney's mortality began circulating. Allegedly, the Beatles had covered up the bassist's decapitation in an automotive accident since November 1966. Now the story broke worldwide.

College and underground radio hosts debated the story for weeks, asking listeners to call in with clues throughout October 1969. Some found evidence in song lyrics. John described the car accident on *Sgt. Pepper's* "A Day In The Life" ("he blew his mind out in a car"), and begged Paul to return and "open up his eyes" on the White Album's "Dear Prudence." Spin the records backward and you heard even more—in "Revolution #9," for instance, "a man says 'turn me on dead man.'"

Others inspected the films and album covers for visual clues. Paul's cold blue uniform on *Sgt. Pepper's* contrasts with the warm tones of the other three; he wears a patch with the acronym, OPD, or "officially pronounced dead"; George points at a lyric, "Wednesday morning at 5 o'clock," allegedly Paul's time of death. On *Pepper's* cover and on *Magical Mystery Tour*, over Paul's head hover hands, supposedly an occult symbol for marking the dead; there's the black flower on Paul's lapel; there's the figure of The Walrus, an Inuit symbol (allegedly) for the afterworld. On the White Album, John at one point even sings: "Here's another clue for you all: the Walrus was Paul."

These hints culminate on *Abbey Road*. Its cover depicts a resurrected Paul walking out of step with the priestly Ringo, grave-digger George, and Christ-like John. The title "Octopus's Garden" refers to London slang for a cemetery, where Paul had been buried. "I Want You (She's So Heavy)" depicts the disinterment. Side Two's "Sun King" refers to Paul's resurrection ("here comes the Sun King / everybody's laughing"), as this mop-top Lazarus assumes his rightful place next to John.[42] It's all there, isn't it?

"It was not some 'x-marks-the-spot' clue," one fan later recalled. "You could sort of hear it, but you couldn't. It was like you were seeing the tip of the iceberg of a larger reality."[43]

~

In early October, police raided Barker Ranch. Members of the commune had set fire to some construction equipment a few weeks earlier, for reasons unknown. The commune had been disintegrating; even longtime members began abandoning the group.

The authorities rounded up nearly everyone who remained. But not Manson. And when the cops returned a day later, Charlie nearly escaped a second time, too. He had secreted himself away in a cupboard, too small—the cops thought—to be a hiding place. But a stray strand of hair, outside the cupboard's door, gave him away.

~

The person who really helped spread the "Paul Is Dead" story nearly gave the whole thing away, and at the most inopportune time. A local New York station planned a mock trial to investigate the claims, charging attorney F. Lee Bailey with considering the evidence and cross-examining witnesses. One of these witnesses would be Fred LaBour, a college student who wrote an early account in the *Michigan Daily* that went viral.

He confessed to the hoax just before they went live. "Well, we have an hour of television to do," Bailey told him. "You're going to have to go along with this."[44]

~

Charlie and the rest of the group rode along in the back of a pickup truck, over the dirt track leading back to town. He allegedly told the two white cops that, if they were smart, they'd soon take off for the desert. A race war was coming.

In Independence, the authorities fingerprinted Charlie. And they booked him—as "Manson, Charles M., aka Jesus Christ, God."[45]

IN A CELL AT THE BRAND WOMEN'S PRISON, Sadie Mae Glutz (t/n Susan Atkins) talked too much.[46] Sadie told Virginia Graham and Ronnie Howard (t/n Veronica) that she had been with the group that broke into *that house*. She told them other things, too. That she had stabbed the actress, Sharon Tate. That she had tasted her blood.

This happened on or about the sixth of November. Atkins later suggested she told these tales to look tough, to scare off any hardened criminal who might want to hurt her. She was playing crazy, as Charlie had during his prison days, a strategy the group had used before. Like when they got booked back in April 1968, and everyone swallowed the drugs they were holding, and the police took that iconic mugshot of Charlie, the Rasputin visage soon staring out at millions of Americans from beneath the bold white banner reading, *The Love and Terror Cult*, on the cover of *Life* magazine. That April night in 1968, a stoned fifteen-year-old Dianne Lake just sang and sang in the cell, any Beatles song that came into her head. *I want to hold your hand! For the benefit of Mr Kite!*[47] *He's a real nowhere man!*

Virginia and Ronnie weren't too sure what to make of this slight person. She appeared to be experiencing a psychotic break with reality; it's difficult to imagine what these conversations with Sadie would have looked or sounded like. Descriptions of other commune members at this time invariably related glassy-eyed stares, suggesting that drugs—and perhaps, Manson—continued to exercise a hold on body and soul for quite some time.

Sadie talked and talked, and at some point, Virginia and Ronnie started to listen. Luckily for Sadie and her commune friends, they didn't quite believe her at first—and then, the people that Virginia and Ronnie told didn't quite believe them, either.

~

"The thing is that nobody believes in anything any more and human beings have a great need to believe," the *Stone*'s resident critic, Ralph Gleason, wrote a month later, just as the grand jury convened to charge Sadie, Katie, Leslie, and Charlie with seven counts of murder. He's writing about the Beatles' *Abbey Road*, of course, and the purported death of Paul McCartney, as well as the motorcycle accident that Bob Dylan allegedly suffered in 1966—not the commune or Helter Skelter or any of the other conspiracies then going to seed all over the California underground.

Why don't we believe? The critic invoked a theory in vogue at the time. "If you remove or destroy man's objects of belief (as God has been removed and destroyed) then man will invent other things in which to believe. The Beatles are only a part of it, though an important part. There has been deep religious significance in the reaction to all the artists, from Ray Charles on. The laying on of hands, the necessity to touch, the icons and the idolatry."

When this basic human need goes unmet, the trouble begins. Says Gleason: "And when, as with the Beatles, there is an absence of personal manifestation in Candlestick Park or Shea Stadium, then the faithful give free rein to loose imaginative play and mythology fills the void."[48] (Though compare Gleason's analysis with psychologist Rollo May's speculation that the political unrest of 1968 should be blamed on "a myth gap." The stories Americans share, and the truths such stories contain, thought May, just don't pack the same punch anymore.[49])

That's why the recent, fervid belief in the Masked Marauders doesn't surprise the critic. In October, the *Stone* had published a fake review of an album recorded—allegedly—by Bob Dylan, Mick Jagger, John Lennon, and Paul McCartney. The hoax spoofed the vogue for so-called supergroups; as the hoax gained momentum, Jann Wenner even paid for soundalikes to quickly record some tracks. The false Jagger sounds passable; the imitation Dylan, farcical. Their cover of "Season of the Witch" rivals Donovan's original in daftness. And Gleason marvels that, even after the hoax had been revealed, many *Stone* readers refused to believe they'd been fooled. Some even told the critic that *he* was wrong. "They *will* believe," Gleason writes, "no matter what you say." Yet this situation shouldn't overly alarm us. The critic dismissed fears that we are "lost in a new dark age, mindless and irresponsible in a non-linear world built on flashes and hits and visions." He refuses to lose sleep over a growing lack of trust in institutions, or even the rampant circulation of what he terms "disinformation."

Why worry? These are just signs of the times, so to speak, easily absorbed by a generation primed to believe that just about *anything* might be real. "Nothing it too far out in today's world," Gleason concluded. "Miracles are standard operating procedure and the divine is commonplace. If man can set foot on the moon, why can't thousands of people involve themselves in a conspiracy to conceal the death of Paul yet reveal it by obscure and intricate clues? After all, there *was* a fool on the hill, or a man on the grassy knoll, wasn't there? And isn't everything a conspiracy, trial or not?"[50]

~

In Death Valley, deputies began collecting evidence; they would soon visit the Spahn Movie Ranch. They collected bullet casings and weapons, car parts and tools, the field telephones strung up to safeguard against intruders. They photographed the dwellings after ransacking them, capturing mattresses laid side by side, albums and album inserts pasted around as if upon teenaged bedroom walls.

On 25 November, according to official records, law enforcement officers removed a cabinet door at Spahn Ranch covered in graffiti. "Happy." "Peace" (with the "eace" filling the elongated P). "Love." "Hi Collie I love you" (with a small heart dotting the "i" in Colleen's nickname). "Elves." "Nothingness." A few lines from one song:

1234567
ALL GOOD CHILDREN
(Go to Heaven?)

And another:

HELTER
SCELTER
IS
CO
MI
NG
DOWN
FAST

~

If rock was going to start a revolution, Ralph Gleason—riffing off C. Wright Mills ("a kind of rock'n roll sociologist")—thought he knew how.

Rock had become "serious," Gleason wrote, had "risen through imitation and eclecticism into individuality." And there lies the revolutionary potential of rock. A number of "groups are now creating the music out of their own experience, out of their own heads and in the process are also creating a life style which is going to change America."[51]

The key phrase here must surely be *out of their own experience*. Representations of social reality, derived from the individual experiences of the musicians, provided models for listeners to not only consume, but to *live*. Imagine a kind of feedback loop between recordings and lived experience, a loop that sustained itself, prefiguring potential futures that demand a revolutionary break with the past. "The truths in which we need to believe are all inside us," Gleason wrote, "and that message is being sent back to us again and again by the poets and the musicians who, whether they are conscious of it or not, are the true religious figures of this New Time." (A notion the prosecution soon alleged Manson and the commune to have believed.)

This way of approaching "truths," Gleason continued, has consequences for how we listen to the music. "It makes no difference if the Beatles insist that what they say is simple and without hidden meaning. The point is *how it applies to us*." The authentic meaning of the text, at least when it comes to rock, Gleason seems to argue, emerges primarily through an individual's personal reading, whether credible or not. And according to the critic, the Sixties had made this situation possible: "When, as in this present time, the institutions and the heroes and the Gods of civilization crumble, and one needs no particular door to perception to see them crumbling all around, then something must take their place," Gleason concluded. "Hopefully it will be something positive." Then he offered a warning. "Sometimes, in the absence of a positive thing in which to believe, negativity becomes paramount and rumors and mythology and speed paranoia conspiracy theories rush in like a Wasatch Zephyr to fill the void."[52]

~

As poetic as that last image sounds, "a Wasatch Zephyr," if you don't know, refers to an interstate passenger train with a terminus in California, just south of San Francisco.

The quotidian too often obscures the poetic, so we should be mindful not to efface all things magic. Consider the cabinet door, on which Country Sue (t/n Susan Bartell) along with a woman named Colleen Sinclair had inscribed those Beatle lyrics. They had not gone to the desert with the other commune members, but remained at the Spahn Movie Ranch. "We were writing down the words to a song we liked," Sue later told an interviewer. "Period. Nothing scary."[53]

The lyrics, of course, had been taken from the songs "You Never Give Me Your Money" and "Helter Skelter." The Beatles released the White Album's "Helter Skelter" in November 1968, but *Abbey Road*—and its Side B medley, featuring the nursery-rhyme conclusion to "You Never Give Me Your Money"— only appeared in October 1969, after most of the commune had left for the desert. If Sue and Collie scrawled all the messages at the same time, then they must have done so after everyone associated with those two nights in August had split. Does it matter that two months separated the crimes from the door in time?

Bugliosi only found out about the door in May 1970. "You mean for five months, while I've been desperately trying to link the killers to Helter Skelter," he scolded one investigator, "you've had this door, with those very words printed on it, the same bloody words that were found at the LaBianca residence?" The door provided key physical evidence linking the commune to the murders. Within the narrative of *Helter Skelter*, its discovery shows that, if not for Bugliosi's tireless work in bringing order to the chaos of the police investigation, Charles Manson and the Family would have walked free. Because the bumbling investigators, riven by internal squabbling, had made a real dog's breakfast of the case, at least according to Bugliosi. Forgive them, as they're only men. And man, as we know, is only too fallible.

~

Ralph Gleason, as correspondents to the *Stone* sometimes noted, could be fallible, too. One reader pointed out that Gleason claimed (falsely) that Jefferson Airplane never played a bad show (which the letter writer believed showed Gleason's "habit of 'adopting' a rising group and then basking in their success"). Gleason had also praised *Magical Mystery Tour*, which he pointed out could only be seen as "at best, an expensive Home Movie."

"It is my belief that a music critic should have a fundamental knowledge of music," the correspondent concluded. "If Mr. Gleason has one, he has done an admirable job of concealing it."[54]

~

Investigators broke the case in the middle of November, when Virginia and Ronnie finally got someone to listen to the tales that Sadie told them. The pieces now began quickly falling into place: the two nights of mayhem, the bloodthirsty commune, the powerful, Svengali-like leader. (The significance of the White Album came later.)

Someone called Beach Boys manager Nick Grillo, and he secured the tapes from all their recording sessions with Manson. Fromme allegedly visited Dennis soon after. "The music is his best defense," a commune member, possibly Lyn, wrote in a letter to the *Berkeley Barb* in early 1970. Wilson told Fromme he had given the tapes to the district attorney's office; at least that's what he said to a few friends, though this has never been corroborated.[55]

~

Around this time, Squeaky allegedly called Apple Records, too. And members of the commune began making plans to release an album of Charlie's songs.

~

The sleeve for that album used the *Life* magazine cover that, in December, devoted pages and pages of coverage to the commune. Someone disappeared the third letter in LIFE for the cover, leaving the words LIE: The Love and Terror Cult. Someone erased the subheadings, in white against Charlie's shoulder-length black hair, too. These had read:

The man who was their leader
The charge of multiple murder
The dark edge of hippie life

~

How could this have happened? Here's one possible explanation: "There are societies which swallow people up, namely anthropophagic societies, and societies which vomit people out—anthropoemic societies," proposed psychiatrist David Cooper. "In the traditional psychiatric hospital today, despite the proclamation of progress, society gets the best of both worlds—the person who is 'vomited' out of his family, out of society, is 'swallowed up' by the hospital and then digested and metabolized out of existence as an identifiable person.

This, I think, must be regarded as violence."[56] Just replace "hospital" with any other totalizing institution, such as "prison" or "school" or "work."

And here's a second, possible explanation: "Considerable technical advance during this period, accompanied by a gradual deterioration of mores, orientation, and social institutions, terminating in mass psychoses in the sixth decade."[57]

~

In an editor's note on the "strange story of Charlie Manson and his brood of nubile flower children" from that upcoming December 1969 issue of *Life* magazine, reporter Judy Fayard explained how she and a colleague, photographer Vernon Merritt, nearly stumbled over the story in the days *before* the Manson Family became headline news. What should we make of this instance of propinquity?

"Luck—good and bad—figures mightily in a story of this kind," she said. "Merritt and I had been to Death Valley on a different story about 10 days before the Manson thing broke, and when it did I called a friend I had made there and asked if he'd heard of this desert commune. 'Sure,' he said. 'Why didn't you ask?' Now that is bad luck."

NO SENSE MAKES SENSE.

On or around the eighteenth of November, The Investigation: Phase Two—as Bugliosi and ghostwriter Curt Gentry subtitled this part of their book—began. The reader of *Helter Skelter* now encounters a blow-by-blow reenactment of preparations for the trial, prefaced by that quote from Charlie, "No Sense Makes Sense," allegedly one of his cryptic mantras.

Bugliosi learned about the commune after two detectives came to the Hall of Justice in Los Angeles to brief the District Attorney's office. These two officers related the sensational account of Sadie's cellmate, Ronnie Howard.[58] The story sounded unbelievable. It included details about the August murders, but also at least a dozen others, including one beheading. Ronnie had also learned that Sadie followed a man who claimed to be both Jesus Christ and the Devil. And she learned about something called "helter skelter," which she did not quite fully understand. She thought it meant that "you have to be killed to live."[59]

~

Imagine hearing these stories for the first time; a normal person might feel shock, disorientation. Yet by the time *Helter Skelter* appeared on bookstore shelves in late 1974, the entire sordid narrative had already come out, in lurid detail—and over, and over again. Few readers wouldn't have known the plot of "the Manson Family Murders."

When your readers know the key plot points before they happen, you need either to offer new information, however scanty, or new interpretations, however fanciful. All that said, prior knowledge is not at all a problem. In fact, this situation makes true crime—as a genre—possible. Authors (and their complicit readers) expect to relitigate and revisit and revise and reread, adding bits and pieces of information every now and then, or recasting the same old "facts" in the bracing light of their new interpretations.[60]

Back in the printed world of *Helter Skelter*, Vincent Bugliosi seems to have anticipated this problem. He acknowledged that the reader would have arrived at this point in the book with a great deal of knowledge. Yet he insisted on repeating elements of the story not merely for the sake of narrative continuity, but also to put on the record his own feelings about (and role in) their discovery. It's a remarkable moment of self-reflection, albeit a reflexivity couched in self-flattery and false modesty.

"By now the reader knows a great deal more about the Tate-LaBianca murders than I did on the day I was assigned that case," Bugliosi begins. "In fact, since large portions of the foregoing story have not been made public before this, the reader is an insider in a sense highly unusual in a murder case. And, in a way, I'm a newcomer, an intruder. The sudden switch from an unseen background narrator to a very personal account is bound to be a surprise. The best way to soften it, I suspect, would be to introduce myself; then, when we've got that out of the way, we'll resume the narrative together. This digression, though unfortunately necessary, will be as brief as possible."[61]

~

On the same day a California grand jury indicted Manson and three commune members, Apple announced that John and Yoko would back a documentary on James Hanratty, a convicted rapist and murderer who had been one of the last British citizens executed in 1962. Dubbed the "A6 Murderer" by the British press,

Hanratty had received an unusual level of support from conspiracy-minded persons convinced that someone else committed the crimes.

During this period, people from across the political spectrum advocated for those convicted of even the most heinous acts. Conservative writer and editor of the *National Review* William F. Buckley, for instance, worked for years to free Edgar Smith, convicted of kidnapping and murdering a teenaged hitchhiker in New Jersey. He published an article re-examining the case in *Esquire* magazine, "The Approaching End of Edgar H. Smith, Jr.," and he found him a literary agent; Knopf would publish Smith's autobiographical debut, *Brief Against Death*, in 1968. Buckley even hired the team of lawyers who secured Smith's release from prison three years later. Then there's Truman Capote's depiction of Perry Edward Smith in the true-crime novel, *In Cold Blood* (1965). Convicted of killing five members of a family in America's heartland, Smith receives a remarkably sympathetic portrait. A litany of traumas shaped Capote's Smith: an abusive father, an alcoholic mother who sometimes did sex work, imprisonment for petty crimes. The portrait does more than simply explain the childlike murderer; verging on the exculpatory, it nearly absolves him of all blame.

This rhetorical strategy can later be found in sympathetic coverage of Manson, which invariably focused on his difficult upbringing: his mother had also been a sex worker; he too had experienced sexual violence in juvenile detention facilities; he spent most of his life in penal institutions. Manson's final release from prison in 1967 became an essential element, what earlier we termed the inaugural event of this mythos, in all future narrations of his story: on the day of his parole, and after collecting his few belongings—some clothing, petty cash, and a battered guitar—he begs to go back inside. Manson does not want, maybe cannot really understand, freedom.

If additional context cannot fully absolve such men of their crimes, these advocates claimed, it at least explains their capacity for committing such atrocities. And of course, these three examples shared something else. Each featured a powerful white man advocating for a blue-collar man convicted of abusing and killing women. And perhaps even more significantly, all three advocates were dead wrong. The convicted persons, later evidence affirmed, had been guilty of committing their crimes.

~

At the beginning of December, the authorities held a press conference announcing that they had in custody suspects in the Tate-LaBianca killings. A week later, a grand jury indicted five members of the commune, including Manson, largely on evidence from Sadie and two "untested informants": biker Danny DeCarlo, as well as Bobby Beausoleil's longtime girlfriend, Kitty Lutesinger.

Beausoleil's trial for the murder of Gary Hinman, entering its third month, would end in a hung jury. Jurors couldn't agree on finding him guilty of first-degree murder, a crime then punishable by death in California, or a lesser charge.

~

Now Bugliosi began collecting evidence to support the seven counts of first-degree murder. He wanted to learn how the commune functioned as a group. A group's dynamics would not necessarily matter to a prosecutor, but because Manson did not directly kill anyone, Bugliosi needed to construct a case that relied on sociological appeals to group dynamics—and philosophical appeals to the nature of free will. That is to say, Bugliosi needed to prove that Charlie brainwashed his followers.

In one passage in *Helter Skelter*, Bugliosi meets in his office with Squeaky and Sandy. Their comportment, he claims, astonished him: "They seemed to radiate inner contentment. I'd seen others like this—true believers, religious fanatics—yet I was both shocked and impressed. Nothing seemed to faze them. They smiled almost continuously, no matter what was said. For them all the questions had been answered. There was no need to search any more, because they had found the truth. And their truth was 'Charlie is love.'"[62]

In addition to the sexist premise of the overall "brainwashing" thesis, there's a leering prurience in these pages, a prurience we've encountered before. The "girls" smile "enigmatically" at one another in response to a question about whether Charlie was really Jesus Christ; there's something almost erotic about the scene (though maybe this reveals more about me than I'm willing to admit). Bugliosi feels there's "a little-girl quality to them, as if they hadn't aged but had been retarded at a certain stage in their development." He claims that Squeaky tried to shock him by describing ("she was quite graphic") sex with George Spahn. How does that detail accord with an earlier impression from Bugliosi, that these were "little girls, playing little-girl games?" The prosecutor presents the act with octogenarian George as fact, part of an overall accretion of details suggesting something sordid about sex and control. (Fromme seems to have been playing a game with the pervy prosecutor. She and other members later expressed real anger at this particular revelation—calling it a lie.)

"I talked to them for a long time, asking specific questions now," Bugliosi continues, "but still getting pat answers. On asking where they were on a certain date, for example, they'd reply, 'There is no such thing as time.' The answers were both non-responsive and a guard. I wanted to get past that guard, to learn what they really felt. I couldn't." (Should we expect persons in this situation to *let down their guard*, so to speak? Nevermind that we often struggle to really know even our closest, most intimate friends and partners.)

"I sensed something else," the prosecutor continues. "Each was, in her own way, a pretty girl. But there was a sameness about them that was much stronger than their individuality. I'd notice it again later that afternoon, in talking to other female members of the Family. Same expressions, same patterned responses, same tone of voice, same lack of distinct personality. The realization came with a shock: they reminded me less of human beings than Barbie dolls."

At this point, note that Bugliosi combines details from multiple interviews with Leslie, Ruth Anne, Dianne, Nancy, and Catherine (or as he renders the list, "Leslie, Ouisch, Snake, Brenda, Gypsy").* He finds their answers to be "rehearsed," which evidenced to him not conspiracy so much as "a cohesion, a kind of cement, that held them together." Bugliosi here foreshadows a key narrative thread: explaining how that cement worked will occupy much of the rest of the prosecutor's chronicle.

~

While John and Yoko never completed a book or documentary about Hanratty, they did stage a happening to raise awareness about his innocence, appearing on stage silent and motionless, covered in a sack, or bag. Bagism in action.

---

* We earlier learned that Bugliosi selectively distinguishes an individual's "true name" in the text. Here we should note that he also includes at the beginning of *Helter Skelter* a lengthy "Cast of Characters," just like you would find for a play. The entries look like this:

Minette, Manon. Alias used by Family member Catherine Share.

Or this:

Wildebush, Joan, aka Juanita. Was with Manson's advance group at Barker Ranch; left Family and eloped with Bob Berry, Paul Crockett's partner.

And can sometimes be quite long:

Brunner, Mary Theresa, aka Marioche, Och, Mother Mary, Mary Manson, Linda Dee Moser, Christine Marie Euchts. First girl to join the Manson Family; had a son by Manson; was involved in the Hinman murder and the Hawthorne shootout.

"What's Bagism? It's like a tag for what we all do," John told David Frost around this time, "we're all in a bag, you know, and we realized that we came from two bags—I was in this pop bag going round and round in my little clique and she was in her little avant-garde clique going round and round and you're in your little tele[vision] clique and they're in their . . . you know? And we all sort of come out and look at each other every now and then, but we don't communicate. We all intellectualize about how there is no barrier between art, music, poetry. But we're still all: 'I'm a rock and roller,' or 'He's a poet.' So we just came up with the word so you would ask us what bagism is. And we'd say, 'We're all in a bag, baby!'"

"You know, this life is speeded up so much," Yoko added, "and the whole world is getting tenser and tenser because things are just going so fast, you know. So it's so nice to slow down the rhythm of the whole world, just to make it peaceful. So like the bag, when you get in, you see that it's very peaceful and your movements are sort of limited. You can walk around on the street in a bag."

Of course, you don't really know who is in the bag; they never reveal themselves. Sometimes it wasn't John or Yoko. At the Hanratty event, for instance, Lennon later revealed that "it wasn't us in the bag, it was somebody else."[63]

~

And with the publication of the *Life* magazine cover story on December 19, a singularly coherent narrative about the Manson Family took flight. It's remarkable just how fully fledged the story emerged.

"Long-haired, bearded little Charlie Manson so disturbed the American millions last week—when he was charged with sending four docile girls and a hairy male acolyte off to slaughter strangers in two Los Angeles houses last August—that the victims of his blithe and gory crimes seemed suddenly to have played only secondary roles in the final brutal moments of their own lives," Paul O'Neil wrote. "The Los Angeles killings struck innumerable Americans as an inexplicable controversion of everything they wanted to believe about the society and their children—and made Charlie Manson seem to be the very encapsulation of truth about revolt and violence by the young."[64]

Such long sentences. The first requires sixty-three words, and the second, forty-two, and if six and three make nine, then four and two make six, and if six turned out to be nine, well—what then? Then there's that strange word, *controversion*, alongside a carelessly imprecise but curiously specific repetition ("the American millions" versus the "innumerable Americans"), suggesting we should not dwell too much on numerological significance, especially when the numbers seem too obvious. Deeper revelations need not always lurk beneath the surface.

The journalist interviewed David Smith at the Haight-Ashbury Free Clinic, who offered a diagnosis. "Most of Charlie's girls, in the opinion of a San Francisco psychiatrist who encountered them, were 'hysterics, wishful thinkers, seekers after some absolute' who came to regard Charlie as a high priest, 'all-powerful, all-knowing.'" In a breakout on the following page, Dr. Smith receives a half-column alongside that other Dr. Smith, the ex-parole officer Charlie called Jubal, t/n Roger.

Here David claimed that the group broke down the middle-class morality of new members primarily through sex, not drugs. "That way he was able to eliminate the controls that normally govern our lives." He described the group's violence in general terms, as "not the kind of 'escape' violence we see in the Haight but a psychotic, Rasputin-like violence." And he posed the question that everyone would begin to ask: If Charlie could grow a group so large, appeal to so many young seekers, what does that say about the youth of America? "If we're going to pin a psychiatric label on Charlie's girls, then we'd have to say there are hundreds of thousands of kids in this country who are also mentally disturbed."[65]

Roger then called Charlie "the most hostile parolee I've ever come across." In a previous period, he suggested, Charlie would've been back in prison a few months after release. Not so now. "You have a very transient, mobile delinquent population, and many of them end up in scenes like this," he said. "They pick up the rhetoric and sort of blend in and manipulate the scene." How many scenes? How many master manipulators? "There are a lot of Charlies running around, believe me," Roger warned. "He's just one of several hundred thousand people who are released from prison after a shattering, soul-rending experience, not prepared for anything except to go back on the streets and do more of the same—but bigger."[66]

What role did sex and drugs play? What does this tell us about our young people? How many dropouts might murder? How many gurus might be exercising their Rasputin-like power over the young at this very moment, a hidden parasitic force bleeding the body politic dry? So many questions. And no real answers, only snatches and fragments from the frontline, a nearly full paragraph, maybe a half-column, summarizing the nature and extent of the problem, the repetition in the two men's accounts numbing any impulse to dig down into even the most sweeping assertions. Here's just one example to illustrate what I mean:

> Criminals and ex-cons have discovered a new sort of refuge in the last couple of years: they grow hair, assume beads and sandals, and sink—carnivores moving in with the vegetarians—into the life of hippie colonies from the East Village to Big Sur. Charlie Manson went to San Francisco's Haight-Ashbury and, with an exquisite sort of diplomatic skill, adopted the local coloration as a means of controlling, utilizing and dominating the impulse-ridden, drug-directed "kids" he discovered there. Most of the kids were female—who had come to escape a cynical society or to seek "reality and freedom." Charlie billed himself as a "roving minstrel" come to fulfill their dreams with magic, strike off the chains of male chauvinism and lead them to the promised land—although in fact he regarded them as squaws, treated them like cattle and excommunicated those who complained.[67]

Dropouts and runaways, easy prey for the Pied Piper figure, an exploiter without equal. Vegetarians, overrun by the carnivores. But did this happen? In this case, or in others?[68]

And it's remarkable, too, just how quickly the threads related to Charlie's rap came to be reported—without parsing their contradictions, without situating them in any sort of context. Charlie exited prison functionally illiterate, we learn, yet on the streets "now he read the Bible and tracts on the quasi-religion Scientology, decided that the Book of Revelation had predicted the Beatles, learned to play the guitar and assumed he could compose music. One of his lyrics consisted solely of the words, 'You know, you know, you know . . .' He left prison in March 1967, ready to give new meaning to the old saw: a little learning is a dangerous thing."[69]

~

On visiting the Spahn Movie Ranch, Bugliosi found a scene that impressed on him a kind of "unreality," a scene that seemed an appropriate setting for what "might have been the plot of a horror film." Diegetic music issued from a cheap transistor radio in old George Spahn's "shack," Sonny James singing "Young Love," a detail almost too on-the-nose, as this had been the term Charlie allegedly used for his girls. Young loves then began emerging from the dwellings on the property as Bugliosi's group searched for bullet casings that could tie Manson to the crimes.

At one point, a few "odd sounds" began emerging from an old doghouse. Bugliosi peered inside to find two animals and, apparently, "a toothless, white-haired old woman of about eighty." Here's how Bugliosi, or perhaps a ghostwriting Gentry, summarized his impressions with an authorial flourish of understatement: "It was a very strange place."

~

At a recent dinner party, a historian asked: "You don't really believe in all those hallucinations you write about, do you?"

"I believe in them," I replied, "as much as I believe in the one I'm having right now."

This exchange didn't happen to me, but there's no reason why it couldn't have. It allegedly occurred at a faculty get-together at UCLA in the 1970s; the quip is anthropologist Carlos Castaneda's.[70]

How DARE YOU put a picture of Charles Manson on the cover of a national magazine. This is a glorification of one of the most horrible crimes ever committed. If there are more murders like this, you will have contributed to them." Who signed this Letter to the Editors, which appeared on page 18A of the January 23, 1970, edition of *Life* magazine? Believe it or not: "John Cassavetes, Universal City, Calif."

~

The night holds terror for us all sometimes, and I'm certainly wary of digging too deeply into particular topics. But as Bugliosi's investigation case relied on certain unconventional methods, we might at least relate a final example or two for context.

"Why do you hate your father?" Bugliosi asked Steve "Clem" Grogan, quoting from a psychiatrist's report.

"I'm my father and I don't hate myself," Clem apparently responded.[71]

Don't take Bugliosi's voice for anything other than what it must be: an author (with Curty Gentry) crafting a case (or a plot, with all the forward momentum that term implies). That author invites us to psychoanalyze "the girls," and maybe

Clem and Tex and Charlie, too. But most of us, if we are honest, will admit we are simply not qualified to do that.

But what if we turned the tables on Bugliosi? If we decide those quotes tell us more about him than the commune? Or about the social order he represents, the People of the State of California? If we make the typical, modern move toward interpretation, toward fashioning a deep reading?

~

"I'm dying a little every day," Clem told a prison psychiatrist. "My ego is dying and knows he's dying and struggles hard. When you're free of ego you're free of everything . . . Whatever you say is right for yourself . . . Whoever you think I am, that's who I am."[72]

~

Who is in the bag?

6

December 1969 to February 1972

or, Child of the State

On the eighth of December, members of the commune appeared before the grand jury. Atkins would soon be isolated from the general population, placed in an observation ward, Cellblock 4000, mostly alone with her thoughts. But before that, her testimony provided the state's most compelling evidence. "I've given up sacred information to outsiders and betrayed my own people," Atkins recalled thinking. "I'm going to be fingered from both sides. The world will never understand me. They will hate me. Charlie, Pat, Leslie, Tex, Mary—they will all hate me. They will never trust me. What am I going to do?"

In return for Susan's testimony, the prosecution (allegedly) agreed not to seek the death penalty. "I just didn't know what I would do from hour to hour," she remembered. "But I agreed to the deal. At least I wouldn't die."[1]

~

Police conduct had complicated the investigation from the very beginning. "It looked ritualistic," one officer had told journalists. Someone thought it might be a drug burn. Another called it a "typical fag murder."[2] This kind of speculation caused real problems. So many "poly keys," small details only the real killers would know, had been revealed to the public, compromising the effectiveness of lie detector tests. And toward what ends? "There is no knowing," as Ed Sanders put it, describing one such leaked detail, "what led reporters to print or officers to say that Sebring was wearing a black hood over his head. There is a great difference between a light-colored bloody towel and a black hood."[3]

The strange nature of the crime scene itself also caused problems. "Everything was weird," wrote Sanders. "There was that bloody flag. There were those blood-barefoot prints on the sidewalk to the driveway. There was a blood soaked purple scarf found by Frykowski."[4] There were a pair of spectacles, too, allegedly planted as a false clue.⁵ Then there was the fact that officers had tracked blood all over the front porch. But after their marks had been counted, there remained "an evident bloody boot-heel print on the flagstone front porch that was not made by the police. Whose is it?"⁶ The cops didn't know.

~

"Susan," the prosecutor asked at the grand jury, "did Charlie oftentimes use the word 'pig' or 'pigs?'"

"Yes."

"How about 'helter skelter?'"

"Yes."

"Did he use the word 'pigs' and 'helter skelter' very, very frequently?"

"Well, Charlie talks a lot," Sadie replied. "In some of the songs he wrote, 'helter skelter' was in them and he'd talk about helter skelter. We all talked about helter skelter."

"You say 'we'; are you speaking of the Family?"

"Yes."⁷

~

"The Beatles confuse you with what they say," Manson allegedly told one of Gary Hinman's friends, who reported this statement to the two men who authored *The Garbage People* (1970), an early, sensationalized look inside the commune. "You get programmed from the front or programmed from the back. Music doesn't know time. Music is soul. And you can bring it in from the back. I can sing a song right now and when it's over you forget the words, the music, but it stays in your infinite unconscious. And then a few months later you hear a song and it'll end with the same kind of riff . . . It's the same. You forget the words and yet in the back of your mind, what it *means* comes back to you . . . And this is what the Beatles do, they confuse you with cadence, and program you in the back, behind the beat, and that is what stays with you. Dig?"⁸

~

Just after relating the grand jury testimony, the narrative in Susan's memoir breaks, skipping from December 1969 to March 1970—three whole months. During this period, the prosecution had allowed members of the commune to visit Susan. The girls brought messages from Charlie. And then, Manson himself appeared.

Even with her attorney and a deputy sheriff alongside, Susan felt nervous, maybe even "frightened." Here's what allegedly happened.

"Charlie looked at me with his piercing eyes early in the conversation and spoke to my insides. 'Sadie, are you afraid of the gas chamber?'"

"I knew he was pressing me as to why I had talked. 'No, I'm not afraid of it now,' I said, smiling. In that instant I was back under his control. I knew it, and he knew it."

With that agreement in place, the two began planning. The guru spoke in "a kind of double-talk, with real words dropped in every now and then," impenetrable to the outsiders, though Atkins understood, could read between the lines. She fired her lawyer, disavowed the grand jury testimony, lost the immunity deal, and dropped plans for an insanity plea. According to *Helter Skelter*, the entire meeting lasted fifteen minutes.[9]

~

Helter Skelter angered officers who felt that Bugliosi portrayed them as bumbling, stumbling idiots. Think Keystone Cops, from the slapstick silent films of the 1910s. Or compare Scotland Yard's fictional Lestrade, unseeing and so unknowing, to Baker Street's Holmes, so sensitively attuned to what's really going on, able to see what others cannot.

This idea becomes something of a leitmotif in *Helter Skelter*, allowing the narrator, Bugliosi, to overcome hardships unnumbered before facing off with Manson himself, evil incarnate. If the casting of a villain requires a hero, then that hero's development requires obstacles.

~

Atkins, and later biker Danny DeCarlo, told Bugliosi that Charlie interpolated the phrase "helter skelter" into his own songs. But these specific words don't appear on tracks attributed to Charlie and the commune, though because Bugliosi didn't put any of Charlie's own lyrics into evidence, you would need to listen to the music to find this out. In the thousands and thousands of pages of transcripts, the official record of what really happened, you won't find a single line.

~

Could lyrics from the desert songs have been put into evidence? From the "hundreds of hours" of recordings in the Beach Boys vault? The recordings that Wilson allegedly gave to the district attorney's office?

NOW CHARLIE SOUNDED A DEFIANT NOTE. "The news media," he told reporters, "have already executed and buried me."

On 14 December, the *LA Times* had published a six-thousand-word account by Susan not only detailing the killings, but also suggesting their motive (instilling fear in the Establishment) and mechanism (brainwashing and hypnotism). This narrative formed the basis for the first of many Manson books, *The Killing of Sharon Tate*, billed as an "Exclusive Story by Susan Atkins, Confessed Participant in the Murder," and published in January 1970.

"There's no one in Los Angeles," one legal expert said, "who doesn't already think Manson and his people are guilty." A columnist at the *LA Times* wondered whether there ought to be a law "that lawyers will not become literary agents for clients accused of felonies, and another that journalists will not enter into actions for exclusive rights to the accused."[10]

~

Published accounts accused the commune—variously called "a nomadic band," "a hate-oriented, cult band of hippies," "a 'family,'" or just "a cult"—of all sorts of things. Their victims numbered nine, or possibly eleven, or maybe "dozens." In San Jose, authorities investigated links to the murder of two teenagers, Kathy Snoozy and Deborah Furlong.[11] In Los Angeles, investigators began re-examining the deaths of Doreen Gaul and James Sharp, two young people associated with the Church of Scientology and the Process Church. They also investigated the November suicide of commune member Christopher Jesus, aka Zero, t/n John Haught.[12]

These and other mysteries proliferated.* Journalists reported that "Manson had visited the Benedict Canyon estate leased by the actress [Sharon Tate] when

---

* According to official accounts, for instance, Zero had allegedly been playing Russian roulette at a house in Venice Beach. Cappy, Bruce, and Little Patty were there, too. And another young man, apparently, who described finding Zero alongside a person whom, according to other accounts, was Country Sue. "She told me: 'Jesus shot himself,'" Jerry Cohen reported in the *LA Times* on December 10, 1969. "But she had this strange far-away smile on her face, as if she were saying to me: 'His time had come, time for me to shoot him.' You have to understand what those people believe—'That you

Doris Day's son, Terry Melcher, lived there." After Melcher rejected Manson's plea for a record deal, one journalist now theorized, the cult leader targeted the home as a "symbol of rejection."[13]

In "Hollywood Slayings Suspect Beat Way Oddly from Social Outcast to Hippie Guru," a journalist quoted Manson referring to himself as "a roving minstrel" and "a walking musician."[14] Another called him an "evil Pied Piper."[15] Still another account revealed that the Beach Boys had purchased for $25,000 the copyrights to two songs (though, as far as we know, the group only recorded "Cease To Exist," renamed "Never Learn Not To Love"). They had even invited him to "accompany [them] to Texas in the spring of 1968 for two engagements there." The trip, of course, never materialized.[16]

~

Picked up just outside Copeville in November 1969, a good six hours' drive from where Manson might have made that Texas debut, Tex Watson now languished in jail. Because he enjoyed independent counsel, Tex's future trial would be split from Manson's.

You may recall learning that lawyer Bill Boyd also petitioned against extradition by arguing that, given the sensationalistic coverage, his client could not receive a fair trial in California. As you'll also recall, the petition failed. The hundreds of pages of newspaper and magazine articles, clipped and collated, in my mind filling great big thick binders to overflowing with grainy images and words and headlines, headlines so big and thick and black you couldn't have helped but see them on the newsstand, had not persuaded the courts.

With repetition the enemy of concision, and our genre—nonfiction—now requiring a move toward conclusions, we'll leave this failed gambit, and the image of those binders.

~

Squeaky prepared to release an album, a collection of demos, really, that would be distributed by Great White, the California-based bootleg company best remembered for Dylan's Basement Tapes. Had Fromme found more tapes, what album might have been possible? In one story, an inebriated Dennis Wilson, filled with black bile and self-recriminations, had cast recordings of Charlie

---

are me, and I am you'—to realize how their minds, interlock, how she could have killed him and then said he did it."

Manson into the surf sometime in the late 1970s. True or not, chances are those tracks, allegedly polished by famed Los Angeles session musicians, the Wrecking Crew, will never be heard.

Though every now and then "lost" albums can be found. There's the recreated *SMiLE*, finished decades too late by Brian Wilson. Then there's Brian's collaboration with Stephen Kalinich, *A World of Peace Must Come* (1969/2008), recorded in August 1969 but released only forty-nine years later. After an introduction of pure multitracked Beach Boys' bliss, Kalinich's spoken words sparkle darkly, suggestively: "Below the façade of the Candy Face / Lies the destruction of the race / Of all mankind."

Then there's "Be Still," a reworking of the Dennis-penned ditty from *Friends* (1968), the Beach Boys album released just as Charlie's friends moved into 14400 Sunset Boulevard. On this track you can hear the drummer chatting with Kalinich, then playing a bit of organ while the poet declaims: "Know that like the flower takes the sun and wind and rain and eventually blossoms / Your life too must go through many changes."

~

The story of the blossoming of the commune between 1967 and 1969 now began to be told. The fullest accounting from these early days came at a press conference with Paul Watkins, Brooks Poston, and Paul Crockett shortly after the arraignments.

"The whole thing," journalists quoted Watkins to have said, "was held together by black magic. You don't believe it? Well, it really exists, and it is powerful. We could show you." Charlie believed, journalists quoted Poston saying, "that he—and all human beings—are God and the devil at the same time. He believes all human beings are all part of each other."

"You see what that means," journalists then have Crockett interjecting, interpreting this diffuse notion. "It means that human life has no value. If you kill a human being, you are just killing a part of yourself. So it's all right." Charlie "developed virtual hypnotic power over his tribe" journalists reported. "This sort of power takes a long time to work an effect," Crockett averred. "Motions are tied to emotions. Certain motions create certain responses if you know how to use them."

Now the reader comes to the key takeaway from the press conference, helpfully summarized: that "Manson's talent as a musician and a songwriter magnified his hypnotic hold on the group." Brooks quoted a snippet of song, seemingly to suggest the musical mechanism facilitating this command. "There is no good, there is no bad," Manson allegedly sang, "There is no crime, there is no sin."

Here's how one journalist described the import of these lines: "That lyric, the three men suggested, embodies the philosophy Manson tried to instill in his followers."[17]

~

Music figured prominently in these early print accounts. "One day a little man came in with a guitar and started singing for a group of us in that place where we were living, in Haight-Ashbury in San Francisco," Susan said. "Even before I saw him, while I was still in the kitchen, *his voice just hypnotized me—mesmerized me*. Then when I saw him, I fell absolutely in love with him. I found out later his name was Charles Manson. But he had other names, too, and so would I."

By the end of her life, Susan would ultimately narrate this encounter an auspicious three times, with this above narration in the *LA Times* (December 14, 1969) published first. And why did Susan follow Charlie?

"He gave me nothing but love, complete love, gave me the answers to all the questions I've ever had in my mind. This whole world and everybody and everything in it has been God's game, and that game is just about to come to an end. Judgment Day for every human being on the face of the earth is coming."[18]

~

In Texas, Bill Boyd recorded Tex Watson's narration of the commune's life, those two nights in August, and—allegedly—other murders. A few years later, Tex shared the tapes with a man named Chaplain Ray, who helped him write *Will You Die For Me?* (1978). Few others have heard them.[19]

~

Allow the piles of documents and tapes, real and imaginary, heard and unheard, to evoke another image: the twenty-six bound volumes of the unabridged edition of the Warren Commission's report on the assassination of John F. Kennedy as they must have appeared, piled high and dog-eared, on the suburban California dining room table of Mae Brussell.

By her own account, Brussell had little interest in current affairs until 1966, when she encountered a news story about the investigation into those famous six seconds in Dallas. The housewife quickly acquired a full set of the official reports, referencing and cross-referencing their pages. She began subscribing to major newspapers and journals, too, referencing and cross-referencing these, too, seeking out concordances and patterns, instances of propinquity longing for connection.[20]

Brussell's pile of books and files would not have looked much different from the corpus of materials, bristling with bits of colored paper and scrawled notes, burying my desk. Something about the Manson case, incidentally, aroused her sixth sense for deeper meanings, too. By that time Brussell had a weekly radio program that charted the hidden world of conspiracies. The government may have been involved in forming the Manson commune, Brussell told listeners, as part of their experiments with mind control. They may have actually instigated the murders in order to discredit the counterculture.[21] (Paul Krassner later noted that the case demonstrated a "propagandistic horror that benefits nobody but the police state."[22]) Most people would dismiss such suggestions as unhinged. Or worse: as conspiracy theory.

~

Lawyers in Los Angeles began teasing their own theory. "Can a person under hypnosis be persuaded to commit murder?" asked Ralph Dighton for the *LA Times*. Speculation about this potential trial ploy now ran rampant. "If the defense is going to be hypnotism, I don't think the defendants have a chance," an expert told Dighton. "No one can be forced under hypnosis to commit murder unless that capacity was already in their essential nature."[23]

~

Stories about the commune quickly entered an occult economy of the lurid and sensational, an economy that—through my use of these stories—has inevitably leached into this book. "Look, it's quite simple," Sandy soon would tell *Rolling Stone*. "If we give away all our stories in interviews, we are going to have nothing to put in our book. I thought we were going to put it all down and get a publisher to give us a big chance."[24] A journalist named Lawrence Schiller helped broker the sale of Susan Atkins' confession, the one sold worldwide as *The Killing of Sharon Tate* (1970). He also soon claimed to represent Manson, as well as "a book of Mansonania [that the commune members] have been working on . . . [and that] includes some of Manson's song lyrics, poems, metaphysics and stories about various raids."[25]

Schiller had by this time a few other scoops under his belt. He had published the final interview with Jack Ruby, the man who killed JFK's assassin, Lee Harvey Oswald. His photographs depicting the dangers of LSD had illustrated the *Life* magazine article that, some say, helped lead to its criminalization. He also published a book debunking conspiracy theories about the JFK assassination. He was at the Ambassador Hotel the night Sirhan Sirhan shot Robert F. Kennedy in 1968.

~

In 1967, the Central Intelligence Agency invented the term "conspiracy theory," or at least began concerted efforts to stigmatize "conspiracy theorists," possibly as a means to discredit Warren Commission skeptics.[26] (Or so some people believe.)

~

"But there is another, far more powerful influence which may be seen here: brainwashing," journalist Ralph Dighton had continued. "Under long-term confinement, deprivation and brutality, which I understand may have been operative in this case, suggestive influence may be brought to bear which will *completely change a personality*. A victim of such treatment can be forced to commit a crime under duress."

Those italicized words evoke a constellation of ideas about the integrity of an individual's personality, conceived here as something unitary and coherent, as requiring protection, something that can be developed, yes, but also as something we risk losing.

~

"Charlie would, in effect, conjure up a vision detrimental to her in his mind," Susan's lawyer Richard Caballero told reporters, "and then transfer it to her mind and then she would know if she is marked."[27]

"I think she's just trying to talk her way out of it," Susan's father told the media. "She's sick and she needs help." Mr. Atkins had last seen Susan in September 1968, when she and "at least two other members of the cult" stayed with him for just over a week. "I thought they were just a slap-happy bunch of kooks, dumb hippies—not killers. And now the horror has come. And I know where she's been. Everywhere people died when they were there."[28]

What might a father have done differently? In Florida, a well-meaning mother petitioned a local judge to declare her adult, hippie son incompetent. "Testimony at the sanity hearing indicated that the subject's beliefs about 'love and nonviolence,' his atheism, and personal conduct brought him into conflict with his father," an article in *Rolling Stone* summarized.

But on appeal, the decision had been overturned. "The mother had clearly been moved," the ruling noted, by a "sincere desire to save the appellant from a life of waste and degradation, and, by medical treatment, to have him restored as a useful member of society." But the fact that he "lived the life of a 'hippie' . . . in the sincere belief that his way of life was preferable to that of his parents and the great majority of those comprising our society"—that does not mean he is insane.[29] At least not legally speaking (though perhaps providing evidence for the notion that "mental illness is a form of collusion, by which we elect others to live out the chaos we refuse to confront in ourselves").[30]

~

The distinction between insanity and evil, we might also agree, represents a social construct, not a legal one. Even had Atkins been brainwashed, she must have had buried deep inside her a seed of hate that Manson had uncovered, nurtured, tended. "We discount the Svengali influence these days," as one psychiatrist told Ralph Dightman, "but it is entirely possible that a Trilby might somehow let a Svengali know of suppressed hatred for society and then excuse her actions by blaming them on him."[31]

LSD could have been used as a tool for unearthing a deeply held cruelty. "This drug has been proven to have a powerful effect in deterioration of the personality," another expert, a psychotherapist, told Dightman. "People who have used it are more likely to express any antisocial wishes buried in their unconsciousness. The user tends to think in a primordial, atavistic manner which may lead to behavior that society finds horrible and savage."[32]

People who take LSD tend to express antisocial desires, this statement suggests, which through an unnamed mechanism can be found beneath the surface of their conscious minds. These desires, the figurative language implies, live deep underground. Under the influence of acid, the statement continues, people's minds tend toward primitive patterns of thought. And primitive patterns of thought, it follows, engender actions abhorrent to others.

Note the value-laden terms: primordial, atavistic, and savage, glossed here with the term "primitive." And note too how the psychoanalytical cloaks itself in the anthropological. The ego slips, allowing the unconscious free reign, so that civilization may fall, allowing the re-emergence of the primitive. As described by the psychotherapist, the end result appears to be strikingly similar to what psychedelic voyagers themselves had been seeking: the mirror reversal of the straight world. It's just that in the straight world, that stripping away of civilization disintegrates the personality. While through countercultural practices of the self, it leads to self-actualization, to the revelation of a truer, more authentic self. And, of course, the annihilation of a false one.

~

A day or so after Zero's suicide, a musician named Mark Ross brought filmmaker John Hendrickson to see the bloodied bedroom. Ross had invited the commune members to crash at 28 Clubhouse Avenue, where Zero died, a few weeks earlier; he would later change his name to Aesop Aquarian.[33]

At the time, Hendrickson had been shooting his first feature film, about the second coming of Jesus. Mark (t/n Aesop) played the role of a hippie Christ returned to violent, protest-torn contemporary Southern California. Hendrickson intended the film, which remains uncompleted, to be fictional. The filmmaker's unofficial account of Zero's death soon circulated far and wide through the California underground: Zero had been purposely killed, maybe because he seemed unreliable, and perhaps during a quasi-ritual sexual encounter (shot once in the temple while achieving orgasm, a deadly kind of sex magick).[34]

Sometime soon after this encounter (days, or maybe weeks, and possibly following the indictments), commune members invited the filmmaker to the Spahn Movie Ranch. Lyn drove to Los Angeles to request Charlie's permission for filming. With permission granted, Hendrickson began documenting the remaining members of the commune over the next eighteen months at both Chatsworth and in Death Valley. He recorded their songs, too.

~

"The idea that the killers and victims were strangers," longtime Manson researcher Dennis LaCalandra has summarized, "is perhaps the biggest lie told to conceal the truth about what happened." In his explanation, Watson—an up-and-coming drug dealer—drove the violence, providing a link between the victims (especially Bernard Crowe, Gary Hinman, Woytek Frykowski, and Jay Sebring) and the commune.

Could the killings have been drug burns gone wrong?[35] Manson researchers often cite a December 1969 interview in the *LA Free Press* with Preston Guillory, a sheriff with the Los Angeles Police Department, who posed this theory.[36] The *Berkeley Barb* reported that the commune had bought 63 kilos of bum marijuana at Cielo Drive—and the killings had been retribution. The person who reported that rumor also warned that "if Manson were to be made a scapegoat, this would signal the beginning of a general reign of terror against hippies."[37] "The coke market went crazy" directly after the murders, another countercultural journalist later reported in a cover feature titled "Charles Manson: Lifestyle on Trial?"

"The state claims that little Charlie somehow exercised enormous psychic power & control over the members of his family, that they were virtually his slaves and would, robot-like, do anything he commanded, even (and especially) kill," the journalist continued. "He had them hypnotized, is the way the papers usually expressed it . . . The state's claim—*most* of the state's claims—is absurd on the face of it, a tale cribbed from a movie. It's impossible, or as nearly so as makes no difference, for a man to exercise that degree of hypnotic control over that many people for so long."[38]

~

Conspiracy, such an evocative word, derived from *con* + *spirare*, meaning "to breathe together as one." Imagine a group huddled together, their faces darkened, conspiring as a single organism, breathing together, in and out. And isn't that what we have been doing, albeit at a remove in time and space? The rate of my breath steadily increases as words appear on the screen before me, until something jams the mechanism and my autonomic system fails. Surely you have been breathing, in and out, while reading this page? Quite literally conspiring, with me.

Charley doesn't tell people what to do," the open letter to the *LA Free Press* stated. "They do what they want to do." The commune freely shared love, not to mention money and food. When you are living in such a situation, you do what comes naturally. No one can force that. Just imagine if we all lived lives structured so.

The letter goes on and on, and toward the end, its author begins to falter, perhaps unable to express what cannot be put into words. But words at last do come: "the only defense left to Charles Manson IS THE MUSIC." Charlie writes "songs of the desert, of revelations, of things happening right now, of children as old as the moon."

"There will be no question when you meet this man," the letter writer concluded. "He says it all when he sings. He is a hole in the infinite—and infinity has no 'philosophy,' it just Is."[39]

~

If there existed any philosophy, Vincent Bugliosi later claimed, then Charlie had instrumentalized it for menticide, brainwashing. "On the hot summer night of August the eighth, 1969, Charles Manson, the Mephistophelean guru who raped and bastardized the minds of all those who gave themselves so totally to him," Bugliosi told jurors in his closing argument in late 1970, "sent out from the fires of hell at Spahn Ranch three heartless, bloodthirsty robots and—unfortunately for him—one human being, the little hippie girl Linda Kasabian."[40]

~

Throughout the early months of 1970, the commune and Manson continued to provide fodder for fictionalized and semi-fictionalized stories, offered up by a diverse cast of characters with an equally diverse set of motivations. A person going by the name "Blaine" reported getting caught up in a Death Cult that involved Manson, devil worship, and sadomasochism in the Haight during the Summer of Love. He claimed to have brought the story to one editor, who promptly called the police, before deciding to take his tapes and notes off to work into a novel.[41] Rock critic Richard Meltzer, poking fun at those claiming intimate, firsthand knowledge of Manson, published a spoof in *The Realist* titled "Charles Manson Was My Bunkmate." ("I didn't see [what was coming] then," Meltzer winked, describing their teenaged acquaintance at a reformatory, "but I can piece it all together").[42] Not everyone got the joke.

Manson himself began considering how the story might be filmed. After all, as the singer allegedly told actor Dennis Hopper during a prison visit in June, "his whole life had been acting out a movie, but there hadn't been any movie cameras there."[43] Would Hopper have played him?[44]

Attorney Marvin L. Part, entertainment chairman for the Los Angeles Bar Criminal Bar Association, penned by far the strangest fictional representation, a musical spoof titled *Oh! Calcourta!*[45] "The Family That Slays Together, Stays Together," an emcee announced. Lawyers performed a song titled "Death Valley," and another, "Defendant Manson," sung to the tune of "Gee, Officer Krupke" from *West Side Story*. Part had briefly represented Leslie Van Houten; he claimed to have been horrified by her tape-recorded interrogation after the Barker Ranch raid. "I knew right away this girl has no will of her own," Part later told journalist Ivor Davis. "She's insane in a way that is almost science fiction."[46]

In the lyric to "Defendant Manson," Part imagines "the County Jail . . . overcrowded with lawyers, wanting to help Charles Manson sell his books and records":

> Defendant Manson, let's both use our head
> Like why should Susan Atkins be making all of the bread
> There's plenty of money
> We'll both make a pile
> And we can share it, family style
> Family style
> Family style
> Family style
> Share it family style,
> All the bread, we'll share it family style—

Did Part have a particularly mercenary lawyer in mind? The press had recently reported that George E. Shibley—a leftwing activist who made his name defending Mexican-American teenagers during the zoot suit riots of the 1940s, and now represented assassin Sirhan Sirhan—had opened negotiations with record companies on Manson's behalf. An album would include "a number of protest songs and numbers Manson improvised," all taken from tapes recorded prior to the arrests. Shibley "declined to name the record company." Funds raised from album sales, the report stated, would go to Charlie's defense team.[47]

Judge William B. Keene, appointed to oversee the upcoming trial, attended *Oh! Calcourta!*, reportedly sitting in the front row. Someone told *Rolling Stone* he "appeared to enjoy the skit." When Manson filed an affidavit of prejudice in May, Keene stepped down without protest.[48]

As Judge Keene chortled, *Rolling Stone* announced its "Annual Awards for Idiocy, Evil, and Profundity in the Arts and Culture." John, "his wailing wife Yoko," and the Plastic Ono Band received the "Electric Skiffle Jam Band of the Year Award." Crosby, Stills, Nash, and Young received "Best New Group of the Year." Aretha Franklin received the "Can Blue Men Sing The Whites? Award" for a covers album of songs by the Beatles, the Rascals, and the Rolling Stones. The "Three Best Hypes of the Year?" Vice President Spiro Agnew, the Masked Marauders, and Paul McCartney's Death Rumor.

Paul lived on, though the Beatles soon came to an end. While promoting a solo album in April, Paul told the press the group had split. What was the final straw? Arguments about money? Paul's condescension? Or just growing up, and growing apart? (At just this moment, the mainstream press began reporting the White Album might have "supplied a 'script' for the Tate and LaBianca murders," and that investigators believed "members of Charles Manson's hippie clan were *Beatle addicts*, even to the extent of papering walls of their various dwellings with Beatle posters."[49])

John's partisans often claim that Paul's overly saccharine productions soured things, and watching the group's efforts to record "Maxwell's Silver Hammer" during the *Get Back* sessions does seem to show a band on the verge of giving up the ghost, so to speak. McCartney detractors sometimes single out this lyric, about a murderous character on trial for killing a series of people with a hammer, as a particularly galling example of his bad taste. Consider this rhyme, for instance. The *quizzical* first victim "studied *pataphysical* science in the home."

~

"I know the truth," Charlie told journalist Steve Alexander at *Tuesday's Child*, "the truth is in no word form. It just is. And everything is the way it is because that's the way love says so. And when you tune in with love, you tune in with yourself. You know, that's not really a philosophy, that's a fact and everybody who's got love in their hearts knows that. Okay?"[50]

A lengthy excerpt from this interview covered half of the back of *LIE: The Love and Terror Cult*, released in March 1970. Charlie's old friend Phil Kaufman released the album through his makeshift label, Awareness Records. (A Scientology reference, or just a commune term?) Three songs—"Sick City," "Look At Your Game, Girl," and "Eyes of a Dreamer"—had been taken from the 1967 demo; the other ten songs came from the August 1968 session at Gold Star

Studios organized by Gregg Jakobson.[51] Kaufman pressed two thousand copies; only three hundred sold in the first three months.[52]

"If you've got anything else to say, just keep talking," Alexander prompted, as reproduced on the back cover of *LIE*.

"Yeah, okay, if anybody wants to listen," Charlie responded. "I realize everybody's got their own message, dig? But I can't tell anybody nothing they don't already know. But I can sing for them and I got some music that says what I like to say if I ever had anything to say."

~

Founded in 1948, the Collège de 'Pataphysique fostered "learned and inutilious research." The field's founder, Alfred Jarry, intended the prefix to indicate "that which is above metaphysics." The most well-known definition calls pataphysics "the science of imaginary solutions."[53]

~

As the investigation progressed, the commune, following a period of disintegration, began stabilizing. A hard core of followers now acted as go-betweens, connecting Charlie, Sadie, Leslie, and Katie to the outside world. They began intimidating witnesses, allegedly setting fire to Paul Watkins' camper as he slept, and later dosing commune member Barbara Hoyt with an LSD-laced hamburger.[54]

At Spahn Ranch they recorded some of the desert songs, with Clem on lead vocals backed by Gypsy, Cappy, Brenda, Ouisch, Squeaky, and Sandy. The director Hendrickson made several early recordings in late 1969, which have never been released; they later rerecorded the desert songs during the trial. We know this because on one rolicking folk cover, "Get On Home," a young woman—perhaps Sandy, or Gypsy—sings: "When you see the children, with X-s on their heads / If you dare to look at them, soon you will be dead." Several commune members kept vigil outside the Hall of Justice in the summer of 1970. And in solidarity with the defendants, they had carved into their foreheads X-s. They even crawled in protest nearly a mile on hands and knees one day, too, making themselves a messy, bloody spectacle.

~

"Even in the hands of the most careful storyteller," cautions Kat Rosenfeld, writing about the true-crime genre in general, "there's no nonautobiographical version of these stories that isn't at least a little bit exploitative."⁵⁵ And as we have seen, the autobiographical versions can be exploitative, too.

~

In March 1970, director Monroe Beehler released the first of many exploitation films about the Manson Family, *Love and Murder in the Commune*. A pioneer in gay film, Beehler may have been after a quick buck; the film played at only a handful of adult theaters. "The Unbelievable Manifesto of the Assassin Cult! Worship Him! Kill for Him! Die for Him! Make Love for Him! A Film Document that Blow-torches the Whole World!. . .Depicting the Shocking Cult of Desert Animalism and Sex Cruelty Climaxed by Death!"

The exploitation continued. *Tuesday's Child* presented a long-haired, clean-shaven Charlie on its cover with the banner, "Man of the Year." (Manson found himself in mixed company: while *Rolling Stone* named John Lennon its Man of the Year for 1970, *Time* named Middle Americans its Man and Woman of the Year.) A second cover featured a cartoon Charlie, beneath a placard reading "HIPPIE," nailed to a cross.⁵⁶ Members of the radical Weather Underground Radical allegedly adopted a four-finger salute in homage to the fork left in one of the commune's victims; activist Bernardine Dohrn, in an offhand comment that trailed her ever since, said "the Weathermen dig Charles Manson."*

As above, so below. Those in the underground saw in the commune what they wanted to see. And all the while, David Dalton and David Felton had been working on a story that *Rolling Stone* would publish in June, just before jury selection for the trial began. The thirty-thousand-word cover story included a visit to Spahn Ranch with the commune's remaining members; a lengthy, sympathetic jailhouse interview with Charlie; firsthand accounts of the music from Dennis Wilson's inner circle; even an inside look at the investigation from a member of the prosecutor's office, whom they codenamed Porfiry, after the detective in Dostoevsky's *Crime and Punishment*.

---

* Among the speeches and statements, attendees at this forum sang "Weatherman songs, high camp numbers such as 'I'm Dreaming of a White Riot,' 'Communism Is What We Do,' and "We Need A Red Party." Spirited chants broke out, too: 'Women power!' 'Struggling power!' 'Charlie Manson power!' 'Sirhan Sirhan power!' 'Red Army power!' 'Power to the People!' 'Off the pig!'" Reported in "Year of the Fork?," *The Fifth Estate* (January 22, 1970), pp. 12–14. Not all radicals agreed. "What if Manson is innocent?" one person asked in *Quicksilver Times* (February 9–19, 1971), p. 18. "Why such faith in the pigs and the pig press to believe it all, to start a myth? More important, why so willing to adopt as your hero this creature defined not by your movement, or any people's movement, but by the cops, the Los Angeles sensationalist journalists?"

When Felton and Dalton arrived at the jail to interview Manson, they encountered a young man tripping. Clem recognized them. But how?

"Spirals," he explained. "Spirals coming away . . . circles curling out of the sun."

"A hole in the fourth dimension," the authors responded.

"A hole in all dimensions," Clem replied, before taking them in, with Squeaky, to see Charlie. He's a "cajun Christ," the journalists write, Little John the Conqueror or an Elf King. They ask about his album and his songs.

"I never really dug recording, you know, all those things pointing at you. Greg would say, 'Come down to the studio, and we'll tape some things,' so I went. You get into the studio, you know, and it's hard to sing into microphones. Giant phallic symbols pointing at you. All my latent tendencies . . . My relationship to music is completely subliminal, it just flows through me."

Charlie had been pantomiming sex during the response. Now the journalists asked about specific lyrics. "Once you give in to paranoia, it ceases to exist. That's why I say submission is a gift, just give in to it, don't resist. It's like saying, 'Tie me on the cross!' Here, want me to hold the nail? Everything is beautiful if you want to experience it totally."

Felton and Dalton here and there insert a parenthetical explanation about how to read these statements. "Charlie's rap is super acid rap—*symbols, parables, gestures, nothing literal,* everything enigmatic, resting nowhere, stopping briefly to overturn an idea, stand it on its head, and then exploit the paradox." Next he's talking about the coyote; now about the child. "The death trip is something they pick up from their parents, mama and papa. They don't have to die. You can live forever. It's all been put in your head."

Everything we need, Charlie explained, we have in our own minds. We just need to cut through the programming, the words that keep us bound in submission, the language occluding the truth of experience. "The whole fucking system is built on those words, the church, the government, war, the whole death trip," Charlie continued. "The original sin was to write it down."[57]

~

Another article at this time seemed to anticipate the prosecution's case. Attributed to Y. Lee Freeman and published in *The Argosy*, the article allegedly related several days in the life of the commune as seen through Freeman's eyes. "I met the Family of Charles Manson in a place that was nowhere," he began, "the ghost of a ghost town."

Freeman met the group in May 1969. He described seeing how Satan's Slaves, the biker gang, "were held together by Manson's hypnotic personality and his understanding of certain fundamental drives: tribal unity, sex, music and religious revelation." Manson sounded like "an old country preacher." After a few days, the preacher revealed his true identity. "All my women are witches," he said, "and I'm the devil you know, Y. Lee."

"Sure," Freeman responded.

"No, I really am," Manson replied. "I'm indestructible." There's a war coming, and the Blacks know it—that's why they've started organizing. White people need to recognize this, too. "That's why the Family is starting to get bigger," Manson continued. "When the time comes, we'll be ready."[58]

~

In second part of their article, subtitled "Porfiry's Complaint," Felton and Dalton related an overview of the crimes as described by "a prosecutor . . . [who] works in the District Attorney's office, investigates crimes, prepares cases and occasionally appears in court."

Manson "had this crazy philosophy that the world was coming to an end," Porfiry explained, and he began preparing the commune for the revolution. They needed guns and dune buggies to make their escape to the desert. But the killings, the prosecutor seemed to suggest, probably had little to do with the philosophy. Instead he offered two motives: copycat killings in order to free Bobby Beausoleil, jailed for the murder of Gary Hinman, or revenge killings to scare the producer Terry Melcher, who had broken his word.[59]

~

Back in *The Argosy*, Freeman attempted to resist Charlie, but finds this impossible. Charlie wanted Freeman's car, and he wanted to move the commune into the part of the Spahn Movie Ranch where Freeman had been staying.

Canonical accounts note that Charlie's group had wanted to move into the dwellings occupied by a group of hippies sometime in 1968. But by the period allegedly described here—after the revelations of the White Album—those hippies were long gone. If Freeman's account accurately describes events in 1968, then preaching about a race war must have emerged much earlier than usually suggested, as Atkins suggested to us on page 101.

A biker named "Jingles" at one point offered acid; Freeman took it, but later realized "he gave me a PCP dog tranquilizer." The ritual that would frighten Freeman away from the Ranch now begins.

"Later, I find myself standing in front of Charles Manson, with about twenty-five people of his tribe sitting around, listening to tapes of Charlie playing on guitar, and singing the way-out songs he wrote." The tape stops, and Charlie speaks, "his voice . . . still in rhythm with the music."

"I knew you would come, Y. Lee," Charlie said. "Why have you tried to resist us?"

A "strange ceremony" ensued.

"Who do you think I am, Y. Lee?"

"You're the wizard," a drugged Freeman replied. "The magician."

"I can do anything because I am holy. I am God."

At this point "everyone rises and we all form a circle, walking and swaying as Charlie chants; 'We are all one, it is all love. Everything is love . . . .'"

Freeman becomes aware that commune members have been emptying his bedroom of books; he takes up the books, his "most precious possessions," and begins throwing them into a burning fire. He takes money from his pocket and hands it to Charlie, who throws it into the fireplace. Here's how Freeman summarized the experience: "So Charles Manson took my possessions from me by destroying my will and taking charge of my mind. But he did not get from me what he wanted most: my identity. When I awoke, dazed, the next day, there was still a little voice inside that said, 'I am Y. Lee Freeman.'"[60]

~

What does Manson's story explain? One potential answer concerned how the murders revealed something important about the counterculture. Here's how David Felton and David Dalton put it in their lengthy feature:

> One is tempted to say that Manson spent 22 of his 35 years in prison, that he is more a product of the penal system than the Haight-Ashbury. But it cannot be dismissed that easily. Charles Manson raises some very serious questions about our culture, whether he is entirely part of it or not. For actually we are not yet a culture at all, but a sort of pre-culture, a gathering of disenchanted seekers, an ovum unfertilized. There is no new morality, as *Time* and *Life* would have us believe, but a growing awareness that the old morality has not been practiced for some time.

The right to smoke dope, to pursue different goals, to be free of social and economic oppression, the right to live in peace and equity with our brothers—this is Founding Fathers stuff. In the meantime we must suffer the void, waiting for the subversives in power to die, waiting for the old, dead, amoral culture to be buried. [. . .]

Felton and Dalton counterposed the West Coast counterculture to the mainstream, asking whether "our culture" yet has form, a coherent morality. They concluded that it did not—and that this absence of direction had created an opportunity for someone like Charlie.

"This smiling, dancing music man offered a refreshing short cut," Felton and Dalton argued, "a genuine and revolutionary new morality that redefines or rather eliminates the historic boundaries between life and death." It's a bitter, maybe ironic conclusion—for of course, put into practice, Manson's revolutionary ethos leads only to self-destruction.

~

A month after *The Argosy* article appeared under "his" name, "Freeman" wrote into the *LA Free Press*. The magazine never sent him proofs, the author claimed, and among the 2,500 words or so, only about 250 were his. The paper invented the section on the race war. And that strange passage reproduced in full just pages ago, about "taking charge of my mind," seeking to steal "my identity?" Fabricated, not Freeman's words.

"Sensationalism, yellow press, one-sided views—whether Charlie's innocent or guilty," this Freeman wrote, "the farcical cry of a fair trial rings true only in the ears of those conditioned to respond to symbols geared to the manipulation of their psyches." In other words, Freeman hasn't been brainwashed—but those who believe this made-up story have. "The basis for the American Judicial System is individual responsibility," the wily Freeman continued. "If the system succeeds in proving that Charlie is guilty of the crime of controlling other peoples' minds, then the next logical step is the indictment of the military, of industry, of churches, of anyone with a collective idea."

In reality, Charlie figured as a character in a novel he had been writing, *The Indescribable Adventures of Y. Lee Freeman*. Now Freeman addressed Manson directly: "I'm impressed by our challenge of the basic premises of the American Judicial System: memory as a valid instrument for legal evidence, the role of judge as dictator, and the desire to defend oneself as without formal legal training."

And then, just before quoting lyrics by Manson and Sonny Boy Williamson, Freeman implored readers to consider the admonition of Lord Kṛṣṇa to His devotee Arjuna from the Bhagavad Gita: "A person is considered still further advanced when he regards honest well-wishers, affectionate benefactors, the neutral, mediators, the envious, friends and enemies, the pious and the sinners all with an equal mind."[61]

~

So what did the story of one Y. Lee Freeman in the *Argosy* actually tell readers?

~

And just who was "Porfiry?"

~

In the final section of the *Rolling Stone* article, subtitled "Super Ego vs. the Id," Felton and Dalton discussed the social and legal implications of the upcoming trial. It's a confusing section, because the two authors seem to slip between simply reporting Manson's words and endorsing them.

Manson argued that the courts had scapegoated him. "The fiction is in the assigning of guilt to one party, even the isolation of one crime, within a society that perpetuates itself through both mental and physical violence," the authors wrote. "Justice can be done only if the jury could consist of everybody in society so the court can expose *all* the connections between *all* events simultaneously. Since this is a physical impossibility except through electronic media, the court must proceed as if events took place isolated from the society in which they took place, and once that fiction has been established, it is easy to find villains in individuals. [...] By accepting this without question, our legal system is guilty of just what Manson claims: It is a form of theater in which real victims are found for sacrifice. And if we have allowed our legal system to become theater, we are already in the area of magic."

Our seemingly rational system has been constructed on occult foundations, the journalists suggested, with troubling implications for us all: "We are under a spell; the courts, the government have mesmerized us with documents, facts, fetishes to keep our minds off what is really happening. [...] The judicial system actually perpetuates crime because it is incapable of dealing with psychological reality or the true climate of the society."

~

"Histories, then, are not only about events but also about the possible sets of relationships that those events can be demonstrated to figure," Hayden White later wrote. "These sets of relationships are not, however, immanent in the events themselves, they exist only in the mind of the historian reflecting on them."[62]

If we can imagine something, whether an object, or a person, or perhaps even an event, we may describe it, even when, like the hircocervus of the ancients, that thing does not exist. Recognizing that truth claims may be mounted differently within contrasting genres, and that this may give rise to competing "truths," does not mean we're letting anyone off the hook. Weighing the evidence on the whole, here's what I think.[63] The commune had a small group of tightly bound members at its center, who gamboled and played with metaphysical practices and languages. They also had a larger group around them, which came to include bikers and figures such as Tex Watson, who was not with them for large parts of the time. The group had some apocalyptic ideas about society, and some of these ideas were quite racist; they believed very much in the power of music—and in particular, rock music.

At some point, a series of events began that set in motion these violent acts. Tex burned drug dealer Bernard Crowe, which heightened paranoia within the group; Bobby screwed up a robbery with Gary Hinman; Tex and other group members tried to get him out of prison with a copycat killing, and then a second one: so much ineptitude and criminal naivete, fueled by the use of methedrine by Tex and Sadie, and channeled through the druggy haze of Manson's diffuse philosophies.

~

"Throw away words from your mind," Manson wrote in a letter to the countercultural *LA Free Press*, which diligently covered his perspective. "Know and know you know and everything is the way it is 'because' that's the way God says so and it and you are perfect and all will work out if you love it all."[64]

CHARLIE STOOD, turning his back to Judge Older. Leslie, Sadie, and Katie followed suit. So the court sent them to empty rooms on another floor, to listen in on the jury selection process remotely via speakers. Would jurors interpret their mimicry as evidencing Charlie's domination? Could their removal jeopardize a conviction on appeal? Bugliosi was not sure.[65] Before the afternoon session, Katie appealed to the judge for their return to the courtroom.

"We should be able to be present at this play here," Katie told Judge Older.

He duly returned them. And each again stood, turned their backs, and were removed.

~

Attorneys questioned two-hundred and five people, dismissing all but eighteen (the twelve jurors plus six alternates), and generating four-thousand-and-five-hundred pages of transcripts detailing their beliefs about capital punishment, the Bible, the counterculture, rock music, race, the generation gap. These eighteen souls will be sequestered from the public, Judge Older announced, for three to five months. As it turned out, they holed up in the Ambassador Hotel nearly nine months.

Rosemary Baer found out her husband, sixty-one-year-old John, an electrical technician, would be serving from a television newscast. She later published a memoir of the trial, *Journal of a Pseudo-Juror*, which included her visits to the courtroom, the hotel, and to church with members of the jury. After the jury returned a guilty verdict the following February 1971, Rosemary at one point relates, she and John found themselves discussing Gnosticism.

"I've been doing a lot of thinking," John said. "Young people, mentioning no names, talk about living in the now; living in love, forgiveness and understanding; living together and sharing resources. It's death to the ego. Like the early days of Christianity. Be not anxious for the morrow."[66] The two then discussed a Bible verse: about courage, and letting gof those things we cannot control.

"Maybe this kind of courage goes by the name of foolhardiness," Rosemary concluded. "But we prefer to live without fear. Fear takes too much energy. We need to save our strength for our moral struggles. That we act in ignorance, superficiality, prejudice, hatred or folly—now *that* is something to fear. (Why do I saw *we*? This matter of life or death isn't my decision. Is it?)"[67]

~

Is it?

~

Defense attorney Paul Fitzgerald allegedly told a newsman the chosen jurors would be "excellent for the defense—no engineers, administrators, bankers or slide rule logic people on the jury who always come to mathematical conclusions."[68]

In addition to Fitzgerald, representing Krenwinkel, the defense team now also included Ron Hughes, Daye Shinn, and Irving Kranarek. Hughes lived in a friend's garage; journalists dubbed him the "hippie" lawyer. He hanged out with members of the commune, possibly prior to the murders, at least according to one account. He would be found dead, possibly murdered by the group, before the jury returned a verdict.[69] Shinn represented Atkins; *Time* described him as "a former used-car salesman of Korean descent, who specializes in immigration cases for wealthy clients seeking Mexican maids," suggesting that "Manson took him on mainly to handle movie, record and publishing rights."[70] Kranarek, representing Manson, had a reputation for obstruction and what Bugliosi would call "dilatory tactics." That means he often caused delays.

District attorney Aaron Stovitz took a lower profile after Judge Older cited him for breaching the court's gag order for the *Rolling Stone* interview. (Porfiry was Stovitz. Or rather, Stovitz was Porfiry.) He would be kicked off the case in September after telling journalists what he really thought about a delay caused by Susan's stomach pains. "It was a performance," he said, "worthy of Sarah Bernhardt."[71]

~

The trial began at the end of July. Charlie arrived in court bearing a crude X carved into his forehead; Katie, Sadie, and Leslie followed suit. Bugliosi's opening statement laid out the prosecution's case against Manson: that "everyone in the Family was slavishly obedient to him; that he always had the other members of the Family do his bidding for him; and that eventually they committed the seven Tate-LaBianca murders at his command."[72]

In addition to the mechanism, mind control, Bugliosi also explained the motivation. "Besides the motives of Manson's passion for violent death and his extreme anti-establishment state of mind, the evidence in this trial will show that there was a further motive for these murders, which is perhaps as bizarre, or perhaps even more bizarre, than the murders themselves. Briefly, the evidence will show Manson's fanatical obsession with Helter Skelter, a term he got from the English musical group the Beatles."

Manson told the commune that the Beatles had been communicating to him through their lyrics, that these lyrics secretly affirmed Manson's bizarre philosophy. "To Charles Manson, Helter Skelter, the title of one of their songs, meant the black man rising up and destroying the entire white race; that is, with the exception of Charles Manson and his chosen followers, who intended to escape from Helter Skelter by going to the desert and living in a bottomless pit, a place that Manson derived from Revelation 9, a chapter in the last book of the New Testament."[73]

~

The palest ink proves more reliable than the most powerful memory, Bugliosi advised jurors. People often attribute this "ancient Chinese proverb" to Confucius; it dates back at least to the Qing Dynasty. Make good notes, the prosecutor meant to say, so when you deliberate, you'll have a record of key testimony. Though notes can only be as truthful, of course, as the testimony itself.

~

Defense attorney Paul Fitzgerald called Bugliosi's description of Helter Skelter "a truly preposterous theory." It really is, if you think about it. And what should we think about it? In an influential study of genre fiction published not long after the trial's conclusion, theorist John Cawelti makes the common-sense observation that human beings seem to have an inborn need to transform events into socially recognized genres.[74] The story modes we choose, however, depend on underlying cultural needs. There's a kind of organic, even symbiotic, relationship between people and the stories they choose.

Does the Helter Skelter narrative excavate the hidden, subterranean desires of ordinary Americans? Does its role in the birth of the true-crime genre tell us something about our collective needs? And what does it say about us that we keep telling and retelling the Helter Skelter story, over and over again? Note that this functionalist theory of genre depends on a conception of a society in a state of equilibrium, or at least potentially able to enter such a state, where the constituent parts comprising our "culture" articulate to ensure the proper functioning of the whole. A social body in good nick or, mixing metaphors, a well-oiled machine. Each element seems to fit seamlessly into the whole; no puzzle pieces remain at the end of the game.

As Linda Kasabian prepared to take the stand, she received a final directive: buy a new dress to replace her long, white homemade frock. Joan Didion, at Sybil Brand to interview Kasabian (she had been pondering a book on the young woman), went out to select a more demure cut. The surreality of the moment was, of course, not lost on the journalist.

"In this light all narrative was sentimental," Didion later wrote. "In this light all connections were equally meaningful, and equally senseless. Try these: on the morning of John Kennedy's death in 1963 I was buying, at Ransohoff's in San Francisco, a short silk dress in which to be married. A few years later this dress of mine was ruined when, at a dinner party in Bel-Air, Roman Polanski accidentally spilled a glass of red wine on it. Sharon Tate was also a guest at this party, although she and Roman Polanski were not yet married. On July 27, 1970, I went to the Magnin-Hi Shop of I. Magnin in Beverly Hills and picked out, at Linda Kasabian's request, the dress in which she began her testimony about the murders at Sharon Tate Polanski's house on Cielo Drive. 'Size 9 Petite,' her instructions read. 'Mini but not extremely mini. In velvet if possible. Emerald green or gold. Or: A Mexican peasant-style dress, smocked or embroidered.' . . . At her own wedding in 1965 Linda Kasabian had worn a white brocade suit. Time passed, times change. Everything was to teach us something. At 11:20 on that July morning in 1970 I delivered the dress in which she would testify to Gary Fleischman, who was waiting in front of his office on Rodeo Drive in Beverly Hills. He was wearing his porkpie hat and he was standing with Linda's second husband, Bob Kasabian, and their friend Charlie Melton, both of whom were wearing long white robes."

The men could wear long white robes, but pig-tailed Linda couldn't wear the long white frock? Too cultish? (Or not coltish enough?) Didion has already made the leap, of course, and articulates the incongruity: "Long was for Bob and Charlie, the dress in the I. Magnin box was for Linda. The three of them took the I. Magnin box and got into Gary's Cadillac convertible with the top down and drove off in the sunlight toward the freeway downtown, waving back at me."

To this point, we have expended nearly eighty thousand words examining that basic insight: that "all narrative was sentimental," and "all connections . . . equally meaningful, equally senseless." Summarizing the sequence that began with the dress she bought as Jack Kennedy bled to death, and concluding with the dress she bought as Linda prepared to help send Manson and several commune members to the gas chamber, Didion wrote this: "I believe this to be an authentically senseless chain of correspondences, but in the jingle-jangle morning of that summer it made as much sense as anything."[75]

~

The approaches to storymaking examined throughout our book—whether from Castaneda and Cawelti and White on genre and narrative, or Laing and Cooper on the possibility of making an account of ourselves, or Didion and Vonnegut on the radical subjectivity of journalism, or Anger and Calvino and Kandel on the art of mythmaking (and the myth of artmaking)—emerged within, through, against, and in spite of the very conditions that gave rise to the commune itself, its music-making and its experiments in the arts of living. Hayden White sued the Los Angeles police department, for instance, while conceiving and writing *Metahistory*; agents had infiltrated UCLA's campus by posing as students, attending class and making notes, using public funds for illegal, covert intelligence gathering.[76] And as we've just learned, Joan Didion even bought the dress that Bugliosi's star witness wore on the stand.

~

On the stand, Kasabian proved a credible witness under questioning from Bugliosi. She described the orgies; she described the Beatles connection. She explained her understanding of Helter Skelter. Bugliosi opened by asking her to confirm her knowledge that, if she testified, she would be granted immunity from first-degree murder charges.

"Besides the benefits which will accrue to you under the agreement," Bugliosi continued, "is there any other reason why you have decided to tell everything you know about these seven murders?"

"I strongly believe in the truth," Linda replied, "and I feel the truth should be spoken."

The defense attempted to poke holes in Linda's credibility. The drugs, the hundreds of LSD trips. Her unusual marriage arrangement, the unseemly admission that she liked the sex. "I was not really together in myself," she told the defense attorney Fitzgerald. "I was extremely impressionistic . . . *I let others put ideas in me.*"

On cross-examination from Ronald Hughes, Linda revealed that she felt herself to have extrasensory perception. Charlie, she also claimed, dominated her through his vibrations.

"Do you feel that you are controlled by Mr. Manson's vibrations?" asked Hughes.

"Possibly."

"Did he put off a lot of vibes?"

"Sure, he's doing it right now."

"May the record reflect, Your Honor, that Mr. Manson is merely sitting here," Hughes stated.

"He doesn't *seem* to be vibrating," Kranarek added.

Linda admitted to using drugs that, Hughes suggested, in their quantity and diversity may have impaired her ability to distinguish fantasy from reality.

"You have testified that you have had trips on marijuana, hash, THC, morning-glory seeds, psilocybin, LSD, mescaline, peyote, methedrine, and Romilar, is that right?"

"Yes."

"And in the last year you have had the following major delusions: You have believed that Charles Manson is Jesus Christ, is that right?"

"Yes."

"And you believed yourself to be a witch?" Hughes prodded.

"Yes."

"Your Honor, I have no further questions at this time." Linda's testimony took a full seventeen days, during which time her husband, Robert Kasabian, and friend, Charles Melton, split, and another witness, Randy Starr, the Spahn Ranch foreman and a stuntman known for his "death drags," where a runaway horse dragged him by the neck, passed from natural causes—an ear infection—just shy of his fortieth birthday.*

~

The countercultural press wrote that Linda Kasabian appeared to be "something of a pathological liar, has been all her life, is even famous for it in her own circles," and that her star turn had been engineered toward nefarious ends. "The point of all this is that the Tate-LaBianca Trial is a political trial—and that next to none of our political heads seem to have recognized it as such."[77] That Manson had been allowed to wear his usual clothes in court suggested that whoever was

---

* Starr's gun had been used in the commission of the murders. After commune members tossed it out the car window, speeding away from Cielo Drive, an eleven-year-old had found it in his yard. He took care not to touch the grip, so as to not obscure any fingerprints. A fan of *Dragnet*, the boy knew standard police procedure.

pulling the strings behind the scenes wanted to indict the counterculture itself: "the police and the media team up to present straight Amerika with their image of a 'typical hippie': fantastic sex life, heavily involved with drugs, a depraved killer underneath."[78]

"It was perfect," an editorial in the *Berkeley Tribe* explained. "Here was their murderer. He looked like the Devil himself, and then there was all that dope, all that sex, those orgies with teenagers. [. . .] What happened next sealed his fate. The media got hold of it and proceeded to further sensationalize the Tate-LaBianca murders. . . . He became, to middle-amerika, the symbol of dope-crazed freaks running lose, murdering people. . . . The trial itself was an empty formality, a way of making legitimate, premises that would never stand up in any kind of equitable system."

Not that we should valorize Manson, the editorial cautioned. If he had any politics, they veered toward individualism, even fascism; and in any case, Manson was "a fuck-up: he never could get anything together." But the commune's treatment showed what could happen to anyone seeking to make life more livable outside the constraints of straight society. "We ARE all outlaws in the eyes of Amerika and most of us are vulnerable to being railroaded one way or another. As the price of living outside the mainstream of pig Amerika increases, so will the busts, the harassments, the penalties."[79]

~

As Kasabian took the stand, a group of countercultural activists invaded Disneyland. Jerry Rubin had visited Manson in prison and praised him in the press. Now his Yippies—members of the absurdist Youth International Party—overwhelmed the amusement park.

The group gathered at Sleeping Beauty's Castle, then marched down Main Street. After failing to enter Disneyland's City Hall, several occupied Tom Sawyer's Island, getting high and running up the Viet Cong flag. Chants accompanied their march: cheers for Ho Chi Minh—and for Charlie Manson.[80]

~

MANSON GUILTY, NIXON SAYS—Charlie flashed the newspaper headline toward the jury, giving most of them just enough time to read the big black bold letters before a bailiff snatched it away. Daye Shinn spent a night in jail for handing the paper to Manson; Judge Older ultimately decided that, even though the President of the United States had declared Charlie to be guilty of the crimes, the jury had not been prejudiced.

"We told the world Manson is a reflection, yet even President Nixon, a lawyer, publicly declared Manson 'guilty, directly or indirectly,' before the trial was over," Squeaky Fromme wrote in 1977, introducing a book about the commune that would never be published. "Believe it or not, Rome stumbled over the truth in one bastard."[81]

~

How do you fight the state? Can ordinary people struggle against systemic forces arrayed against them? The following ideas come courtesy of Abbie Hoffman:

Question: How to deal with an impersonal federal marshal?
Answer: Squirt him with chemical LACE, a high-potency sex juice that will make him pull off his clothes and make love. [...]
Question: How to infiltrate the very highest levels of the military industrial complex?
Answer: Attend one of Tricia Nixon's teas, and bring enough LSD for all the honored guests.

Hoffman might have succeeded, aided by a dropout from Tricia's alma mater, Finch College, Grace Wing—better known as Grace Slick of the Jefferson Airplane. Tricia had invited former classmates to the White House for a reception, and Slick claims she, an incognito Hoffman, and six hundred micrograms of LSD in powdered form nearly passed through security. "Entertainers gesture a lot, we're flamboyant," Slick later told an interviewer, "and I could just gesture over Richard Nixon's teacup, and drop the acid in."[82] One pill makes you smaller; security turned the two away. (An FBI memorandum on the April 24, 1970, incident noted that "a weekly hippie type newspaper," the *East Village Other*, had recently quoted Slick as stating "I prefer not to kill people, but I'd like to destroy as much property as possible."[83])

~

A parade of witnesses now testified about life at Spahn Ranch: T. J. Walleman, Barbara Hoyt, Juan Flynn. Tex Watson even visited; he had been hospitalized shortly after his return to California, wasting away by refusing to eat. At one point, Charlie threatened the judge, leaping over the desk. Sadie, Katie, and

Leslie were reported to have begun "chanting something in Latin."[84] The court appointed security details to members of the prosecution.

~

At the end of September, a wildfire swept through Chatsworth, obliterating the Spahn Movie Ranch. Yet another sign of the apocalypse, commune members told journalists.

~

Bugliosi would soon call Gregg Jakobson to the stand. But what if he had called other Beach Boy collaborators to bear witness at this trial?

"And will you state your full name for the record."

"Stephen John Kalinich, citizen of Earth."

"Mr Kalinich, will you read into the record these lines from the first track of the album you recorded in Brian Wilson's bedroom on the twenty-second of August of last year?" Kranarek might have asked. "From your poem, 'Candy Face Lane?'"

"Yes," Kalinich coughed, before reciting: "The nuclear age of violence and rage / Waits and waits for a Wonderful Sage."

"And Mr Kalinich, who is this Wonderful Sage? Who were you and Brian expecting?"

"Objection!"

"Okay, who were *you* expecting to come and 'turn the page?'"

"Objection! Your Honour, I don't see how this question is relevant."

"Fine, I'll withdraw it. Mr Kalinich, do you see the Wonderful Sage here in this courtroom today?"

~

Shortly after Manson made his great leap at Judge Older, Virginia Graham took the stand. Once there she admitted withholding evidence from Sadie's confession the previous year. Her grisly revelations broke worldwide on the ninth of October.

The Family had a "hit list" of celebrities. They allegedly planned to carve "helter skelter" in Liz Taylor's forehead. Then they'd cut out her beautiful violet eyes, sending them—along with Richard Burton's penis—to Eddie Fischer. Sadie allegedly planned to slit the throat of Tom Jones while fucking him; the girls would allegedly flay Frank Sinatra alive. They'd allegedly make purses from his tanned skin to sell in local head shops.[85] Allegedly.

~

The final major witness to be called, Gregg Jakobson, took the stand on the sixteenth of October. At the trial, prosecutor Vincent Bugliosi used Jakobson to establish the link between Manson's group, their ideology, and the Beatles. His testimony lasted three days.

"Did Mr. Manson ever discuss with you the recording group called the Beatles?" Bugliosi asked.

"Yes," Jakobson replied.

"And their role, if any, in the scheme of life?"

"Many times." [. . .]

"What were his feelings about the Beatles? What did he say about them?"

"He believed that they were prophets and they were prophesying Helter Skelter if you were listening to them, if you were tuned in. That is what they were prophesying. They were the leaders of the movement, within the words and context of their songs." [. . .]

"Would you say he indicated that he worshiped them?"

Here Manson's lawyer, Irving Kranarek, interjected: "I will object on the grounds of freedom of religion, your Honor, on the First Amendment Right."

"Overruled," the judge says. "You may answer."

"I don't know about worship. He thought an awful lot of the Beatles. They were—well, he thought an awful lot of them."

Bugliosi established, at length, that the commune owned a copy of the White Album, that the commune often listened to the Beatles, that Manson, "without having the lyrics in front of him," as the prosecutor revealed, "he would quote them verbatim." He then established that the group interpreted songs by the Beatles, introducing Manson's alleged readings into evidence through extended questioning of Jakobson.

"Directing your attention to the second verse," Bugliosi asked, "'Have you seen the bigger piggies in their starched white shirts.' Did he say who the bigger piggies in the starched white shirts were?"

"Again," Jakobson replied, "it was the establishment."

"Who were the bigger piggies? Were they the older people in the establishment?"

"Yes," Jakobson agreed. "Sure."

"I don't want to put any words in your mouth now," the prosecutor clarified. "Did he say the bigger piggies were the older members of the establishment?"

"No, he didn't say that the bigger piggies were the members of the establishment," Jakobson said. "The establishment is the establishment. It stands by itself."

Here and there, Jakobson gets tripped up. "You testified earlier as to what Mr. Manson said the Beatles meant by the word 'Piggies' in that particular album," Bugliosi at one point later prompted. "Did Mr. Manson ever tell you what he meant by the word 'pigs?'"

"Well, I am sorry," Jakobson replied. "Before, what I said was, it wasn't my interpretations of what the Beatles meant, it was Charlie's interpretation of what the Beatles meant."[86]

~

Melcher briefly took the stand, as did a photographer named Hatami who testified that he saw Manson at the Cielo Drive home. The home's owner, Rudy Altobelli, testified as well. And so did Brooks Poston and Paul Watkins.

Paul Fitzgerald told the press that he would call John Phillips and Mama Cass of the Mamas and the Papas. He said that he would call John Lennon, too. (The ex-Beatle had been in Los Angeles for primal therapy at the clinic of Dr. Janov during the trial's summer months, though he was not subpoenaed.) Who else didn't the defense team call to the stand?

~

"Please state your name for the court," the bailiff might have said.

"David Crosby."

In later decades, Crosby became an elder statesman of the Sixties, a grandfatherly presence espousing all sorts of liberal pieties. But at this point in time he had just left the Byrds, where Terry Melcher had produced him, after tensions reached a head at the Monterey Pop Festival when he commandeered the microphone to spout conspiracy theories about the Kennedy assassination. His new group, Crosby, Stills, Nash, and Young had recently released *Déjà vu* (1970).

Kranarek's line of questioning seemed opaque over the first three hours.

"When did you first meet the Family?"

Charlie gives Crosby a big smile.

"Uh, I'm not sure that I have. No."

"Do you see anyone in the courtroom today that you recognize as having met in 1967 or early 1968?"

He looks around, and sees Cappy, Catherine Gillies. "Yes, but Cathy—that's the name I knew her as, when she was hanging out with the Buffalo Springfield—I don't think at that time she or anyone else had heard of Charlie Manson."

"When was the last time you say Ms Gillies?"

"Uh."

Now the questioning might have shifted to lyrics.

"Where do your ideas for song lyrics come from, Mr Crosby?"

"Um—"

"Objection, first amendment rights."

Kranarek might laugh, hearing Bugliosi try his tack. "Please come to the point, Mr Kranarek," Judge Older might have said. "What is the purpose of this question about song lyrics?"

"It's to establish the identity of the narrator in the songs written by the witness, your honor." As an example, Kranarek might now introduce the lyrics to "Triad."

"When you sing, 'One and one and one makes three,' can you explain to the court the theme, the deeper meaning behind that phrase?"

"Objection."

"Sustained."

"Does 'one and one and one makes three' refer to a *ménage à trois*?"

"What's that?"

"Three people engaging in the sexual act."

"Oh, sure."

"The narrator of the lyric seems to be persuading someone to join a group marriage situation. Is that narrator you, Mr. Crosby?"

"Objection."

"You sing: 'Sister-lover, water brother—and in time, there may be others.' Can you explain those references?"

"Objection, I don't see the relevance of these questions."

"Overruled, but please come to the point Mr Kranarek."

"I'm asking where these references come from."

"Well, sister-lover—I mean, that's just how we talk. Not a literal sister, mind you, but in a metaphorical sense—like we're all brothers and sisters, you know?"

"You mean in the sense of a family."

"Yeah, like a family."

"And 'water brother?'"

"Oh, that's just an image."

"Where did you take that image from, Mr Crosby?"

"Well, the science fiction writer, Robert Heinlein—he writes about 'water brothers' in a novel, *Stranger in a Strange Land*."

Charlie maybe smiled broadly at Crosby, showing his teeth, as he leaves the stand for a short recess before cross-examination. Maybe Crosby looks away, not meeting the eyes of Cappy, who—having left her vigil outside the courtroom on the request of Kranarek—might have been seated behind the defense table. When Crosby returned, would Bugliosi have pushed on the question of authorship? Probably not. Why put into jurors' heads the idea the idea that rock lyrics should not be taken literally?

Would Bugliosi have attacked Crosby's credibility? "I'm now going to read from a transcript of your remarks on stage at the Monterey Pop Festival in June of 1967. On that day, you performed with a guitar group called the Buffalo Springfield. Is that correct?"

"Yes."

"Here is what you said: 'When President Kennedy was killed, he was not killed by one man. He was shot from a number of different directions by different guns. The story has been suppressed, witnesses have been killed, and this is your country, ladies and gentleman.' Do you stand by this statement?"

Or should Kranarek have called John Lennon to the stand? Or John Phillips? Mama Cass died before she would have been called, murdered by the CIA, some conspiracists would say, for her role in a Hollywood drug operation.[87]

~

Should the defense have called expert witnesses on the music? "Rock's the first head music we've had since the end of the baroque," one such expert had recently claimed. "By itself, without the aid of strobe lights, day-glo paints & other sublimaginative copouts, it engages the entire sensorium, appealing to the intelligence with no interference from the intellect." The following "principles" might then have guided jury members in their consideration of testimony:

> That rock is an intensely participational & nontypographic art form, a forerunner of something much like McLuhan's covertly projected spherical society.
>
> That far from being degenerate or decadent, rock is a regenerative & revolutionary art, offering us our first real hope for the future (indeed, for the present) since August 6, 1945. [. . .]

That rock is a way of life, international & verging in this decade on universal; and can't be stopped, retarded, put down, muted, modified or successfully controlled by typeheads, whose arguments don't apply & whose machinations don't mesh because they can't perceive (dig) what rock really is & does.

And finally: "That rock is a tribal phenomenon, immune to definition & other typographical operations, and constitutes what might be called a 20th Century magic."[88]

~

Dianne Lake would be the final commune member to testify, in November, followed by two psychiatrists, a Dr. Deering and a Dr. Skrdla. LSD neither caused brain damage, they explained, nor impaired memory. Someone taking LSD can distinguish the real from the unreal, as well as right from wrong. After a weekend recess, the prosecution spent most of Monday entering into evidence three hundred and twenty exhibits: the crime scene photos, maps, weapons and rope, and of course, the Beatles White Album—Exhibit 228. And then, just before five p.m., the prosecution rested.

~

The defense never called a witness. But the three female defendants now shouted that they wanted to testify. "Sadie, Katie, and Leslie wanted to take the stand and testify that they had planned and committed the murders—and that Manson was not involved!" Bugliosi summarized. "Charlie had tried to explode his bombshell, but the attorneys for the girls had managed to defuse it, at least temporarily. Standing up against Manson for the first time, Ronald Hughes said, "I refuse to take part in any proceeding where I am forced to push a client out the window."[89]

~

If Manson had a proper defense, Ed Sanders wrote at the time, he might have been able "to walk free and book himself into the Troubadour. Well, none of this team of defense attorneys could quite swallow that scenario. So, tentatively, as attractive as putting Mama Cass upon the witness stand might be, the defense decided to rest, when the day should come to present their case."[90]

~

"You wish to retreat!" cried the Byrd.

"No, resist!" came the reply.

AFTER THE DEFENSE RESTED on the nineteenth of November, lawyer Ronald Hughes went missing, and in the interim, Charlie provided the court with, in effect, a defense. "He rambled, he digressed, he repeated himself, but there *was* something hypnotic about the whole performance," wrote Bugliosi. "In his own strange way he was trying to weave a spell, not unlike the ones he had cast over his impressionable followers."[91]

~

The *LA Free Press* printed Manson's statement in full, thousands of words reproduced over seven pages. "We are reproducing the transcript in its entirety because we believe that the people of the free world who believe in our American system of jurisprudence have a right to hear what will probably be a condemned man's last and only appeal for his freedom," an editorial prefaced the transcript. "Now you must be Manson's jury, for he has no defense other than the testimony that follows."[92]

~

With the disappearance of Ronald Hughes, the court adjourned so his replacement, Maxwell Keith, could read the thousands upon thousands of pages of transcripts created over the previous seven months.[93]

Across the country, John Lennon and Yoko Ono sat down with *Rolling Stone* editor Jann Wenner in New York City for a lengthy interview that later appeared across two issues of *Rolling Stone*. Lennon eulogized his old group, the Beatles; he discussed what he understands to have been the political stakes and social significance of rock 'n' roll; and he offered his take on the Manson trial.

"I don't know what I thought when it happened," Lennon told Wenner. "A lot of the things he says are true: he is a child of the state, made by us, and he took their children [in] when nobody else would."

"Of course," Lennon added, "he's cracked all right."

~

When Clem had taken the stand, Bugliosi sparred with him. At one point, the prosecutor tried to pin down a timeline for the second night in August. But the most cracked member of the commune failed to offer a specific enough answer.

"No, I don't carry a watch," Clem said. "I am not always timing everything." Now believing that Clem (t/n Steve) had entangled himself in an untruth, Bugliosi pressed the point, inadvertently revealing an important truth about testimony itself.

"Well, Steve, the three female defendants in this case have previously testified that Linda got out of the car with Tex Watson, and then came back to the car later and drove away with you and Sadie. Do you care to change your testimony at this point?"

Bugliosi asked this because truth, within the context of the courtroom, emerges almost entirely through concordances. That is, truthful statements can be judged as such because other statements or evidence corroborate them. But what if that's not the truth game someone has decided to play?

"Do I care to change—? Just because they say that doesn't mean anything," Clem replied. "What does that mean to me? Am I supposed to change my whole story because they said that?"[94]

~

Toward the end of Charlie's statement, Judge Older had interrupted him, asking him if he had anything else to say, or could the court adjourn.

"I have killed no one and I have ordered no one to be killed," Manson said. "I may have implied on several different occasions to several different people that I may have been Jesus Christ, but I haven't decided yet what I am or who I am."

Some called him Christ, Manson said. In prison his name had been a number. Some now want a sadistic fiend, and so they see him as that. So be it. Guilty. Not guilty. These are only words. "Mr. Bugliosi is a hard-driving prosecutor, polished education, a master of words, *semantics*. He is a genius. He has got everything that every lawyer would want to have except one thing: a case. He doesn't have a case. Were I allowed to defend myself, I could have proven this to you."[95]

~

Closing statements came quickly, traded back and forth between the defense and the prosecution. In the last week of December, Bugliosi spoke. Then Fitzgerald, Shinn, Kranarek, and Keith.

Defending Leslie Van Houten, Maxwell Keith pointed out the most obvious problem. "If you believe the prosecution theory that these female defendants and Mr. Watson were extensions of Mr. Manson—his additional arms and legs as it were—if you believe that they were mindless robots, they cannot be guilty of premeditated murder." How could they demonstrate *malice aforethought*, as required by first-degree murder, if—as Bugliosi claimed—they had been puppets?

"And these people did not have minds to make up," Keith inveighed, accepting the prosecution's premise. "Each of the minds of these girls and Mr. Watson were totally controlled by someone else."

"Baa-aa like sheep," Manson allegedly told the commune at Spahn Movie Ranch, according to Leslie in a television interview decades later. And guess what? "Every single one of us did it exactly at the moment that he said it."[96]

~

On the thirteenth of January in 1971, Bugliosi began his final summations.

"The Family, the Family that lived at Spahn Ranch in the very, very, last analysis, was nothing more than a closely knit band of vagabond robots who were slavishly obedient to one man and one man only, their master, their leader, their god, Charles Manson. Within his domain, his authority and power were unlimited. He was the dictatorial maharajah, if you will, of a tribe of bootlicking slaves who were only too happy to do his bidding for him."

Bugliosi continued: "Charles Manson's Family preached love but practiced cold-blooded, savage murder. Why was that so? Because Charles Manson, their boss, ordained it. If Manson had wanted his Family to be singers in a church choir, that is what they would have been."[97]

~

On the twenty-fifth of January, the jury returned a verdict. They had not deliberated long. Their two requests had been to visit the Tate and LaBianca houses, and to acquire a record player on which to play the White Album, which had been entered into evidence without actually having been broadcast in court.

The verdict was unanimous. Guilty. The sentencing phase stretched into March. The parents of the convicted spoke in defense of their daughters (though Susan Atkins's father refused to come); an expert called Leslie "a psychologically loaded gun which went off as a consequence of the complex intermeshing of highly unlikely and bizarre circumstances."[98] There existed a seed of rage inside her, the psychologist stated, a kind of hate, that had expressed itself through the murders.

~

On the ninth of February in 1971, a major earthquake shook Southern California. Manson caused it, remaining commune members told journalists.

~

A few months later, a fan named Curt Claudio visited John Lennon's estate at Tittenhurst. Born in California in 1948, Curt began taking LSD while attending the University of California at Davis. He soon came to understand that the Beatles were communicating with him directly through their songs.[99] You can see Claudio and John together in the documentary *Imagine,* which was only released in its full form in 1988; the scene was cut from the earlier 1972 TV special.

After speaking with John, Curt returned to California, disillusioned with the ex-Beatle but still seeking answers to life's big questions. At one point, "he wanted to go into the wilderness like Jesus did," his brother later recalled. "Forty days and forty nights." He returned a few days shy of three weeks with a message. "You know, Jesus is going to come back to Earth again."

"I know," his brother said.

"I'm him," Curt said.

Claudio's visit occurred nine years, six months, and twelve days before Lennon's death.

~

At the end of March, the jury voted for the death penalty, and in April, the four defendants were formally sentenced. (Their sentences would be commuted to life in prison following the abolishment of the death penalty in 1972.) There would be more trials. But this largely concluded the general public's interest in legal proceedings against the commune, if not in their story.

~

In the months and years to follow, individuals associated with the commune continued to have major entanglements with the law. Brenda, t/n Nancy Pitman, would go to jail for the murder of a woman named Lauren Willett; a number of commune members went to prison for killing Shorty Shea. Sandy and others would be jailed for robbing a gun store in Hawthorne, California, the hometown of the Beach Boys. The most spectacular trial would be for Lynnette Fromme, who pointed a gun at President Ford in Sacramento in 1975. She would be sentenced to life imprisonment.

~

Managed by Paul Crockett, Paul Watkins and Brook Poston toured the West Coast as Desert Sun over the next decade or so. Poston still makes music; Watkins passed away from cancer in the late 1980s. Did they ever refute Manson and the commune? They testified, unlike other commune members. But they also continued to play Manson's songs into the early 1980s.

Terry Melcher released a solo album, *Melcher* (1974) to lukewarm reviews. Dennis Wilson released his masterpiece, *Pacific Ocean Blue* (1977), six years before he drowned off the coast of California. Bobby Beausoleil remains in prison; he continues to release music as of this writing.

~

Manson nearly died in 1984, when another inmate at Vacaville poured paint thinner over his head and set him alight. He spent much of that decade heavily medicated, though cassettes of songs he wrote at this time, smuggled out over the years, have been released over the past three decades to little interest.

But interest in Manson—the story, and the person—has rarely flagged. That's allegedly why a fiancé, along with a confidant on the outside, a man who had joined the commune just months after the August 1969 killings, schemed to acquire Manson's body after his death in 2017. They wanted to have it taxidermied. To exhibit as a tourist attraction.[100] Allegedly.

~

So it goes.

It seems so obvious, Susan Atkins later wrote, "with the benefit of hindsight, that on display were three young women clearly not in their right minds who were in slavish obedience to a madman. Every defendant in the case was mentally and spiritually sick, deeply ill. We were not to be excused; we were guilty. But we were desperately sick, legally so, and all the authorities refused to acknowledge this. We were treated as though we were intelligent masterminds."[101]

~

"Manson was an avid follower of the Beatles and believed that they were speaking to him across the ocean through the lyrics of their songs," Bugliosi told jurors in his opening statement. "In fact, Manson told his followers that he found complete support for his philosophy in the words of those songs."

What about the music? What about Helter Skelter?

"It means confusion, literally," Manson said during the trial. "It doesn't mean any war with anyone. It doesn't mean that some people are going to kill other people . . . Helter Skelter is confusion. Confusion is coming down around you fast. If you can't see the confusion coming down around you fast, you can call it what you wish."

Dare call it conspiracy?

"Is it a conspiracy that the music is telling the youth to rise up against the establishment because the establishment is rapidly destroying things? Is that a conspiracy? The music speaks to you every day, but you are too deaf, dumb, and blind to even listen to the music . . . It is not my conspiracy. It is not my music. I hear what it relates. It says 'Rise,' it says 'Kill.'"[102]

~

"I know why Charles Manson did what he did," Dennis Wilson said at some point in the 1970s. "Someday, I'll tell the world. I'll write a book and explain why he did it."[103]

~

"Why blame it on me? I didn't write the music."[104]

Epilogue

The Invention of the Sixties

"The swirling hallucination of the sixties," one commentator later wrote, "had climaxed in the ultimate 'summer bummer,' and it all made a grotesquely twisted sense."[1] And it all made sense, two other authors suggest, because "the Manson murders were the logical culmination of the counterculture's project of throwing off the shackles of conscience and consciousness, the grim flowering of the id's voodoo energies."[2] Or as another person, this one an eyewitness to the madness, concluded: "The sixties' myth of peace, harmony, and free love had been shattered by a blood-soaked orgy of murder and mutilation."[3]

In these and other narrations of the Sixties, the Tate-LaBianca murders function as a terminal event: a natural endpoint, the moment where *what is* merged wholly with *what must be*, and nevermind that an absent author must naturalize this endpoint, reframing event as inevitability.[4] You will find the most famous invocation of this sense of "the Manson murders" in the closing pages of a much-celebrated essay by Joan Didion.

"Many people I know in Los Angeles believe that the Sixties ended abruptly on August 9, 1969," Didion wrote in *The White Album* (1979), "ended at the exact moment when word of the murders on Cielo Drive traveled like brushfire through the community, and in a sense this is true. The tension broke that day. The paranoia was fulfilled." Didion goes on to explain that a more personal conclusion came, for her, just shy of eighteen months later, on cleaning out from a new home by the sea the detritus of the Sixties—a Scientology pamphlet, a copy of *Stranger in a Strange Land*. She reflects often on the people and persons from that period, we learn, and on her own strange intersections with its protagonists, evincing so many moments of propinquity—"but writing has not yet helped me to see what it means."[5]

~

Writing in *Fusion* as Charlie, Sadie, Katie, and Leslie sat in jail awaiting their trial, countercultural commentator Wayne McGuire predicted a massive, worldwide schizophrenic breakdown, a collapse of the social order through which Charles Manson would become a major American folk hero.[6] And in a sense, haven't these two predictions—the breakdown, and the mythologization—come to pass?

First the breakdown. Consider the broader shift in the West as to how we should best make sense of our world. We once knew that we were accurately experiencing reality insofar as we had freed ourselves from the repressions of our past. As neurotic subjects, we desired to become whole again, to strip away the hang-ups keeping us from seeing the world *as it really is*. (A skeptic could argue that our desires have always been illusory—nothing if not loves' nonesense, to invoke the poet, wrap'd up in thick clouds.)[7] What if neuroticism, thinkers from the 1960s onward have asked, has not been our primary sickness? And the cure was never a talking therapy?

Now the mythologization.[8] The story of Charles Manson has certainly passed into the realm of myth, albeit in multiple, contradictory ways. There's the success of the Helter Skelter prosecution, with its remarkably effective literary division between the lone psychopath and the rational community, between the disorder of the counterculture and the order of middle America.[9] Then there's the broader triumph of the true-crime impulse, a compulsion to make sense of someone like Manson, to fit all the rumors and stories and details and anecdotes into an overarching narrative, and to do this repeatedly, over and over again. Yet myth, like all narrative forms, wrenches from the chaos of lived experience only an attenuated, simplified kind of order. To layer meaning into the amorphous, quotidian messiness of lives once lived, myth requires characters. Myth needs events, too, whether observed and phenomenal, or (less often) pataphysical and extrasensory. Successful we call he who excavates truth from the raw materials of so-called lived experience, bringing that truth to the surface, and in so doing *makes it make sense*, rendering experience not merely legible, but also consequential.

That could be why William F. Buckley praised Vincent Bugliosi as "the counter-guru, if not the successful *exorcist*, of the strange disease which some people fear is rooted in the American social *dis*-order—and spreading."[10] The prosecutor was sitting on stage at Buckley's *Firing Line* in early 1975 to discuss the recently published *Helter Skelter*. In footage from the show, Bugliosi looks nervous; he pitches forward with a start when the lugubrious Buckley says that word, "exorcist." But should that word have startled Bugliosi? Because surely that's any author's deepest desire: to draw from his subject the truth, just as a devil might be drawn out and purged from the spiritually sick.

~

In taking the form of an emotional purging, Didion's essay related impressionistic moments from about 1966 to 1971. While it's worth reading in full, you can still feel the full weight of the essay's fatalistic final words—cited above, on the failure of the act of writing to help the author make sense of the world—if you know its opening line: "We tell ourselves stories in order to live."

Objectivity, not to mention truth, does not seem to figure in here. "We interpret what we see, select the most workable of the multiple choices," continues Didion. "We live entirely, especially if we are writers, by the imposition of a narrative line upon disparate images, by the 'ideas' with which we have learned to freeze the shifting phantasmagoria which is our actual experience."[11] Perhaps no one captured as evocatively as Didion this problem, what we might call the invention of the Sixties. It's the suspicion that the truth may not exist, or at least may not be accessible to us. It's the suggestion that we should write history as satire, as "a drama dominated by the apprehension that man is ultimately a captive of the world rather than its master, and by the recognition that, in the final analysis, human consciousness and will are always inadequate to the task of overcoming definitively the dark force of death, which is man's unremitting enemy."[12]

And yet we almost never narrate "the Sixties" in that satirical mode. Who would dare tell the story of the Beatles, the Beach Boys, and Charles Manson's commune in such a way? Certainly not me; the best I could manage in the foregoing chapters has been a healthy dose of irony. At least an ironic emplotment has the effect of enforcing a measure of critical distance. Though irony accomplishes this, as we have seen, through its tendency "to engender belief in the 'madness' of civilization itself and to inspire a mandarin-like disdain for those seeking to grasp the nature of social reality in either science or art."[13] And this approach, too, has its drawbacks.

~

This belief, that disdain: these tendencies surely describe how the subjects of this book approached their world. The commune members and their fellow travelers, I mean, but also the critics, authors, journalists, academics, and musicians we have encountered within the preceding chapters. Rather than refuse the tools these protagonists have gifted us, whether in the name of "objectivity" or something equally misguided, why not use them?[14] Because the raw materials from which we must draw in examining the late 1960s and its afterlives surely point us toward more skepticism about the natural order of things, not less. "Don't forget this was a period," the author of one account of the Manson saga quotes an eyewitness saying, "when many of us had a hard time sorting fact from fiction."[15]

If we take this statement as a challenge, as an injunction to ferret out the truth about *what really happened*, we fail to uncover its real meaning. Why not instead affect a kind of mandarin-like disdain? Or try on that belief in the madness of civilization? And so we have. Such an approach has allowed us to play along with that invention of the Sixties, those rapidly proliferating postwar truth games: not to reveal "the truth" about our not-so-distant past, but to uncover the hidden origins—in paperbacks, magazines, films, and of course, records—of the post-truth world we live in today.

"I speak and speak," as a historical explorer once said, imagining the circulation of stories about his exploits, "but the listener retains only the words he is expecting." He imagines how a sympathetic listener might understand his story, spoken directly and simply and in the first-person; how it might later "make the rounds" of gossips and chinwags in town; how an author of adventure stories might render its plot points; how later in life, he himself might turn it into memoir. And he comes to a conclusion.

"It is not the voice that commands the story: it is the ear."[16]

A Note On Reading *No Sense Makes Sense*

To REALLY UNDERSTAND a piece of writing, you must grasp its unity. And that unity can be grasped only by discovering how a work is one—and in that same moment, many. This advice can be found in Mortimer J. Adler's classic *How to Read a Book* (1940), overhauled for publication in 1972 with Charles Van Doren. And it's an example of the central problem underlying *No Sense Makes Sense*: namely that, during the so-called American century, an exegetical impulse—characterized by the compulsion to "read between the lines," to transform all phenomena, written and unwritten, into "texts" that can be parsed—came to dominate how we make sense of our worlds.*

The significance of that problem, as well as its consequences, inflects each page of this book. I have tried to make this precept do double duty: as not only an object for examination, but also as the principle guiding the book's construction. At this point, if you have not done so already, you may wish to finish reading the main text before continuing. Because in a few short paragraphs, this final Note outlines the book's organization, approach, and themes at a glance, letting loose the proverbial cat from its bag.

The main text has been organized according to a handful of writing principles that I have followed (more or less) in good faith. Each chapter functions as an independent entity comprising six sections of balanced lengths. Each interior section comprises as many story-driven scenes as required, organized through a loose, broken-line narrative strategy; every scene includes a reference, sometimes obscured, to Charles Manson, the commune, the Beatles, the Beach Boys, or any combination of these. Any fictional or speculative scenes have been supported in primary sources. Large- and small-scale transitions occur only through explicit and meaningful repetition (that is, of a key word, phrase, image, or character),

---

* Academic works by Rita Felski, Mark Greif, Jessica Grogan, Timothy Melley, Wendy Painting, and Fred Turner provide exemplary models examining these postwar intersections between artistic works, truth, and epistemological claims about personhood. But inspiration for this book came most directly from Italo Calvino, and especially *The Baron in the Trees* (1959), *The Castle of Crossed Destinies* (1969/1973), and the essay collection, *The Written and the Unwritten World* (1983/2023), as well as from Janet Malcolm, and especially *Psychoanalysis: The Impossible Profession* (1981), *The Journalist and the Murderer* (1990), *Iphigenia in Forest Hills* (2011), and the essay collection, *Forty-One False Starts* (2013).

whether logical or apophenic (that is, through an objectively false recognition of patterns or connections).

This concludes the information required to assess the unity-multiplicity aimed at in the structure of the main text; for additional context on my aims and approach, forge ahead.

The construction of this book has followed a handful of underlying theoretical principles. Figurative language suffused the period under examination in general, and this story in particular. And so I have sought where appropriate to present, explore, comment on, and critique figurative language. (Like "the cat" and its "bag," an idiom that some people say derives from a once-common market scam where an unscrupulous farmer substitutes a cat for a more expensive pig. Other people say it's British Royal Navy slang, that officers kept in a sack a whip—a cat-'o-nine-tails—they would use to discipline sailors.)

The narrative not only presents metaphors, speculation, conspiracy theorizing, as well as the generic conventions of gonzo nonfiction and New Journalism, or rock criticism, or the mid-century American novel, but also employs them, willy-nilly. I have aimed to think like an anthropologist parachuted into the postwar United States from elsewhere, like a stranger in a strange land. Such a person would be thunderstruck by the seriousness with which Americans played (and in many cases, continue to play) their truth games. Faced with such a society, an anthropologist might try the oldest trick in the ethnographic playbook: to defamiliarize language and destabilize meaning, seizing opportunities to thunderstrike readers anew. So this is why the narrative has taken the form of a speculative paraethnography, examining the late 1960s and its afterlives through the myriad postwar shifts in how many individuals apprehended and made sense of reality.

These writing and theoretical principles guided the crafting of this book: knowing them may (or may not) support the reading (or rereading) of the main text. To learn what I believe all those pages and pages mean, continue here.

From the foregoing ethnographic pretensions follows the first theme, the commune's mantra, No Sense Makes Sense, so significant it can be found in the book's subtitle (and I had wanted it to be the book's main title). A second theme explores how people perceived order and disorder, approaching the world as a place in turmoil and endeavoring to "set things right." In the modern world, moral claims masquerading as aesthetic claims about order envelop not only popular music, of course, but also jazz, classical music, and other artistic domains and media. This world's inhabitants tend to place themselves within parables about cultivating purposeful disorder as a countercultural art of living (a quintessentially progressive response), or about the necessity of reestablishing norms in the face of social disintegration (an avowedly conservative one). Techniques for cultivating alternatives, at least in this book's retelling, emerge from seekers; efforts to reintroduce a measure of order tend to come from people who believe that, while the world has become complicated, serious persons can find and implement solutions. But that suggests too stark a contrast between the two positions. From their complementarities and disjunctures we can, perhaps, discern the emergence of larger lessons about the politics of belonging in the postwar world.

A final theme examines how people began problematizing reality, proposing that—for a diverse cast of characters, and in sometimes unexpected ways—reality became unmoored, replaced by a new object, experience. How do we ground ourselves in a world seemingly no longer subject to the strictures of objective reality? When consensus failed, in its place there appeared new techniques of selfhood demanding we learn about ourselves, that we shed the mantle of civilization that cloaks our senses, deadening us to what is *really* real, what we could see if only we opened our eyes.

These themes might have been explored using any number of approaches. But I chose an affectively fraught postwar moment that generated an unwieldy corpus of materials, and which played a major role, outsized in proportion to its actual significance to most Americans, in the post-Woodstock imagination. I hope that the resulting narrative—about the musical lives of Charles Manson and his commune—has worked as a kind of scaffolding for approaching the intersections between popular music and postwar debates about truth in the 1960s and beyond. All I ask is that you read with an open mind. You don't, of course, have to believe a word of it.

Acknowledgments

"Few books today are forgivable," R. D. Laing wrote in 1967, introducing what might be considered a philosophy of the present. "Black on the canvas, silence on the screen, an empty white sheet of paper, are perhaps feasible."

If this book can be forgiven, then it's thanks to those who supported my writing and revising. For reading and commenting on portions of the manuscript, I'm grateful to Isobel D'Cruz Barnes, Michael Christoforidis, Krishan Meepe, Nicholas Sotir, and B. R. Tochka. A special thank you to Kyle Devine for comments on a full, early draft that much improved the final version, and for conversations and encouragement along the way. Thank you to Stephanie Shon for her as-always indefatigable research assistance. Special thanks to Leah Babb-Rosenfeld and the crack Bloomsbury team for their advice and support.

A sabbatical from my usual duties at the University of Melbourne, supported by Richard Kurth, Marie Sierra, and Jane Davidson, provided time and resources for researching and writing the first draft. Comments from colleagues and students at our department's postgraduate seminars, as well as from the popular music studies community here in my adopted home at IASPM-ANZ conferences, helped me figure out what I wanted to say, and how I wanted to say it. Thank you to Samantha Bennett, Benjamin Duester, John Encarnação, Tami Gadir, Kerry Murphy, Jadey O'Regan, Padraig Parkhurst, and Sam Whiting for comments that pushed me to refine my approach. For answering several of my queries, thank you to staff members at *Life*, *Rolling Stone*, *Vanity Fair*; thanks to Tom Philo at Gerth Archives and Special Collections for assistance with the holdings related to the countercultural press. Thank you to Althea Greenan for allowing me to reproduce a line from *It Happened In Boston?* as the epigraph. Thank you especially to my colleagues in the Baillieu Library, for their patience and good humor in helping locate some unlikely sources. And finally, my love to the true dedicatee of this book. No author must be / as lucky as me / in having a child (as old as the moon) / who daily reminds / just how thin the line / between this world and others must be.

Notes

Prologue

1. In a review in the countercultural *East Village Other*, Allen Katzman called *The Family* by Ed Sanders, the first serious examination of the commune, "more than just a book about murder, unfettered magic, or instinct unchained, it is the maudlin mirror of American institutional life, Vietnam war games, and public impov[er]ishment of the American soul filtered through the psychotic veins of its truest believers" ("Review," *East Village Other* [October 20, 1971], p. 23). More recently, Jeffrey Melnick's wide-ranging *Creepy Crawling* (2018) presents a comprehensive exploration of the myriad meanings assigned to the group and the murders over the past half century. Recent mainstream biographies that begin from this perspective include Jeff Guinn's *Manson* and Simon Wells's *Coming Down Fast*, as well as a music-focused biography by Tommy Udo, *Charles Manson: Music Mayhem Murder*.
2. Commissioned to write a magazine piece on the commune's music-making and their relationship to the Beach Boys, for instance, Jason Austin Penick initially gave up. "Simply put, the more I researched, the more apparent it became that no accurate version of the story could *ever* be written—there were simply too many contradictory accounts from the people involved for me to separate fact from fiction." He bowed out of the assignment, saying "that there simply was no way that I could ascertain the truth amidst so many fluctuating narratives." Penick later compiled all of these primary source quotes into a lengthy document, "Cease To Exist: The Saga of Dennis Wilson & Charles Manson" (May 25, 2021), "chop[ping] up a collection of quotes and arrang[ing] them into a coherent order, letting the story unfold thusly." Available at https://drive.google.com/file/d/1KiLdR7afoljKOlGMR5xizWTlC75Wvunm/view, accessed October 2024.
3. Described and quoted in Watson, *Cease to Exist*, p. 197.
4. Bugliosi, *Helter Skelter*, p. 218.
5. Major revisionist perspectives include books by Schreck, as well as Emmons, *Manson in His Own Words*; Stimson, *Goodbye Helter Skelter*; and websites such as The Manson Family Blog, The Tate-LaBianca Homicide Research Blog, and The Official Tate-LaBianca Murders Blog. The webmaster of CieloDrive.com curates a major archive of documents, photographs, news stories, and recordings; Michael Channels maintains The Backporch Tapes (TV BPT), an online channel and website collating and commenting on materials related to

the commune then and now. The most significant recent revisionist work is Tom O'Neill's, *Chaos*, which Errol Morris adapted into a streaming special in 2025.
6. Rebecca Fairley Raney, "Manson Family Website: History Rewritten by Losers," *New York Times* (October 21, 1997).
7. "The fear that hovered over Los Angeles in the wake of the August 1969 killings of actress Sharon Tate and six others has, with the passage of a half-century," a recent editorial in the *LA Times* puts it, "evolved into an odd and unseemly nostalgia." Remember the victims, the editorial board argued, but focus your energies on today's problems—not on glorifying "Manson and his sorry followers." Editorial Board, "Editorial: The Odd and Anachronistic Manson Nostalgia," *LA Times* (August 8, 2019). See https://www.latimes.com/opinion/story/2019-08-07/manson-nostalgia-sharon-tate, accessed September 2024.
8. Monroe, *Savage Appetites*, p. 15; emphasis added.
9. White, *Metahistory*, p. 9.
10. On the distinction between romantic and ironic modes of emplotment, see White, *Metahistory*, as well as this book's Epilogue. Theoretical frameworks straitjacket an author, foreclosing particular avenues of inquiry even while opening up others. In this way, theory can be like a pushy lover: "you offer her your hand; she'll take you by the arm." But there's just no way to avoid adopting a framework if you are working in the genre of academic nonfiction.
11. Since the 1970s, "truth" has emerged as a key problem across many academic fields, and especially for authors (like myself) using poststructuralist approaches. This project is not without at least one serious internal contradiction. "To try to show that the search for truth is, for whatever reason, misguided is to try to show, whether we like it or not, that it is true that the search for truth is, for whatever reason, misguided," wrote Alexander Nehamas in 1987, criticizing the poststructuralist project. "In other words, an attack on truth is here being waged, inevitably, in the name of truth. And if the attack is successful, and the search for truth is somehow discredited, then the truth has won out again."
12. Calvino, "Answers to Nine Questions on the Novel" (in *The Written World*), pp. 6–12. The contemporary author, Calvino continued in 1959, should aim to craft works that allow us to "immerse ourselves in them vertically (that is, perpendicular to the direction of the story), with constant discoveries at every layer or level: the human comedy, the historical picture, the lyrical or visionary, the psychological probe, the allegorical and symbolic (including the most diverse allegories and symbols), the invention of its own autonomous linguistic system, the network of cultural references, et cetera [...]." The following chapters represent an attempt to follow this advice; a fuller explanation of this approach can be found in "A Note on Reading *No Sense Makes Sense*."

Chapter 1

1. Interview with Steve Alexander, *Tuesday's Child* (February 1970).
2. Emmons, *Manson in His Own Words*, p. 83.
3. Marynick, *Charles Manson Now*, pp. 183–4; my emphasis.
4. "The Beginning is the Human Be-In," *Berkeley Barb* (January 6, 1967), pp. 1 and 3.
5. "Words in a poem, sounds in movement, rhythm in space, attempt to recapture personal meaning in personal time and space from out of the sights and sounds of a depersonalized, dehumanized world," wrote R. D. Laing in his *Politics of Experience* (p. 37). "They are bridgeheads into alien territory. They are acts of insurrection . . . Wherever and whenever such a whorl of patterned sound or space is established in the external world, the power that it contains generates new lines of forces whose effects are felt for centuries."
6. Photograph by Anders Holmquist in *The Free People*, p. 48.
7. Marin, *The Free People*, pp. 1, 4–5.
8. See Foucault, "The Discourse on Language," p. 215.
9. Following Hayden White, we can consider this moment *the inaugural event* for "the Manson Family murders."
10. Karpis, *On the Rock*, p. 151.
11. Both reports quoted in Bugliosi, *Helter Skelter*, pp. 144–5.
12. This analysis and quotes from Guinn, *Manson*, pp. 72, 74.
13. Versions of this story appear in several sources; my rendering draws primarily from Emmons, *Manson in His Own Words*.
14. See Brown, *The Love You Make*, pp. 172–4.
15. For an intriguing analysis of this encounter and song, see Scott Freer, "Songs of Self-Emptying in the Beatles." Cf. MacDonald, *Revolution in the Head*, pp. 68–9.
16. Quotes from John Lennon's interview with Jann Wenner, "Part One: The Working Class Hero," *Rolling Stone* (January 7, 1971), p. 39.
17. Quoted in Lambert, *Inside the Music of Brian Wilson*, p. 244.
18. See Sánchez, *Smile* and Priore, *Smile: The Story of Brian Wilson's Lost Masterpiece*.
19. See Wilson's July 1970 radio interview with KPFK, reproduced in "Frank Words From Brian Wilson," *Rolling Stone* (September 17, 1970), p. 14.
20. Bugliosi, *Helter Skelter*, p. 226.
21. Seltzer, *True Crime*, p. 38.
22. Kesey, *One Flew Over the Cuckoo's Nest*, p. 8.
23. Emmons, *Manson in His Own Words*, p. 15.
24. Press release for the Human Be-In, January 12, 1967.
25. Dialogue and events in this scene have been drawn from Emmons, *Manson in His Own Words*, pp. 85–99.

26 Bugliosi, *Helter Skelter*, p. 212.
27 For an example, see Wells, *Coming Down Fast*, pp. 73–7.
28 The exchange and lyrics in Emmons, *Manson in His Own Words*, pp. 90–1.
29 Emmons, *Manson in His Own Words*, p. 106.
30 Quoted in Sanders, *The Family*, p. 13.
31 Davis, *High Weirdness*, p. 31.
32 Ibid.
33 Roszak, *Making of a Counter Culture*, p. 205.
34 Ibid., pp. 205–6.
35 Ibid., pp. 208–9.
36 See Atkins, *Child of Satan*, pp. 63–73.
37 Dyrendal, Lewis, and Petersen, *Invention of Satanism*, p. 54.
38 Ibid., pp. 54–6.
39 Atkins, *Child of Satan*, p. 73. Atkins suggests that she danced with LaVey's revue in early 1967, and that after leaving, spent "four months" in the hospital. But the show ran only for a brief time in late July and early August, so the dates in her memoir must be confused.
40 Quoted in *Helter Skelter*, p. 418.
41 See Guinn, *Manson*, pp. 102–4. Fromme (*Reflexion*, pp. 142–4) suggests the meeting occurred later, around the time of their recording session for Universal (see below for discussion of that date). Sanders (*The Family*, p. 39) places this meeting on September 8, 1967 (and the recording session in November).
42 Interpretations by Livsey, *The Manson Women*, pp. 221–5.
43 Faith, *The Long Prison Journey of Leslie Van Houten*, p. 28.
44 Guinn (*Manson*, pp. 144–6) places Manson's meeting with Leslie in Summer 1968, while Sanders (*The Family*, pp. 108–9) and Atkins (*Child of Satan*, p. 104) specify August 1968.
45 Quoted in Livsey, *The Manson Women*, p. 227.
46 Fromme, *Reflexion*, pp. 11–12. This timeline, however, differs from an excerpt from the version of Fromme's memoir published forty-three years earlier. See also the next footnote.
47 This accords with an excerpt from her memoir, "The Memoirs of Squeaky Fromme," in *Time* magazine (September 15, 1975), though that account suggests they met Mary later—which seems to be incorrect, and contradicts her 2018 version of events.
48 For an insider's account and perspective, see Timothy Wyllie, "My Life Inside the Process Church," in *Love Sex Fear Death*, pp. 23–126 and especially pp. 78–9.
49 Sanders, *The Family*, p. 7.
50 Emmons, *Manson in His Own Words*, p. 106.

51 Fromme, *Reflexion*, pp. 26–7.
52 Ibid., p. 45.
53 Though historian Charles Perry, an observer interviewed by Guinn (*Manson*, p. 104), suggests that the meeting had been brief, and the locals glad to see the strange group leave after an unpleasant encounter.
54 Quoted in Fromme, *Reflexion*, p. 70.
55 In Erickson, *Childhood and Society* (1950); see also the analysis in Medovoi, *Rebels*.
56 See Grogan, *Encountering America*.
57 See Makari, *Revolution in Mind*. Competing historical conceptualizations included the mind as mirror of the soul, and the mind as a kind of dream machine.
58 What about the *negative* response to the epistemological condition of our world? For the richly human intratextuality of observers, for instance, such as author Italo Calvino, other postwar commentators would substitute false, suspicious mimicry. Karl Popper labeled that response "the conspiracy theory of society."

"This theory, which is more primitive than most forms of theism, is akin to Homer's theory of society," Popper wrote introducing *Conjectures and Refutations* (1961). "Homer conceived the power of the gods in such a way that whatever happened on the plain before Troy was only a reflection of the various conspiracies on Olympus. The conspiracy theory of society is just a version of this theism, of a belief in gods whose whims and wills rule everything. It comes from abandoning God and then asking: 'Who is in his place?' His place is then filled by various powerful men and groups—sinister pressure groups, who are to be blamed for having planned the great depression and all the evils from which we suffer."

But that's not the way the world really works anymore. Popper believes even the most carefully laid plans of human beings usually fail; it's something of a social law for him. And even when such plans succeed, they have unintended—even unforeseeable—consequences. We err in ascribing too much agency to individuals, a hubris suggesting "that we can explain practically everything in society by asking who wanted it, whereas the real task of the social sciences is to explain those things which nobody wants—such as, for example, a war, or a depression."
59 See Greif, *The Age of the Crisis of Man* and also Melley, *Empire of Conspiracy*.
60 Vonnegut, *Cat's Cradle*, p. 13.
61 Jonah 2:5–6.
62 Jonah 3:10.
63 Sanders, *The Family*, p. 37.
64 Earisman, *Hippies in Our Midst*, p. 36.
65 Underground should perhaps be enclosed in quotation marks. In *Going Underground*, Lara Langer Cohen traces this concept back two centuries: as a physical space and a racialized one, with roots in movements for the emancipation

of enslaved persons in the United States, as well as a figurative one, in the secret society movements of the mid-nineteenth century. In this book's narrative, the metaphor later becomes literal: the commune will, at some point over the next few chapters, allegedly seek out a great hole in the desert, leading to an underground world.

For these reasons, close attention to metaphor matters. As the philosopher Hans Blumenberg has suggested in "Paradigms for a Metaporology," the exploration of figurative language allows us "to burrow down to the substructure of thought, the underground, the nutrient solution of systematic crystallizations, but it also aims to show with what 'courage' the mind preempts itself in its images and how its history is projected in the courage of its conjectures."

66 Earisman, *Hippies in Our Midst*, p. 37.
67 Smith, "Commentaries: Speed Freaks vs. Acid Heads," *Clinical Pediatrics* (April 1969), p. 188.
68 These two can coexist. As Calvino puts it, "my goal is not so much to make a book as to change myself, which I think should be the goal of every human undertaking. You may object that you prefer books that convey a true experience, fully grasped. Well, so do I. But in my experience the motivation to write is always connected to *the lack of something we would like to know and possess*, something that escapes us. . . . What [great authors] convey is a sense of the approach to the experience, rather than a sense of the experience achieved; their secret is in knowing how to keep the force of desire intact." From "The Written and the Unwritten World" (1983); my emphasis.
69 A lightly revised insight from Stew Albert, "Life and Death," *San Francisco Good Times* (April 2, 1971), p. 2.
70 Consider also the development of critics into, as Devon Powers argues, public intellectuals. See Powers, *Writing the Record*.
71 Williams, "Rock is Rock: A Discussion of a Doors Song," *Crawdaddy* (May 1967), pp. 44–6.
72 Fromme, *Reflexion*, p. 29.
73 Emmons, *Manson in His Own Words*, p. 101.
74 Ibid.
75 Manson television interview (1989), reproduced in Wells, *Coming Down Fast*, p. 79.
76 If a history explains something about events that have occurred in the past, then a metahistory reveals something about the uses to which people put history. Either requires particular commitments, perhaps agreements, that channel narratives in particular directions. What should we call a method that rejects history in favor of experience?
77 Atkins, *Child of Satan*, p. 1.
78 Ibid., pp. 4–5.

79 Distinct versions of this meeting can be found in Guinn, *Manson*, pp. 98–9 and Wells, *Coming Down Fast*, p. 72. The only firsthand account can be found in Fromme, *Reflexion*, p. 121.
80 Fromme, *Reflexion*, p. 156.
81 Webber, *Escape to Utopia*, p. 420.
82 Horwitz, *Communes in America*, p. 20.
83 Ibid., p. 151.
84 Voiceover in Whicker, "The Love Generation," BBC (July 1967).
85 Houriet, *Getting Back Together*, p. xiii.
86 There exist remarkably few critical perspectives that point out the basic exploitation at the core of these representations. None of the accounts drawn on so far, for instance, indicate the ages or vulnerabilities of figures involved—such as the fifteen-year-old Darlene.
87 Melville, *Communes in the Counter Culture*, p. 28. Other sources present the dark side of communes. Houriet describes "Oz," a loose knit "family" that "danced in the rain, played music on the roof, and held love-ins down by the creek." But this scene devolved into chaos: bikers swept through, assaulting one young woman, before violence, arson, hepatitis, and protests from the larger community. In a strange instance of propinquity with our commune (see Chapter 5), police raided Oz on 16 August, and they all arrived at jail singing "Yellow Submarine" (*Getting Back Together*, pp. xxix and xxxi).
88 Atkins, *Child of Satan*, pp. 7–8.
89 Earisman, *Hippies in Our Midst*, p. 17.
90 Smith thought so, too. He co-published an article, "The Group Marriage Commune: A Case Study," in the *Journal of Psychedelic Drugs* (1970) with co-author Alan J. Rose. Rose conducted participant-observation with the group; researcher Tom O'Neill in *Chaos* has suggested that he became a member for a time. Smith and Rose describe the group's leader, "Charlie," as "an extroverted, persuasive individual who served as absolute ruler of this group marriage" as well as "probably . . . an ambulatory schizophrenic" (p. 116).
91 Smith, *Love Needs Care*, p. 256.
92 Ibid., p. 259.
93 Ibid., p. 261.
94 For a richly speculative account suggesting ties between the commune, the two Smiths, and secret government programs, see O'Neill, *Chaos*, especially pp. 305–7, 323–3, and 332–8. O'Neill reads some of the passages in *Love Needs Care* as "gingerly public-relations efforts" (p. 307).
95 This quote comes from pp. 205–6 of my 1968 paperback edition of Heinlein's *Stranger in a Strange Land*. For an etymology and critical discussion of this term, see McGiveron, "From Free Love to the Free-Fire Zone."

96 Fromme, *Reflexion*, p. 19.
97 My paraethnographic approach draws heavily from contemporary authors in approaching characters in this book as what George Marcus in *Para-Sites* (p. 3) called "other sorts of experts with shared, discovered, and negotiated critical sensibilities.".
98 This coincided with the moment when, as some individuals claimed, the position of the "intellectual" disappeared. Intellectuals formerly imagined what society might be, but they had become "almost exclusively concerned with measuring and analyzing what it is." Melville, *Communes in the Counter Culture*, p. 30.
99 Keith Altham, "Interview with Dennis Wilson," *Rave* (September 1969).
100 Calvino, *The Baron in the Trees*, p. 142.

Chapter 2

1 Dialogue in this opening section is transcribed from *Charles Manson: The Complete September 11, 1967 Session*, available on CD and also uploaded at https://youtu.be/VkpNngNVb-Q?si=XAzr6x_2jqqojhWC, accessed July 2024.
2 See Guinn, *Manson*, pp. 124–5, who draws on Felton and Dalton, "Year of the Fork" (*Rolling Stone*, June 25, 1970), discussed in Chapter Six.
3 Most authors reproduce this aphorism, a garbled version of a saying attributed to Confucius. The earliest firsthand account can be found in *Time* magazine's "Memoirs of Squeaky Fromme."
4 Interview with Manson, available at https://youtu.be/x-80jmxueXc, accessed July 2024.
5 In a later interview (Wells, *Coming Down Fast*, pp. 93–5), Stromberg describes the collaboration and claims that "Charlie tried to enlist me in his little merry band of psychotics."
6 Emmons, *Manson in His Own Words*, pp. 132–4. Sanders (*The Family*, p. 45) notes that Manson "knew lots" of people; Wells (*Coming Down Fast*, pp. 92–3) reproduces the sadomasochism rumors.
7 Emmons, *Manson in His Own Words*, pp. 131–2.
8 DebS, "Nuel Emmons," The Manson Family Blog (October 26, 2015), https://www.mansonblog.com/2015/10/nuel-emmons.html, accessed July 2024. The author quotes Ben Gurecki, a Manson groupie in contact with him during the 2010s.
9 Lake, *Member of the Family*, p. 122.
10 Emmons, *Manson in His Own Words*, pp. 122–3. Sanders (1971) gives the same story, adding that the woman who invited them was named "Gina." Susan Atkins (1977) writes that a hitchhiker named "Scotty" told them about the house (p. 86).

Dianne Lake (2018) suggests the house had already been named, and that the owner's name was "Ginger." Wells (*Coming Down Fast*, p. 96) suggests one of the commune members named the house, though this seems to be an error.

11 Atkins, *Child of Satan*, pp. 87–8.
12 Lake, *Member of the Family*, p. 122.
13 If it matters, the press release said "musicians," rather than "magicians." See also Brown, *The Love You Make*, p. 276.
14 Cited in Goldberg, *In Search of the Lost Chord*, p. 10.
15 Atkins, *Child of Satan*, p. 81.
16 Fromme, *Reflexion*, p. 190.
17 Atkins, *Child of Satan*, p. 93.
18 Fromme, *Reflexion*, p. 191.
19 Sanders, *The Family*, pp. 45–6.
20 See Hultkrans, *Forever Changes*.
21 Sanders, *The Family*, p. 47; also Wells, *Coming Down Fast*, pp. 63–7.
22 Lipton, "Anger's Anguish," *Berkeley Barb* (October 6–12, 1968), p. 8.
23 Lipton, "Lucifer Gone; Anger Offers Reward," *Berkeley Barb* (September 29 to October 5, 1968), p. 3.
24 When did Beausoleil meet Manson? According to Wells (*Coming Down Fast*, p. 63), they met in San Francisco the previous year, around the time Manson encountered the Process Church. Guinn (*Manson*, p. 126) and Atkins (*Child of Satan*, p. 91) place the meeting in Los Angeles in late 1967, as does Sanders (*The Family*, p. 126), who specifies Topanga Canyon.
25 Reagan, "A Time for Choosing" (October 27, 1964), available at https://www.reaganlibrary.gov/reagans/ronald-reagan/time-choosing-speech-october-27-1964, accessed July 2025.
26 See Perry, *The Haight Ashbury*, pp. 102–3.
27 From Didion, "Pretty Nancy," reproduced in *Let Me Tell You What I Mean*.
28 Fromme asks this question on p. 129 of *Reflexione*.
29 The preceding six words can be found in Vollmann, *Poor People*, p. 105.
30 This story can be found in most accounts; it functions as a stock narrative device depicting the commune's attitude toward material goods.
31 For versions of this story, see the entries for "Ruth Ann Moorehouse" on cielodrive.com and charlesmanson.com, as well as most biographies of Manson. We can pinpoint when this exchange happened because one of Charlie's relatively rare entanglements with the legal system punctuated this encounter with Moorehouse. Charlie had apparently seduced the preacher's adolescent daughter, Ruth Ann, who left home to join the group. An arrest record dated July 28, 1967, charged Charlie with "interfering with a runaway."
32 Sanders, *The Family*, pp. 46–7; for the date, see Fromme, *Reflexion*, p. 197.

33 Sanders, *The Family*, p. 47, Wells, *Coming Down Fast*, p. 103.
34 Advertisement section, *Berkeley Barb* (October 6–12, 1968), p. 12.
35 Refer to the 1971 poem by Philip Larkin, "This Be The Verse," or consider your own personal experiences.
36 "Under Gresham's law of biography," suggests Janet Malcolm, "good stories drive out true ones." From "Edward Weston's Women," *New York Review of Books* (December 5, 2005).
37 Atkins, *Child of Satan*, p. 91.
38 Fromme, *Reflexion*, p. 201.
39 Sheff, "John Lennon and Yoko Ono," *Playboy* (January 1981), reproduced at http://www.beatlesinterviews.org/dbjypb.int4.html, accessed July 2024.
40 Ibid.
41 This radio broadcast came to be interpolated on the evening of September 29, 1967; the actor voicing those words taken from the BBC Third Programme was John Bryning. See Lewisohn, *The Complete Beatles Recording Sessions*, p. 128.
42 Capote, "Then It All Came Down" (in *Music for Chameleons*), p. 218.
43 Carlin, *Catch a Wave*, p. 141.
44 Guinn (*Manson*, p. 127) mentions the rehearsal in passing; see also Wells, *Coming Down Fast*, p. 107.
45 A collection of information about Knapp can be found at "The Milky Way, The Corral Night Club in Topanga Canyon, and Ernie Knapp" (June 24, 2015) on The Tate-LaBianca Homicide Research Blog, available at https://www.lsb3.com/2015/06/the-milky-way-corral-night-club-in.html, accessed July 2024.
46 Fromme, *Reflexion*, p. 213.
47 For a description and skeptical overview of this memo, see Tom Bethell, "Was Sirhan Sirhan on the Grassy Knoll?" *The Washington Monthly* (March 1975), reproduced at https://www.jfk-assassination.net/bethell.htm, accessed July 2024.
48 For a more sympathetic approach, see how Adam Curtis describes and employs this method in the six-part documentary *Can't Get You Out of My Head* (2021).
49 See Lambert, *False Witness*, but also the more conspiratorial Mellen, *A Farewell to Justice*.
50 See Taylor, *As Time Goes By*, p. 38.
51 Wenner, "Rock and Roll Music," *Rolling Stone* (December 14, 1967), p. 16.
52 Fromme, *Reflexion*, p. 207.
53 Watkins, *My Life With Charles Manson*, pp. 3–4.
54 Scene and dialogue related in Watkins, *My Life With Charles Manson*, pp. 10–13. He dates this March 16, 1968; other firsthand accounts suggest he met the group in February.
55 "Beatles OK Maharishi Film," *Rolling Stone* (November 23, 1967), p. 6.

56 "Donovan: The Rolling Stone Interview," *Rolling Stone* (November 23, 1967), p. 12; emphasis added.
57 Kloman, "Maharishi Meets the Press," *Rolling Stone* (March 9, 1968), p. 8.
58 "George and Ringo: The Rolling Stone Interview," *Rolling Stone* (February 10, 1968), p. 12. "God didn't die for long in America," wrote Naomi Lowinsky a few years later. "The generation that broke with middle class values in the sixties, that went scampering after Timothy Leary as though he were the Pied Piper, turning on or dropping out en masse, now has wandered into religion. Whether they've chosen Charlie Manson, Jesus, Christ, or Meher Baba as their prophet, they're on their way to God." "Try a Morehouse?" *Berkeley Barb* (February 4–10, 1972), p. 6.
59 Watkins (with Guillermo Soledad), "Author's Note" to *My Life With Charles Manson* (1979); I adapted these words toward my own ends in the Prologue.
60 "Maharishi Has Hopes for SRO Crowds," *Rolling Stone* (May 11, 1968), p. 4.
61 Kurt Vonnegut, "Yes, We Have No Nirvanas," *Esquire* (June 1968), pp. 78–9.
62 See https://beatles.fandom.com/wiki/Spiritual_Regeneration, accessed July 2024.
63 See Brown, *The Love You Make*, pp. 282–91.
64 Lake, *Member of the Family*, p. 171.
65 Frazer, *Golden Bough*, pp. 104–5.
66 Adapted from Revelation 14:2–3.
67 "George and Ringo: The Rolling Stone Interview," *Rolling Stone* (February 10, 1968), p. 13; my italics.
68 Lake, *Member of the Family*, p. 186.
69 Genesis 3:14.
70 Lake, *Member of the Family*, pp. 186–7.
71 Sanders, *The Family*, p. 44.
72 For one account of how it began, see Genesis, Chapter 2.
73 See Guinn, *Manson*, p. 2.
74 Williams interview with Anderle, "Brian: Part I," *Crawdaddy* (April 1968), pp. 17–22; my emphasis.
75 The folk-rock duo Blackburn & Snow released the Crosby-penned single "Stranger in a Strange Land" in December 1966.
76 This phrase was popularized by a largely self-taught clinician named Coué in the first decades of the twentieth century.
77 Hubbard, *Dianetics*, p. 19.
78 Ibid., p. 30; emphasis added. It's important to note that this is not Hubbard is quite clear on this point. "Now when we get into such capabilities people are liable to believe that we have entered the field of mysticism and spiritualism," Hubbard writes. "But an inspection of these fields demonstrates the people in them not to be very able."

79 A man named Lafayette Raimer allegedly organized the small study group at McNeil Island that Manson attended. An internal Scientology Church document from 1978 seems to suggest that Manson had been subjected to approximately 150 hours of auditing, a substantial amount; the provenance and authenticity of that document have been questioned.
80 See Wyllie, *Love Sex Fear Death*.
81 Feral House has reissued the Sex, Fear, and Death issues in a collection, "Propaganda and the Holy Writ of The Process Church of The Final Judgment."
82 The commune lived around the corner from the Process Church headquarters on Cole Street in San Francisco, a propinquity-driven argument first posed by Sanders (*The Family*, pp. 80–96).
83 In his 1993 memoir, Kaufman suggests Manson looked like "Frankie Laine," singer of "Shadow of Your Smile"—in a documentary interview filmed nearly three decades later, he hums the song. See Kaufman, *Road Mangler Deluxe*, p. 64 and the documentary film *Music From an Unsound Mind* (2019, dir. Tom O'Dell); for the Atkins story, see *Child of Satan*, p. 2.
84 Bugliosi, *Helter Skelter*, p. 235. "We are all together for a reason," Dianne Lake (*Member of the* Family, p. 148) recalls Charlie saying during a talk-to. "Think about my name, and you will understand my purpose. I am Manson, man son, man's son." This seems to corroborate Bugliosi's account.
85 Bugliosi, *Helter Skelter*, p. 235.
86 Lake, *Member of the Family*, p. 148.
87 Watkins, *My Life with Charles Manson*, pp. 89–90; Atkins, *Child of Satan*, pp. 92, 134. In the late 1970s, Atkins became a born-again Christian.
88 Atkins, *Child of Satan*, pp. 94–5.
89 Bugliosi, *Helter Skelter*, pp. xiii–xix.

Chapter 3

1 Fromme, *Reflexion*, p. 241.
2 Sanders, *The Family*, p. 32.
3 On the American frontier, see Grandin, *End of the Myth*.
4 See Watkins, *The Book of Saints*, p. 269.
5 Revelation 14:2–3.
6 As reported by Lake, *Member of the Family*, p. 217.
7 See Watkins, *The Book of Saints*, p. 86.
8 Jones, *Let Me Take You Down*, pp. 19–20.
9 Ibid., p. 22.

10 Polanski, *Roman*, p. 252.
11 Lake, *Member of the Family*, p. 219.
12 Howard, "Year of the Guru," *Life* (February 9, 1968), p. 53.
13 Bushnell, *Moral Uses of Dark Things*, p. 258.
14 Ibid., pp. 260–1.
15 For a fuller, speculative discussion of this moment, see O'Neill, *Chaos*.
16 The quote here and in the previous paragraph comes from a local television interview filmed in late 1969. Clip available at https://www.youtube.com/watch?v=RZX5lcEbWAM, accessed July 2024. The rock would later be destroyed, according to Michael Channels, by a radical Christian group seeking to exorcise the site. Channels saved some of the rock, which he now sells, broken up in small plastic vials via his website, as a "relic."
17 Kaufman, *Road Mangler Deluxe*, p. 72.
18 Interview with Phil Kaufman, in *Manson* (dir. O'Dell).
19 Fromme, quoted in Clare Booth Luce, "The Significance of Squeaky Fromme," *New York Times* (September 30, 1975), p. 76. Luce's provocatively Freudian analysis of Fromme makes larger claims about the counterculture. "America is now producing a deluge of 'warped souls' and amoral freaks," she writes. "[It] is no 'paradox' that a society which has, helter-skelter, been abandoning its traditional Judeo-Christian moral values, is now producing demons."
20 From a 1998 interview with Manson in Stimson, *Goodbye Helter Skelter*, p. 107.
21 Watson, *Will You Die For Me?*, p. 68.
22 Literature invoking "the game" as metaphor can be found in the field of transactional psychology, though this term gained wider purchase in American society throughout the late 1950s and 1960s (see, e.g., the articles on The Generation Gap in the May 17, 1968 edition of *Life* magazine). It undergirds major sociological theories of society as a field of positions and positions-taking, as typified (for instance) in the work of French theorist Pierre Bourdieu.
23 Berne, *Games People Play*, p. 48. Ed Sanders (*The Family*, p. 30) claims Manson read—and drew inspiration from—this book.
24 Ibid., p. 184.
25 The possibility of a life unmediated troubles the unambitious historian who thinks of himself as nothing more than a glorified middleman, selecting and framing infinitesimal slices of "real life" for readers, mediating—which in certain contexts can mean culling, deleting, or even distorting—reality to fit an agenda.

Here's how conspiracist and far-right libertarian Gary Allen frames the problem of mediation in *None Dare Call It Conspiracy* (1971): "Many college history professors tell their charges that the books they will be using in the class are 'objective.' But stop and ask yourself: Is it possible to write a history book without a particular point of view? There are billions of events which take place in the world each day. To think of writing a complete history of a nation covering even a year is absolutely incredible" (p. 36).

The problem becomes more acute, Allen suggests, when we realize other middlemen keep certain events out of the papers in the name of big business and political power. Moreover, we should be wary of the fact that every author not only sets out to "prove" an argument or thesis, but ultimately succeeds! "But no book is objective," Allen continues. "No book can be objective; and this book is not objective . . . *The information in it is true, but the book is not objective. We have carefully selected the facts to prove our case.*"

26 Watkins, *My Life With Charles Manson*, pp. 23–4.
27 This quote from Leslie Van Houten's 1994 television interview with Diane Sawyer.
28 Turner, *From Counterculture to Cyberculture*, pp. 74–7.
29 Excerpt from Steve Grogan's 1981 parole hearing, reproduced in Stimson, *Goodbye Helter Skelter*, p. 94.
30 In crafting histories, how many of us imagine our jottings—organized, presented, disciplined through the prevailing, agreed-upon apparatus—to express an objectivity that exists outside our selves? What if we dismissed that project as nothing more than an expression of ego? If we asked: "what if it were possible for a work to be conceived beyond the self, a work that allowed us to escape the limited perspective of the individual ego, not only in order to enter other similar selves but to give voice to that which cannot speak—the bird perched on the gutter, the tree in spring and the tree in autumn, stone, cement, plastic . . . ?" In Calvino, *Six Memos*, p. 151.
31 Marynick, *Charles Manson Now*, p. 18.
32 The relationship between Tex Watson, Charles Manson, and Dennis Wilson raises complex historiographical questions. Watson probably knew Wilson and also Terry Melcher before meeting Manson, though Sanders (*The Family*, p. 57) related an "unlikely" story that Wilson met Manson by picking up Watson, who was already in the commune's orbit. Tex Watson's own autobiography includes significant gaps, errors of fact, and misrepresentations. Though perhaps this should not surprise us. "In the case of autobiography, because author and narrator share a name," Janet Malcolm reminds us, "we are only too prone to forget that the latter is a literary construct." In "I Should Have Made Him for a Dentist," *New York Review of Boks* (March 22, 2018).
33 This story can be found in Sanders, *The Family*, p. 131.
34 Watkins, *My Life With Charles Manson*, p. 124.
35 Ling and Buckman, "The Treatment of Frigidity with LSD and Ritalin," *Psychedelic Review* 1/4 (1964), p. 453.
36 Packard, *Hidden Persuaders*, p. 10.

37 See Melley, *Empire of Conspiracy*.
38 "Dylan Record Puts Beatles Up a Tree," *Rolling Stone* (March 9, 1968), p. 4.
39 Noebel, *Communism, Hypnotism and the Beatles*, p. 1.
40 Ibid., p. 7.
41 Ibid., p. 10.
42 Ibid., p. 6.
43 See Lewisohn, *The Complete Beatles Recording Sessions*, pp. 135–9 and pp. 143–4.
44 Griffiths, "Dennis Wilson: 'I Live With 17 Girls,'" *Record Mirror* (December 21, 1968), p. 4.
45 Ibid.
46 Described in Caine, *What's It All About?*, pp. 268–9.
48 Lake, *Member of the Family*, p. 224.
48 Hugh Hefner interviewing Sharon Tate and Roman Polanski at the Playboy Club in London, early 1969. Clip at https://youtu.be/IqkanUm8gVs?si=Ubgak2OQS_iDQAAB, accessed July 2024.
49 Love, *Good Vibrations*, p. 287.
50 Griffiths, "Dennis Wilson: 'I Live With 17 Girls,'" *Record Mirror* (December 21, 1968), p. 4.
51 Quoted in McDonough, *Shakey*, pp. 287–8.
52 Ibid., p. 288.
53 This sentence has been borrowed from the opening to R. D. Laing, "Transcendental Experience in Relation to Religion and Psychosis," *Psychedelic Review* 6 (1965): 7. It represents a larger discourse from the period that argued an epistemological and material underpinning of instability had given rise to key social consequences. "In these circumstances," Laing continues, "we have all reason to be insecure. When the ultimate basis of our world is in question, *we run to different holes in the ground*; we scurry into roles, statuses, identities, interpersonal relations. We attempt to live in castles that can only be in the air, because there is no firm ground in the social cosmos on which to build . . . Each sometimes sees the same fragment of the whole situation differently; often our concern is with different presentations of the same catastrophe" (my emphasis).
54 Brown, *Possess and Conquer*, p. 28.
55 Ibid., pp. 39–40.
56 Ibid., p. 140.
57 Fan fiction from "the Smile Humour Page," "Charlie's SMiLE." https://smilealbum.tripod.com/charlie.htm.
58 Bugliosi, *Helter Skelter*, p. 251.
59 See Belly, "The 275 GTB Man," *eGarage* (January 22, 2015), available at http://egarage.com/car-profiles/275-gtb-man/, accessed October 2024.

60 Sanderson, "An Elaboration of Interests," *SITU Newsletter*, no. 1 (May 1967): 3.
61 Adapted from Watkins, *My Life With Charles Manson*, p. 34.
62 See Penick, "Cease to Exist." Tate-LaBianca lay researcher Dennis LaCalandra has proposed nine separate recording dates; my sense is that he counts several sessions twice.
63 Lake (*Member of the Family*, pp. 23, 7–40) remembers a recording session at Brian Wilson's house in July 1968, but includes details that happened later. She suggests that Manson pulled out a knife at this visit, though Beach Boys engineer places this incident either in March or July 1969; she recalled an argument about the Beach Boys revising the lyrics to Manson's song, "Cease to Exist," but that change didn't happen until September 1968 (and Manson seems to have learned about it in December).
64 Fromme, liner notes to the double CD *Family James* (1997).
65 Ibid.
66 Ebert, "Review: *Wild In The Streets*," *Chicago Sun-Times* (May 20, 1968), available at https://www.rogerebert.com/reviews/wild-in-the-streets-1968, accessed July 2024.
67 Fromme, liner notes to *Family Jams* (1997).
68 Guinn, *Manson*, p. 160.
69 In his autobiography, Phillips doesn't mention hearing the tapes or meeting Manson, though he does describe "incredible, freewheeling openhouse affairs" that included Hollywood stars as well as Terry Melcher, "the Beach Boys and just about every other musical act in the L.A. area. It was not uncommon for our house to bring together in one evening dozens of celebrities from rock and film." See Phillips, *Papa John*, p. 221.
70 Guinn, *Manson*, p. 160.
71 Hunter Davis, excerpt from *The Beatles*, reproduced in *Life* (September 20, 1968), p. 71.
72 George P. Hunt, "Editor's Note," *Life* (September 20,1968), p. 3.
73 Faith, *The Long Prison Journey of Leslie Van Houten*, p. 65.
74 "Correspondence," *Rolling Stone* (February 10, 1968), p. 2.
75 Love, *Good Vibrations*, p. 208.
76 See Atkins, *Child of Satan*, pp. 104–5.
77 Gilmore and Kenner (*The Garbage People*, p. 78) suggest the Beach Boys bought *two* songs, and also invited Manson on tour in Texas.
78 Sandra Good, liner notes to *The Family Jams* (1997).

Chapter 4

1 Watkins, *My Life With Charles Manson*, p. 34.
2 O'Neill, "68' The Incredible Year," *Life* (January 10, 1969), p. 61.

3   This episode occurred just over a decade ago, in a neighborhood just southeast of the train tracks that bisect Flagstaff, Arizona.
4   "The Chicago Police Riot," *Life* (December 6, 1968), p. 38.
5   As quoted in David Horton's *Trickster: The Many Lives of Carlos Castaneda*, episode one; see https://tricksterpodcast.com/.
6   From *Neville* (1960), transcription of Side A, "The Secret of Imagining," available at https://coolwisdombooks.com/neville/1960-neville-goddard-lp-transcript-of-vinyl-record/, accessed July 2024.
7   Watkins, *My Life With Charles Manson*, p. 105.
8   Ibid.
9   Ibid., p. 110.
10 Quote and insight from Kinney, *Dylanologists*, p. 46.
11 Cleave, "How Does a Beatle Live?" *London Evening Standard* (March 4, 1966), p. 10.
12 Gleason, "It Ain't Really Funny," *Rolling Stone* (January 4, 1969), p. 22.
13 Gleason, "Songs Would Do More Than Books," *Rolling Stone* (March 1, 1969), p. 21.
14 Fromme, *Reflexione*, pp. 301–2.
15 Watkins, *My Life With Charles Manson*, pp. 89–90.
16 Sanders, *The Family*, pp. 101–2.
17 Analysis from John Paul Adams, "FIDES," available at https://www.csun.edu/~hcfll004/fides.html, accessed July 2024.
18 Emmons, *Manson in His Own Words*, p. 154; my emphasis.
19 Ibid.
20 Watkins, *My Life With Charles Manson*, pp. 120–1. Interviewed in 1970 for *The Garbage People*, Arlene Barker described the gold record and the approach, but recalled seeing Manson with "a girl" (p. 95). Emmons could have been plagiarizing Watkins, who could have invented the encounter. Or Barker could have been confused.
21 Catton, "What Kind of People Does A Religious Cult Attract?" *American Sociological Review* (22/2), p. 562.
22 Ibid., p. 566.
23 Lake remembers them going to Las Vegas, where they watched *Yellow Submarine*, and claims that Juanita was *with* them; she does not mention hearing the White Album at this point. Lake, *Member of the Family*, pp. 276–7.
24 Watkins, *My Life With Charles Manson*, pp. 135; my emphasis.
25 Fromme, *Reflexion*, pp. 339–40.
26 Watkins, *My Life With Charles Manson*, pp. 133–4.
27 See "The Revolutionary Nature of Richard Hamilton's Final Design," available at https://www.thewhitealbumproject.com/design/, accessed July 2024.
28 Wenner, "Review: The Beatles' White Album," *Rolling Stone* (December 21, 1968).

29 Aronowitz, "Wisdom of Their Years," *Life* (January 31, 1969), p. 22.
30 Ginsberg, *Deliberate Prose*, p. 10.
31 See liner notes, *The Family Jams*.
32 Updike, "Comment," *The New Yorker* (December 9, 1967), p. 51.
33 Bugliosi, *Helter Skelter*, p. 231.
34 Ibid., p. 224.
35 Quotes from Sanders, *The Family*, pp. 129–30; for the December date, see the Jakobson interview in *Music From an Unsound Mind*.
36 Sanders, *The Family*, p. 136.
37 See for instance the post "Who is Charlene Cafritz . . . and what happened to her?" (October 18, 2011) by Katie and Beauders on the Tate-LaBianca Homicide Research Blog, available at https://www.lsb3.com/2011/10/who-is-charlene-cafritz-and-what.html, accessed July 2024.
38 See "Finally Some Late 1960's Image of Charlene Cafritz" (March 5, 2022) posted on the Manson Mythos Blog, available at https://themansonmythos.blogspot.com/2022/03/finally-late-1960s-image-of-charlene.html, accessed July 2024.
39 This phrasing, infamously, from Max Weber's *The Sociology of Religion* (1920).
40 Inscription from Side B of the album, *The Manson Family Sings the Songs of Charles Manson* (ESP-DISK) released in 1986.
41 See Melley, *Empire of Conspiracy*.
42 CBC interview with McLuhan and Mailer, *The Summer Way* (1968), available at https://www.openculture.com/2011/01/norman_mailer_marshall_mcluhan_debate_the_electronic_age.html, accessed July 2024.
43 Watkins, *My Life With Charles Manson*, p. 135.
44 Ibid., p. 136. While the phrasing here suggests the commune did not yet know Melcher, as we will see, this is not really true.
45 Deana Martin, Testimony, "People v. Charles Watson," Monday, August 23, 1971 https://www.cielodrive.com/deana-martin-trial-testimony.php. See also O'Neill, *Chaos*, p. 452, footnote to p. 108, outlining discrepancies in Melcher's accounts. Though unreported in *Helter Skelter*, Tex had attended multiple parties or events at the Cielo Drive home when Melcher lived there. O'Neill (pp. 121–4) also describes finding transcripts of an interview with Danny DeCarlo placing Melcher at both Spahn and Barker Ranches in the weeks and months following the Tate-LaBianca murders.
46 Hunt, "White Tie and Tails," *Life* (June 28, 1968), p. 3.
47 Richman, "The New Rock," *Life* (June 28, 1968), p. 54; my emphasis.
48 Zappa, "The Oracle Has It All," *Life* (June 28, 1968), p. 84.
49 Margaret Mead interview with Irene Neves, "We Must Learn to See What's Really New," *Life* (August 23, 1968), p. 31. Mead also examined this problem in her 1969 book, *Culture and Commitment: A Study of the Generation Gap*.

50 Post, "Letters to the Editors," *Life* (July 19, 1968), p. 4.
51 Billington, "A Ferment of Intellectuals," *Life* Special Issue "'68: The Incredible Year" (January 10, 1969), pp. 96–7.
52 Gentry, *Last Days of the Late, Great State of California*, p. 12.
53 Ibid., p. 390.
54 Adapted from Kandel's "First They Slaughtered the Angels" (1967); this poem first appeared in *Beatitude Anthology* (1960), and in a longer, revised version in her *Word Alchemy* (1967).
55 Lake, *Member of the Family*, p. 282.
56 Ibid., p. 283.
57 Fromme, *Reflexione*, p. 351.
58 Berger and Luckmann, *The Social Construction of Reality*.
59 Davis, *High Weirdness*, pp. 19–20.
60 See Malcolm, *Psychoanalysis: The Impossible Profession*.
61 Marcuse, *Eros and Civilization*.
62 See Tochka, *Rocking in the Free World*, chapters 4–5, for my longer discussion on this point.
63 Laing, *The Divided Self*, p. 42.
64 Text in the reviews has been adapted from Morgan (ed.), *The Letters of Allen Ginsberg* (2008).
65 Lake, *Member of the Family*, pp. 298–9. See also Gilmore and Kenner, *The Garbage People*, pp. 97–8.
66 Fromme, *Reflexion*, p. 374.
67 Ibid., p. 375.
68 Watson, *Cease to Exist*, p. 113.
69 Fromme, *Reflexion*, p. 375.
70 Revelation 9:1–3.
71 Inceoglu, Lango, Jing, Chen, Doymaz, Pessah, and Hammock, "One Scorpion, Two Venoms," pp. 922–7.
72 Mae Brussell provided the first, comprehensive theory about the government's role in discrediting the counterculture. See Chapter 11, "Operation Chaos, from Monterey Pop to Altamont: The CIA's War Against the Sixties Counter-Culture," in *The Essential Mae Brussell: Investigations of Fascism in America*. See also O'Neill, *Chaos*, which builds on and expands this work.
73 Smith, "Traffic in Amphetamines: Patterns of Illegal Manufacture and Distribution," *Journal of Psychedelic Drugs* 2(2), p. 22.
74 See Kinzer, *Poisoner in Chief*.
75 See Collins, *In the Sleep Room*.
76 This description draws from Kinzer, *Poisoner in Chief*, Chapter 8: Operation Midnight Climax.

77 Allen (*Concentration Camps, USA*, 1966) and Bosworth (*America's Concentration Camps*, 1967) revealed that the United States government constructed a system of camps in the early 1950s, following the passage of the McCarran National Security Act (1950). The speculative documentary, *Punishment Park* (1971), demonstrated how Nixon might have used the camps to detain anti-war activists.

78 Abbie Hoffman threatened to dose Chicago during the Democratic National Convention in 1968, and not everyone got the joke. News stories occasionally reported such posturing as serious threats; Deane Romano's classic 1968 book, *The Town That Took A Trip*, revolves around this pulpy plot point.

79 For a synopsis see David Mikkelson, "Did Man Who Used LSD Believe Himself To Be a Glass of Orange Juice?" on Snopes (September 22, 2022/July 10, 1999), available at https://www.snopes.com/fact-check/orange-juice-lsd/, accessed July 2024.

80 Sargant, *Battle for the Mind* (1959, second edition).

81 Cameron, *Life is for Living*, p. 1.

82 See Atkins, *Myth of Helter Skelter*. Published posthumously, this book argues that Manson told different people different things at different times. He told the men they were selling drugs to finance a permanent move to the desert. He told some members, like Fromme and Good, they were becoming eco-terrorists. He told the younger, newer members that a race war was coming.

83 For Watson's description, see "Charles Watson Testimony" (September 1–2 and 28, 1971), reproduced at https://www.charlesmanson.com/testimony/charles-watson/, accessed July 2024; see also Stimson, *Goodbye Helter Skelter* and Atkins, *Myth of Helter Skelter*.

84 See Lewisohn, *The Complete Beatles Chronicle*, p. 278.

85 Thompson, *Hell's Angels*, p. 330.

86 Ibid., p. 11.

87 "The reader extends a kind of credit to the writer of nonfiction which he doesn't extend to the writer of fiction, and for this reason the writer of nonfiction has to be punctilious about delivering the goods for which the reader has prepaid with his forbearance," writes Janet Malcolm. "Of course, there is no such thing as a work of pure factuality, any more than there is one of pure fictitiousness. As every work of fiction draws on life, so every work of nonfiction draws on art. As the novelist must curb his imagination in order to keep his text grounded in the common experience of man (dreams exemplify the uncurbed imagination—thus their uninterestingness to everyone but their author), so the journalist must temper his literal-mindedness with the narrative devices of imaginative literature." From the Afterword to Malcolm's (1990) *The Journalist and the Murderer*, a nonfiction book examining the case murderer Jeffrey MacDonald brought against true-crime author

Joe McGinniss. MacDonald initially blamed his crime, committed in early 1970, on a band of acid-crazed hippies.

88 Beausoleil discussed this at length during a parole hearing in 1985, later writing a statement in 2006 addressing the Capote interview as well as claims that he belonged to the Aryan Brotherhood in prison. For reproductions of the transcript and statement, see George Stimson's essay, "Truman Capote's Credibility" on The Manson Family Blog (October 19, 2015), available at https://www.mansonblog.com/2015/10/truman-capotes-credibility.html, accessed July 2024. "By such foibles is history written," Beausoleil wrote, describing how bits and pieces from misinterpreted stories can give rise to an invented world bearing little relationship to reality.
89 Discussed and quoted in Kinney, *Dylanologists*, p. 55.
90 See Melnick, *Creepy Crawling*, pp. 156–8.
91 Jakobson quoted in Gaines, *Heroes and Villains*, p. 215.
92 Greenan, *Boston*, p. 39.
93 This interpretation has been most strongly posed by George Stimson in *Goodbye Helter Skelter*.
94 Jennings, "Anatomy of a Rumor," *LA Times* (November 30, 1969), p. 22.

Chapter 5

1 Love, *Good Vibrations*, p. 208.
2 Find 1971 Rolling Stone article + cite.
3 Interview with Stephen W. Desper, *Music From an Unsound Mind*.
4 See Desper's replies to comments on the thread, "Manson/Dennis Story" on *The Smiley Smile Message Board*, at http://smileysmile.net/board/index.php/topic,12729.100.html, accessed September 2024. After describing the demo session related above, Desper writes, "Please keep in mind as you read all this, that it happened a couple of weeks BEFORE the 'event.'" He also writes: "I recorded Charles Manson playing several songs during the course of a few days. Those tapes were placed on the tape shelf located under the monitors. During the next few weeks and to my knowledge no one ever requested to hear them. They asked me what I thought of him as a potential talent for the label, but then time ran out. That is to say, before the tapes were ever reviewed by anyone, the murders happened and the tapes were locked away." And finally: "I have often wondered how much my canceling of the demo sessions played in the subsequent unfoldment of events in the follow[ing] weeks, as Charles has said his motive for revenge was primed from his belief that his talents were not appreciated by the label . . . ."

5 Love, *Good Vibrations*, pp. 208–9.
6 Reply by Jason Penick to "New Wing At Bellagio 10542," posted on the *Endless Summer* forum, available at https://endlessharmony.boards.net/thread/543/new-wing-bellagio-10452?page=5, accessed September 2024.
7 One method for understanding this alchemical process would be to create an analytical typology of narrative strategies, as in Hayden White's seminal *Metahistory* (1973), for instance, completed at a desk on the University of California at Los Angeles campus not far from the events found in our book's narrative.
8 See Stimson, *Goodbye Helter Skelter*.
9 This phrase comes from the title of an essay by Chris Lorenz critiquing the narrativism of historians such as Hayden White. "Rejecting the view that the truth of narrative is the by-product of historical research, [historians such as White] simply negate the truth-claim of narrative altogether," Lorenz writes. "This move should be resisted and criticized since the presupposition of the truth of historical narratives is crucial as long as we presuppose that *history is a discipline and not a form of art*" ("Can Histories Be True?" [1998], p. 314; emphasis added).
10 See "Spahn Ranch Search Warrant," reproduced at https://www.charlesmanson.com/vicinity-crimes/spahn-ranch/spahn-ranch-search-warrant/, accessed September 2024.
11 King, *Sharon Tate and the Manson Murders*, p. 38.
12 Ibid., p. 242.
13 None of these claims, reported in various memoirs and news articles over the past fifty years, have turned up credible corroborating evidence.
14 Farrell, "In Hollywood, the Dead Keep Right On Dying," *Life* magazine (November 7, 1969), p. 4.
15 O'Neill, *Chaos*, pp. 125–6.
16 Farrell, "In Hollywood, the Dead Keep Right On Dying," p. 4; emphasis added.
17 Ibid. Though Polanski strongly criticized his late wife's depiction in Quentin Tarantino's film, *Once Upon a Time in Hollywood* (2019), the press reported he planned to make a film (starring Birgit Hamer) about her murder in 1983. "I've been thinking about making a film about my wife's death for years," the *Washington Post* reported. "I now have decided to go ahead. I can never forget the horror, but perhaps this will help." Quoted in "Personalities," *Washington Post* (August 17, 1983), p. B3.
18 Calvino, *Castle of Crossed Destinies*, pp. 87, 75, 91.
19 Ibid., p. 89.
20 See Malcolm, *Journalist and the Murderer*.
21 Vonnegut, "'There's a Maniac Loose Out There,'" *Life* (July 25, 1969), p. 54.
22 Ibid., p. 56.
23 See Edna Buchanan, *The Corpse Had a Familiar Face*, p. 153.

24 Quoted in *Solved! Famous Mystery Writers on Classic True-Crime Cases*, p. 13.
25 See King, *Sharon Tate and the Manson Murders*, pp. 224–5; cf. Didion, *The White Album*.
26 Watkins, *My Life With Charles Manson*, p. 209.
27 Ibid.
28 Ibidi., p. 211.
29 See Thomas Thompson, "A Tragic Trip to the House on the Hill," *Life* (August 29, 1969), pp. 43, 44, 46.
30 Watkins, *My Life With Charles Manson*, pp. 200–1.
31 In 1951, a jury convicted Dr. Drown for "introducing a misbranded device into interstate commerce," a federal charge. A decade later, and with tens of thousands of patients applying her theories and using her equipment, a series of trials for medical fraud finally ended Drown's medical career. "Quackery," the deputy district attorney said in summation, "can kill." See Ralph Lee Smith, "The Incredible Drown Case," *Today's Health* (April 1968).
32 Ibid., pp. 178–80.
33 Avoid showering, for instance, especially when in a weakened state. The water, Drown advised, may wash your magnetism down the drain. As we are all connected through vibrations, we should also take care by exposing ourselves only to positive pulsations. Jazz music, Drown cautioned, may cause cancer; the quiet dignity of an old chestnut such as "A Perfect Day," a bit of 1910 schmaltz by Carrie Jacobs Bond, can do wonders for those suffering from swellings caused by swing. In addition to R. L. Smith's essay, see alsoDrown's 1939 manual, *The Theory And Technique Of The Drown Radio Therapy And Radio-Vision Instruments*.
34 Gary Richardson, "Profile: Paul Crockett," *Psychic* (September/October 1975), p. 31.
35 Interview in Wolf and Wolf, *Voices from the Love Generation*, pp. 29 and 31.
36 See Associated Press, "Tate, Others Killed by Paranoid—Capote" (August 28, 1969), available at https://www.cielodrive.com/archive/tate-others-killed-by-paranoid-capote/, accessed September 2024; Capote repeated this story several times, up to the commune's arrest. See also Jennings, "Anatomy of a Rumor," pp. 46–7, who cites a similar theory from attorney F. Lee Bailey.
37 MacDonald, *Revolution in the Head*, p. 285.
38 Bruce Harris and Steve Harris, "The Beatles Album That No One Will Ever Hear," *Rolling Stone* (September 17, 1970), pp. 26–7.
39 Richardson, "Profile: Paul Crockett," p. 31.
40 Monroe, *Savage Appetites*.
41 Berquist, "True Crime Is Rotting Our Brains," originally published on *Gawker* (October 12, 2021), available at https://medium.com/@emma.berquist/true-crime-is-rotting-our-brains-8c7dea979309, accessed September 2024.

42 See Reeve, *Turn Me On, Dead Man* and Patterson, *The Walrus Was Paul*.
43 Quoted in Glenn, "'Paul is Dead!' (said Fred)," *Michigan Daily* (November 11, 2009), available at https://michigantoday.umich.edu/2009/11/11/a7565/, accessed September 2024.
44 Ibid.
45 Bugliosi, *Helter Skelter*, p. 128.
46 Atkins, *Child of Satan*, p. 161. Discussed in Bugliosi and Gentry, *Helter Skelter*, pp. 78–9.
47 Lake, *Member of the Family*, p. 194.
48 Ralph Gleason, "Are We Lost in a New Dark Age?" *Rolling Stone* (December 13, 1969), p. 21.
49 Quoted in O'Neill, "Mired and Unfettered," *Life* (January 10, 1969), p. 72.
50 Ralph Gleason, "Are We Lost in a New Dark Age?" *Rolling Stone* (December 13, 1969), p. 21.
51 Ibid., p. 9.
52 Ibid., p. 21.
53 Interview with "Country Sue," reproduced by George Stimson in "The Story of the 'Helter Skelter' Door," The Manson Family Blog (June 22, 2015), available at https://www.mansonblog.com/2015/06/the-story-of-helter-skelter-door.html, accessed October 2024. The analysis that follows also derives from Stimson.
54 "Correspondence, Love Letters & Advice," *Rolling Stone* (July 6, 1968), p. 3.
55 Gaines, *Heroes and Villains*, p. 219. "Several nights later [in late November / early December 1969], at Gregg Jakobson's house, Dennis was paid a visit by Family member Squeaky Fromme, who told Dennis that if he didn't give up the tapes Manson had made at Brian's house, she was going to kill him. According to Stanley Shapiro, 'Dennis just scoffed at the whole idea. I said, "Dennis, do you have those tapes?" And he said he had already turned them over to the D.A., which was bullshit.' In fact, when Nick Grillo had heard the news on TV, he locked the tapes in a vault, where they remain to this day."
56 Cooper, *Psychiatry and Anti-Psychiatry*, p. 12.
57 Those words come directly from a timeline published by Robert Heinlein in 1941. This timeline sets out the parameters of the universe in which the author would go on to craft his impressive series of novels and short stories, including, of course, *Stranger in a Strange Land*. Heinlein called this oeuvre a "pseudo-history of the immediate future," a phrase that could also be applied to the publications about Manson that soon began inundating the American public.
58 Bugliosi, *Helter Skelter*, pp. 118–19.
59 Ibid., p. 96.
60 A similar situation, perhaps not incidentally, has long affected the historiography of classic rock. How have the stories we know by heart about the Fab Four, for

instance, shaped contemporary writing about them? Writers sometimes revisit, more rarely relitigate; the usual move has been to sound out the margins, with new books appearing about peripheral figures, reception, or lost recordings. Certain magazines collate lists noting, in top-ten style, any new revelations (usually quite minor). While this is not necessarily a bad thing, we might consider the broader epistemological effect that comes from the proliferation of slightly distinct iterations of the same story, especially within an economy—whether academic, devoted to the study of "popular music," or trade, catering to a book-buying audience increasingly distant in time from those halcyon days of the sixties—that is predicated on novelty.

61 Bugliosi, *Helter Skelter*, p. 117.
62 Ibid., p. 132.
63 Wenner, *Lennon Remembers*, p. 43.
64 Paul O'Neil, "Flattery, Fear and Sex Lured His Girls Into a Sisterhood of Exploitation," *Life* (December 19, 1969), p. 22.
65 Interview with David Smith, "A Doctor and a Parole Officer Remember Manson," *Life* (December 19, 1969), p. 26.
66 Interview with Roger Smith, "A Doctor and a Parole Officer Remember Manson," *Life* (December 19, 1969), p. 26.
67 Interview with David Smith, "A Doctor and a Parole Officer Remember Manson," *Life* (December 19, 1969), p. 26.
68 "It has often been observed that the counterculture, by being ideologically tolerant of other people's trips, presents a good hideout for fugitives, screwballs, and even the criminally insane (after Charlie Manson, most definitely the criminally insane)," wrote Rosabeth Moss Kantner in 1973. "In rural communes this is generally less true than in urban hip ghettos, but almost every commune has experienced such a person or will sooner or later. In some communes he may even be a founding member [. . .]." In *Communes*, p. 151.
69 "The Wreck of a Monstrous 'Family,'" *Life* (December 19, 1969), p. 24.
70 Related in Frank Horton's (2021–2), *Trickster: The Many Lives of Carlos Castaneda*, podcast.
71 Quoted in Bugliosi, *Helter Skelter*, p. 182.
72 Ibid.

Chapter 6

1 Atkins, *Child of Satan*, p. 161.
2 Sanders, *The Family*, p. 302.
3 Ibid.
4 Ibid., p. 304.

5 Bugliosi, *Helter Skelter*, p. 18. Though also consider this moment of propinquity later identified in the countercultural press: "In the film *Chinatown*, a pair of eyeglasses turns out to be an important clue in solving a murder and keeping Jack Nicholson's nose in stitches if not the audience. A pair of eyeglasses turned up mysteriously after Sharon Tate and her friends had been massacred by Tex Watson and his Charlie Manson girl scout troup[e]. Could young widower Roman Polanski be trying to tell us something, or is this just a mild coincidence?" Paul Krassner, "Hooking in Heaven," *Berkeley Barb* (July 26–August 1, 1974), p. 4.
6 Sanders, *The Family*, pp. 304–5.
7 Bugliosi, *Helter Skelter*, p. 247.
8 Gilmore and Kenner, *The Garbage People*, pp. 65–6.
9 Atkins, *Child of Satan*, pp. 163–4.
10 Foley, "'Guilty' Verdict Before the Trial," *LA Times* (January 10, 1970), p. 51.
11 Torgerson, "Cult May Be Linked to Slayings of 2 Girls," *LA Times* (December 18, 1969), p. 3.
12 Cohen, "Possible Links Between Tate, Scientology Murders Studied," *LA Times* (December 10, 1969), p. 1. Jerry Cohen was the ghostwriter who finessed the confession of Susan Atkins into *The Killing of Sharon Tate* (1970), available at https://www.cielodrive.com/archive/possible-links-between-tate-scientology-murders-studied/, accessed October 2024.
13 "5 Killed as 'Symbol,' Cult Member Says" (December 3, 1969), available at https://www.cielodrive.com/archive/5-killed-as-symbol-cultist-member-says/, accessed October 2024.
14 Ibid.
15 "Leader Played Part of Evil Pied Piper" (December 8, 1969), available at https://www.cielodrive.com/archive/leader-played-part-of-evil-pied-piper/, accessed October 2024.
16 "Hollywood Slayings Suspect Beat Way Oddly From Social Outcast to Hippie Guru" (December 4, 1969), available at https://www.cielodrive.com/archive/hollywood-slayings-suspect-beat-way-oddly-from-social-outcast-to-hippie-guru/. The Beach Boys played three concerts in Galveston, Texas, on April 21, 1968, just after Dennis Wilson met Manson; they also played a six-day tour in Texas beginning on February 7, 1969.
17 Powers, "Bizarre Tale of 'Black Magic,'" *LA Times* (December 5, 1969), p. 1.
18 "Susan Atkins' Story of 2 Nights of Murder," *LA Times* (December 14, 1969), p. 1; emphasis added.
19 For an overview of recent efforts to have these tapes released, see Tom O'Neill, "The Tale of the Manson Tapes," available at https://medium.com/law-of-the-land/the-tale-of-the-manson-tapes-324b4a6138d9, accessed October 2024.

20 See Paul Krassner's introduction to *The Essential Mae Brussell*.
21 See especially Brussell, "Operation Chaos: From Monterey Pop to Altamont" (1976/2014), in *The Essential Mae Brussell*.
22 Krassner, "Boil the Prick," *Berkeley Barb* (May 3–9, 1974), p. 2.
23 Dighton, "Can You Hypnotize Person to Murder?" *AP* (December 6, 1969).
24 Dalton and Felton, "The Most Dangerous Man Alive," *Rolling Stone* (June 25, 1970), p. 48.
25 Sanders, "Talk to Charles Manson: $1000 a Crack," *LA Free Press* (June 5, 1970), p. 3.
26 Butter, "There's a Conspiracy Theory that the CIA Invented the Term 'Conspiracy Theory'—Here's Why," available at https://theconversation.com/theres-a-conspiracy-theory-that-the-cia-invented-the-term-conspiracy-theory-heres-why-132117, accessed September 2024.
27 Richard Caballero, quoted in Fox, "Tate Trial Witness Fears Hippie's Mystical Spell," *LA Times* (December 6, 1969).
28 "Susan's Father Doubts 'Spell,'" *LA Times* (December 8, 1969).
29 Summary from *Psychiatric News*, as reported in "Freaky, Yes—Crazy, No," *Rolling Stone* (May 1970).
30 Cooper, *Psychiatry and Anti-Psychiatry*, p. 12.
31 Robert Litman, quoted in Dighton, "Can You Hypnotize Person to Murder?"
32 John Woodbury, quoted in Dighton, "Can You Hypnotize Person to Murder?"
33 Interview with Gary Baum, "The Many Lives and Dying Words of Aesop Aquarian," *The Hollywood Reporter* (July 15, 2022), available at https://www.hollywoodreporter.com/news/general-news/aesop-aquarian-life-story-manson-family-1235180433/, accessed September 2024.
34 This story and information related to Hendrick's relationship to Mark Ross and the commune can be found in *Inside the Manson Gang* (2007), a documentary film purporting to describe how the filming that resulted in *Manson* (1973) came together.
35 See Stimson, *Goodbye Helter Skelter* and Atkins, *Myth of Helter Skelter*, as well as works by a host of lay Manson researchers.
36 Mayers, "Former Sheriff Raps Guns Girls and Grass," *LA Free Press* (December 19, 1969), pp. 2 and 11.
37 Phineas, "Was It Just for a Burn?" *Berkeley Barb* (January 16–22, 1970), p. 3.
38 See "Charles Manson: Lifestyle on Trial?" *The Speckled Bird* (February 8, 1971), pp. 3 and 17.
39 "A Letter from Charles Manson's Friends at Spahn Ranch," *LA Free Press* (February 27, 1970), pp. 6 and 22–3.
40 Bugliosi, *Helter Skelter*, p. 408.

41 Blaine, "Manson in the Hate," *Berkeley Tribe* (January 20–February 6, 1970), pp. 8–9.
42 Richard Meltzer, "Charles Manson Was My Bunkmate," *The Realist* (May–June 1970), pp. 1 and 9–11; quote from p. 9.
43 Quoted in Melnick, *Creepy Crawling*.
44 See Biskind, *Easy Riders, Raging Bulls*.
45 Information and lyrics from "Getting Cute with Manson," *Rolling Stone* (May 14, 1970), p. 10.
46 Quoted in Davis, *Manson Exposed*, p. 232.
47 "Manson Hopes to Sell Record Album For Finances," *Associated Press* (December 26, 1969), available at www.https://www.cielodrive.com/archive/manson-hopes-to-sell-record-album-for-finances/, accessed August 2025.
48 "Getting Cute with Manson," *Rolling Stone* (May 14, 1970), p. 10; Davis, *Manson Exposed*, p. 232.
49 "Theory Links Beatles Album to Murders," *LA Times* (February 6, 1970), p. 17.
50 Taken from ESP-2003 reissue of *LIE*; interview from *Tuesday's Child*, as reproduced on the album cover.
51 According to the insert on the original *LIE*.
52 "What's in it for Charlie Manson?" *Rolling Stone* (April 2, 1970), p. 18.
53 The most active subcommittee of this absurdist Collège was Oulipo, a contraction of *ouvroir de literature potentialle*, a workshop of potential literature, which included luminaries such as George Perec and Italo Calvino. Founder Raymond Queneau famously described members as "rats who construct the labyrinth from which they plan to escape."
54 Davis, *Manson Exposed*, pp. 228–9.
55 Rosenfield, "True Crime Distorts the Truth About Crime," *Reason Magazine* (October 2023), pp. 60–1.
56 Illustration on the cover of *Tuesdays Child* (February 16, 1970) by Robert Williams.
57 Dalton and Felton, "The Most Dangerous Man in the World," *Rolling Stone* (June 25, 1970), pp. 34–5; emphasis added.
58 Y. Lee Freeman, "I Lived with Charlie Manson's 'Family,'" *The Argosy* (May 1970), p. 35.
59 Dalton and Felton, "The Most Dangerous Man in the World," pp. 28–30.
60 Y. Lee Freeman, "I Lived with Charlie Manson's 'Family,'" *The Argosy* (May 1970), pp. 34–7.
61 Bhagavad Gita chapter 6, text 9. https://vedabase.io/en/library/bg/6/.
62 White, "The Historical Text as Literary Artifact," p. 94.
63 In 1871, Rimbaud wrote: "It's wrong to say I think. Better to say: I am thought . . . *I* is an *other*."

64 Letter to the *Los Angeles Free Press* (May 22, 1970), p. 5.
65 Bugliosi, *Helter Skelter*.
66 Baer, *Journal of a Pseudo-Juror*, p. 109.
67 Ibid., p. 111.
68 Related by JFKLN, "The Armadillo Looks at Manson," *The Rag* (August 17, 1970), p. 3.
69 See Davies, *Manson Exposed*.
70 "The Law: Manson's Shattered Defense," *Time* Magazine (November 30, 1970), available at https://time.com/archive/6838369/the-law-mansons-shattered-defense/, accessed October 2024.
71 Quoted in Guinn, *Manson*, p. 366.
72 Bugliosi, *Helter Skelter*, p. 311.
73 Ibid.
74 Cawelti, *Adventure, Mystery, and Romance Formula Stories as Art and Popular Culture*.
75 Didion, *The White Album*, p. 45.
76 See the case White v. Davis (1975), available at https://law.justia.com/cases/california/supreme-court/3d/13/757.html, accessed October 2024.
77 Pentalpha, "Manson," *Speckled Bird* (February 8, 1971), pp. 3 and 17.
78 "Fourteen Ideas on Charlie Manson," *Quicksilver Times* (February 9–19), p. 18.
79 Editorial, "Rosemarys [sic] Baby," *Berkeley Tribe* (January 29–February 5, 1971), p. 4.
80 "Sleeping Beauty if Off Limits," *Rolling Stone* (September 17, 1970), p. 8.
81 From an unpublished manuscript in 1977, reproduced in Schreck, *The Manson File*, p. 164.
82 Interview with Grace Slick by Phyllis Pollack, "If I wasn't Grace Slick, I'd Be Dead," *Counterpunch* (May 29, 2009), available at https://www.counterpunch.org/2009/05/29/quot-if-i-wasn-t-grace-slick-i-d-be-dead-quot/, accessed October 2024.
83 See the "Jefferson Airplane" file, available at https://vault.fbi.gov/Jefferson%20Airplane%20/Jefferson%20Airplane%20Part%201%20of%201/view, accessed October 2024.
84 Bugliosi and Gentry, *Helter Skelter*, p. 335.
85 Journalist William T. Farr broke the story. After refusing to divulge the source, Judge Older held Farr in contempt of court; Farr's first amendment plea would eventually reach the Supreme Court.
86 See the trial transcripts from October 16, 1970. All trial transcripts available at https://www.cielodrive.com/people-v-manson-atkins-van-houten-krenwinkel.php, accessed October 2024.
87 A number of different conspiracy theories related to Mama Cass, alleged relationships with drug dealers, and the Manson Family have been circulated. For

one recent overview, see the Badland podcast, "Mama Cass (Part 1)," available at https://www.disgracelandpod.com/115/mamas-papas-pt-1, accessed October 2024.
88 Chester Anderson, originally printed in the *Oracle* (San Francisco), reproduced in Wolf, *Voices from the Love Generation*, pp. xxxiv–xxxv.
89 Bugliosi, *Helter Skelter*, p. 387.
90 Ed Sanders, "Scenarios be Damned," *LA Free Press* (November 27, 1970), pp. 2 and 19.
91 Ibid.
92 "Manson's Declaration of Innocence," *Los Angeles Free Press* (November 27, 1970), pp. 1, 6, 9–10, 12, 21, 30.
93 Charlie had told Hughes he "never wanted to see him in court again" before that weekend; his corpse turned up months later. Bugliosi hints darkly that a Family member named Lauren Elder, t/n possibly Lauren Willett, committed the assassination.
94 See the trial transcript from March 12, 1971.
95 Quoted in Linder, "The Charles Manson (Tate-LaBianca Murder) Trial," *Famous Trials* (2007), available at https://irlaw.umkc.edu/faculty_works/850, accessed September 2024.
96 Quoted in Karlene Faith, *The Long Prison Journey of Leslie Van Houten*, p. 30; from the Dianne Sawyer television interview in 1994.
97 From Bugliosi's closing argument, January 15, 1971.
98 Noel Hochman, trial transcript from March 11, 1971.
99 See Walsh, "On Claudio: The Man Who Sought Out John Lennon to Ask if His Songs Were About Him," available at https://medium.com/@JahHills/on-claudio-the-man-who-sought-out-john-lennon-to-ask-if-his-songs-were-about-him-c0b34c5d57ac.
100 For one example of this rumor, see Sanderson, "Charles Manson's Fiancée Wanted to Marry Him for his Corpse: Source," *NY Post* (February 8, 2015), available at https://nypost.com/2015/02/08/charles-mansons-fiancee-wanted-to-marry-him-for-his-corpse-source/, accessed October 2024.
101 Atkins, *Child of Satan*, pp. 164–5.
102 See the trial transcript, November 20, 1970.
103 Quoted in Leaf, *The Beach Boys and the California Myth*.
104 See the trial transcript, November 20, 1970; Charles Manson's words.

Epilogue

1 Hoskyns, *Waiting for the Sun*, p. 185.
2 Reynolds and Joy, *The Sex Revolts*, p. 145.

3 Phillips, *Papa John*, p. 303.
4 White, *Metahistory*; my wording here borrows from Harpham, "How Does Literature Teach Ethics?"
5 Didion, *The White Album*, p. 48.
6 McGuire, "An Aquarian Journal," *Fusion* (March 1970).
7 Or perhaps better: "Memory's images, once they are fixed in words, are erased." This claim, found in Italo Calvino's *Invisible Cities* (1972/5), had at one point been intended to serve as this book's epigraph.
8 At one point, the dedication from Nuel Emmons's *Manson in His Own Words* (1986) had been intended as an epigraph for this book, too. As had the cover blurb on the paperback edition of Ed Sanders's *The Family* (1971), a garbled quote from a *New York Times* review: "A *chillingly factual* look at . . . Charles Manson and his zombie-like disciples!" Both would have prepared the reader to consider the processes of myth-making described in the foregoing chapters.
9 Melley, *Empire of Conspiracy*, pp. 135–7.
10 From the opening monologue to *Firing Line* (October 1975), with guest Vincent Bugliosi. Note that even Buckley cannot help but invoke with the non-rational, the magical.
11 Didion, *The White Album*, p. 11.
12 White, *Metahistory*, p. 8.
13 Ibid., p. 37.
14 DeGroot (*Sixties Unplugged*, p. 4) provocatively called for "a history written by someone who doesn't give a damn," arguing (after Louis Menand) that chroniclers of the Sixties often care too much. But intellectual distance does not necessarily lead to ironic or satirical approaches to emplotment (after Hayden White), as pursued throughout the foregoing chapters. "As an intellectual discipline," Raphael Samuel wrote in 1990, "history requires a degree of detachment: the ability to draw contrasts and make connections, to discover a principle of order in the midst of seeming chaos, to explain, or attempt to explain, the whys and wherefores of apparently mysterious acts, to think the unthinkable." "The Return of History," *London Review of Books* (June 14, 1990), available at https://pugpig.lrb.co.uk/the-paper/v12/n11/raphael-samuel/the-return-of-history, accessed September 2024.
15 Director Michael Sarne, quoted in David, *Manson Exposed*, pp. 66–7.
16 From Calvino, *Invisible Cities*.

References

Allen, Gary, with Larry Abraham. 1971. *None Dare Call It Conspiracy*. Rossmoor: Concord Press.
Anthony, Gene. 1980. *The Summer of Love: Haight-Ashbury at Its Highest*. Berkeley: Celestial Arts.
Atkins, Susan, with Bob Slosser. 1977. *Child of Satan, Child of God*. Plainfield: Logos International.
Atkins-Whitehouse, Susan. 2012. *The Myth of Helter Skelter*. N.P: Menelorelin Dorenay's Publishing.
Baer, Rosemary. 1972. *Journal of a Pseudo-Juror*. Waco: Word Bookx.
Berger, Peter L., and Thomas Luckmann. 1966. *The Social Construction of Reality*. New York: Doubleday and Co.
Berne, Eric. 1964. *Games People Play: The Psychology of Human Relationships*. New York: Grove Press.
Biskind, Peter. 1998. *Easy Riders, Raging Bulls: How the Sex-Drugs-and-Rock-'n'-Roll Generation Saved Hollywood*. New York: Simon & Schuster.
Blumenberg, Hans. 2022. "World Pictures and World Models (1961)." In *History, Metaphors, Fables: A Hans Blumenberg Reader*, edited and translated by Hannes Bajohr, Florian Fuchs, and Joe Paul Kroll, 40–52. Ithaca: Cornell University Press.
Brown, Peter, with Steven Gaines. 2002. *The Love You Make: An Insider's Story of the Beatles*. London: Penguin.
Brown, Wenzell. 1975. *Possess and Conquer*. New York: Warner.
Buchanan, Edna. 2010/1987. *The Corpse Had a Familiar Face: Covering Miami, America's Hottest Beat*. New York: Gallery Books.
Bugliosi, Vincent, with Curt Gentry. 1974. *Helter Skelter: The True Story of the Manson Murders*. Norton: New York.
Bushnell, Horace. 1868. *Moral Uses of Dark Things*. New York: Strahan and Co.
Caine, Michael. 2012. *What's It All About?* New York: Random House.
Calvino, Italo. 1959. *The Baron in the Trees*. New York: Random House.
Calvino, Italo. 1973. *The Castle of Crossed Destinies*. New York: Harcourt Brace and Co.
Calvino, Italo. 1974. *Invisible Cities*. New York: Harcourt Brace Jovanovich.
Calvino, Italo. 2016. *Six Memos for the New Millenium*, translated by Geoffrey Brock. New York: Mariner Books.
Calvino, Italo. 2023. *The Written World and the Uwritten World: Essays*, translated by Ann Goldstein. New York: Mariner Books.
Cameron, D. Ewen. 1948. *Life Is for Living*. New York: Macmillan Co.

Capote, Truman. 1965. *In Cold Blood*. New York: Random House.
Capote, Truman. 1980. *Music for Chameleons*. New York: Random House.
Carlin, Peter Ames. 2006. *Catch a Wave: The Rise, Fall, and Redemption of the Beach Boys' Brian Wilson*. New York: Rodale.
Castaneda, Carlos. 1968. *The Teachings of Don Juan: A Yaqui Way of Knowledge*. Berkeley: University of California Press.
Cawelti, John G. 1976. *Adventure, Mystery, and Romance Formula Stories as Art and Popular Culture*. Chicago: University of Chicago Press.
Cohen, Lara Langer. 2023. *Going Underground: Race, Space, and the Subterranean in the Nineteenth-Century United States*. Durham: Duke University Press.
Collins, Anne. I*n The Sleep Room: The Story of the CIA Brainwashing Experiments in Canada*. Toronto: Lester and Orpen Dennys Ltd.
Constantine, Alex, ed. *The Essential Mae Brussell: Investigations of Fascism in America*. Port Townsend: Feral House.
Cooper, David. 1967. *Psychiatry and Anti-psychiatry*. London: Tavistock Publications.
Davis, Erik. 2019. *High Weirdness: Drugs, Esoterica, and Visionary Experience in the Seventies*. London: Strange Attractor Press.
Davis, Ivor. 2019. *Manson Exposed: A Reporter's 50-Year Journey Into Madness and Murder*. Ventury: Cockney Kid Publishing.
DeGroot, Gerard. 2008. *The Sixties Unplugged: A Kaleidoscopic History of a Disorderly Decade*. Cambridge, MA: Harvard University Press.
Didion, Joan. 1979. *The White Album*. New York: Simon and Schuster.
Didion, Joan. 2021. *Let Me Tell You What I Mean*. New York: Alfred A. Knopf.
Dyrendal, Asbjorn, James R. Lewis, and Jesper Aa. Petersen. 2016. *The Invention of Satanism*. New York: Oxford University Press.
Earisman, Delbert L. 1968. *Hippies in Our Midst: The Rebellion Beyond Rebellion*. Philadelphia: Fortress Press.
Eco, Umberto. 2019. "Conspiracy." In *On the Shoulders of Giants*, translated by Alastair McEwen, 243–61. Cambridge, MA: Harvard University Press.
Emmons, Nuel. 1986. *Manson in His Own Words*. New York: Grove Weidenfeld.
Erikson, Erik H. 1950. *Childhood and Society*. New York: Norton.
Faith, Karlene. 2001. *The Long Prison Journey of Leslie Van Houten: Life Beyond the Cult*. Boston: Northeastern University Press.
Foucault, Michel. 1972. "The Discourse on Language." In *The Archeology of Knowledge and the Discourse on Language*, 215–37. New York: Pantheon.
Frazer, James George. 1940. *Golden Bough*. New York: Macmillan.
Fromme, Lynette. 2018. *Reflexion: Lynette Fromme's Story of Her Life With Charles Manson, 1967–1969*. Cobb: Peasenhall Press.
Gaines, Steven. 1995. *Heroes and Villains: The True Story of the Beach Boys*. Philadelphia: Da Capo Press.

Gentry, Curt. 1968. *The Last Days of the Late, Great State of California*. New York: Putman.

Gilmore, John, and Ron Kenner. 1971. *The Garbage People: Story of Charles Manson*. Chicago: Omega Press.

Ginsberg, Allen. 2000. *Deliberate Prose: Selected Essays 1952–1995*. New York: Harper Collins.

Goldberg, Danny. 2017. *In Search of the Lost Chord: 1967 and the Hippie Idea*. New York: Akashic Books.

Graham, John R. 1977. *The MMPI: A Practical Guide*. New York: Oxford University Press.

Grandin, Greg. 2019. *End of the Myth: From the Frontier to the Border Wall in the Mind of America*. New York: Metropolitan Books.

Greenan, Russell H. 1968. *It Happened in Boston?* New York: Random House.

Greif, Mark. 2015. *The Age of the Crisis of Man: Thought and Fiction in America, 1933–1973*. Princeton: Princeton University Press.

Grogan, Jessica. 2013. *Encountering America: Humanistic Psychology, Sixties Culture, and the Shaping of the Modern Self*. New York: Harper Perennial.

Guinn, Jeff. 2013. *Manson: The Life and Times of Charles Manson*. London: Simon and Schuster.

Harpham, Geoffrey. 2009. "How Does Literature Teach Ethics?" *Journal of Philosophy: A Cross-Dicsciplinary Inquiry* 4(10): 1–14.

Heinlein, Robert Anson. 1961. *Stranger in a Strage Land*. New York: Putnam.

Holmquist, Anders, with Peter Marin. 1969. *The Free People*. New York: Outerbridge & Dienstfrey.

Horwitz, Elinor Lander. 1972. *Communes in America: The Place Just Right*. Philadelphia and New York: J.B. Lippincott Company.

Hoskyns, Barney. 1996. *Waiting for the Sun: The Story of the Los Angeles Music Scene*. London: Viking.

Hotchner, A. E. 1976. *Doris Day: Her Own Story*. New York: William Morrow and Co.

Houriet, Robert. 1971. *Getting Back Together:* New York: Coward, McCann and Geoghegan, Inc.

Hubbard, L. Ron. 1955. *Dianetics, 1955!* Silver Spring: Hubbard Dianetic Research Foundation.

Hultkrans, Andrew. 2003. *Love's Forever Changes*. 33 1/3. New York: Continuum.

Inceoglu, Bora, Jozsef Lango, Jie Jing, Lili Chen, Fuat Doymaz, Isaac N. Pessahand, and Bruce D. Hammock. 2003. "One Scorpion, Two Venoms: Prevenom of Parabuthus Transvaalicus Acts as an Alternative Type of Venom with Distinct Mechanism of Action." *Proceedings of the National Academy of Sciences of the United States of America* 100(3): 922–7.

John, Phillips. 1986. *Papa John: An Autobiography*. New York: Dell Publishing Co.

Jones, Jack. 1992. *Let Me Take You Down: Inside the Mind of Mark David Chapman, the Man Who Shot John Lennon*. New York: Villard Books.

Jones, Richard Glyn. 1987. *Solved! Famous Mystery Writers on Classic True-Crime Cases*. London: Xanadu.

Kanter, Rosabeth M. 1973. *Communes: Creating and Managing the Collective Life*. New York: Harper & Row.

Karpis, Alvin. 1980. *On The Rock: Twenty-Five Years in Alcatraz*. Toronto: Beaufort Books.

Kaufman, Phil, with Colin White. 1993. *Road Mangler Deluxe*. Glendale: White Boucke.

Kesey, Ken. 1962. *One Flew Over the Cuckoo's Nest*. New York: Viking Press.

King, Greg. 2000. *Sharon Tate and the Manson Murders*. New York: Barricade Books.

Kinney, David. 2014. *The Dylanologists: Adventures in the Land of Bob*. New York: Simon and Schuster.

Kinzer, Stephen. 2019. *Poisoner in Chief: Sidney Gottlieb and the CIA Search for Mind Control*. New York: Henry Holt and Company.

Laing, R. D. 1960. *The Divided Self: An Existential Study in Sanity and Madness*. London: Tavistock Publications.

Laing, R. D. 1967. *The Politics of Experience and The Bird of Paradise*. Middlesex: Penguin Books.

Lake, Dianne, with Deborah Herman. 2017. *Member of the Family: Manson, Murder and Me*. London: Harper Element.

Lambert, Patricia. 2000. *False Witness: The Real Story of Jim Garrison's Investigation and Oliver Stone's Film JFK*. Lanham: Rowman & Littlefield.

Lambert, Philip. 2007. *Inside the Music of Brian Wilson: The Songs, Sounds, and Influences of the Beach Boys' Founding Genius*. New York: Continuum.

Leaf, David. 1978. *The Beach Boys and the California Myth*. New York: Grosset & Dunlap.

Lewisohn, Mark. 1988. *The Complete Beatles Recording Sessions: The Official Story of the Abbey Road Years*. London: Hamlyn.

Livsey, Clara. 1980. *The Manson Women: A "Family" Portrait*. New York: Richard Marek Publishers.

Lorenz, Chris. 1998. "Can Histories Be True?: Narrativism, Positivism, and the 'Metaphorical Turn.'" *History and Theory* 37(3): 309–29.

Love, Mike, with James S. Hirsch. 2016. *Good Vibrations: My Life as a Beach Boy*. New York: Blue Rider Press.

MacDonald, Ian. 1994. *Revolution in the Head: The Beatles Records and the Sixties*. London: Fourth Estate Ltd.

Makari, George. 2010. *Revolution in Mind: The Creation of Psychoanalysis*. London: Duckworth.

Malcolm, Janet. 1981. *Psychoanalysis: The Impossible Profession*. Lanham: Rowman & Littlefield.
Malcolm, Janet. 1990. *The Journalist and the Murderer*. New York: Alfred A. Knopf.
Malcolm, Janet. 2011. *Iphigenia in Forest Hills: Anatomy of a Murder Trial*. New Haven: Yale University Press.
Malcolm, Janet. 2013. *Forty-on False Starts: Essays on Artists and Writers*. New York: Farrar, Straus, and Giroux.
Marcus, George E. 2000. *Para-Sites: A Casebook against Cynical Reason*. Chicago: University of Chicago Press.
Marcuse, Herbert. 1955. *Eros and Civilization: A Philosophical Inquiry Into Freud*. New York: Random House.
Marynick, Marlin. 2010. *Charles Manson Now*. Montreal: Cogito Media Group.
McDonough, Jimmy. 2002. *Shakey: Neil Young's Biography*. New York: Random House.
McGiveron, Rafeeq O. 2001. "From Free Love to the Free-Fire Zone: Heinlein's Mars, 1939–1987." *Brownsville* 42(2): 137–49.
Medovoi, Leerom. 2005. *Rebels: Youth and the Cold War Origins of Identity*. Durham: Duke University Press.
Mellen, Joan. 2013. *A Farewell to Justice: Jim Garrison, JFK's Assassination, and the Case that Should Have Changed History*. New York: Skyhorse.
Melley, Timothy. 1999. *Empire of Conspiracy the Culture of Paranoia in Postwar America*. Ithaca: Cornell University Press.
Melnick, Jeffrey. 2018. *Creepy Crawling: Charles Manson and the Many Lives of America's Most Infamous Family*. New York: Arcade Publishing.
Melville, Keith. 1972. *Communes in the Counter Culture: Origins, Theories, Styles of Life*. New York: William Morrow and Co.
Monroe, Rachel. 2019. *Savage Apetites: Four True Stories of Women, Crime, and Obsession*. New York: Scribner.
Morgan, Bill, ed. *The Letters of Allen Ginsberg*. Philadelphia: Da Capo Press.
Mungo, Raymond. 1970. *Famous Long Ago: My Life and Hard Times with Liberation News Service*. Boston: Beacon Press.
Noebel, David A. 1965. *Communism, Hypnotism and the Beatles*. Tulsa: Christian Crusade Publications.
O'Neill, Tom. 2019. *Chaos: Charles Manson, the CIA, and the Secret History of the Sixties*. New York: Little, Brown and Co.
Packard, Vance. 1957. *The Hidden Persuaders:* New York: McKay.
Painting, Wendy. 2016. *Aberration in the Heartland of the Real: The Secret Lives of Timothy McVeigh*. Walterville: Trine Day.
Patterson, R. Gary. 1998. *The Walrus Was Paul: The Great Beatle Death Clues*. New York: Simon & Schuster.
Perry, Charles. 1984. *The Haight Ashbury*. New York: Wenner Books.

Phillips, John, with Jim Jerome. 1986. *Papa John: An Autobiography*. Garden City: Doubleday and Co.

Polanski, Roman. 1984. *Roman*. New York: Ballantine Books.

Popper, Karl. 2006. "The Conspiracy Theory of Society." In *Conspiracy Theories: The Philosophical Debate*, edited by David Coady, 13–15. London: Routledge.

Powell, William. 1971. *The Anarchist's Cookbook*. Secaucaus: Lyle Stuart.

Powers, Devon. 2013. *Writing the Record: The Village Voice and the Birth of Rock Criticism*. Amherst: University of Massachusetts Press.

Priore, Domenic, and Brian Wilson. 2005. *Smile: The Story of Brian Wilson's Lost Masterpiece*. London: Bobcat Books.

Reeve, Andru. 1994. *Turn Me On, Dead Man: The Complete Story of the Paul McCartney Death Hoax*. Ann Arbor: Popular Culture, Ink.

Reynolds, Simon, and Joy Press. 1995. *The Sex Revolts: Gender, Rebellion, and Rock 'n' Roll*. Cambridge, MA: Harvard University Press.

Rising, George. 2010. *Stuck In The Sixties: Conservatives and the Legacies of the 1960s*. Bloomington: Xlibris.

Roszak, Theodore. 1968. *The Making of a Counter Culture: Reflections on the Technocratic Society and Its Youthful Opposition*. New York: Doubleday and Co.

Sanchez, Luis. 2014. *The Beach Boys' Smile*. New York: Bloomsbury.

Sanders, ed. 2002. *The Family*. New York: Thunder's Mouth Press.

Sargant, William 1959. *Battle for the Mind: A Physiology of Conversion and Brainwashing*. New York: Doubleday.

Schreck, Nikolas. 1988. *The Manson File*. New York: Amok Press.

Seltzer, Mark. 2007. *True Crime: Observations on Violence and Modernity*. New York: Routledge.

Smith, David E., and John Luce. 1971. *Love Needs Care: A History of San Francisco's Haight-Ashbury Free Medical Clinic and Its Pioneer Role in Treating Drug-Abuse Problems*. Boston: Little Brown and Co.

Stimson, George. 2014. *Goodbye Helter Skelter*. Cobb: Peasenhall Press.

Taylor, Derek. 1973. *As Time Goes By*. London: Davis-Poynter.

Thompson, Hunter S. 1966. *Hell's Angels: A Strange and Terrible Saga*. New York: Random House.

Tochka, Nicholas. 2023. *Rocking in the Free World: Popular Music and the Politics of Freedom in Postwar America*. New York: Oxford University Press.

Turner, Fred. 2010. *From Counterculture to Cyberculture: Stewart Brand, the Whole Earth Network, and the Rise of Digital Utopianism*. Chicago: University of Chicago Press.

Udo, Tommy. 2012. *Charles Manson: Music, Mayhem, Murder*. London: Bobcat Books.

Vollmann, William T. 2007. *Poor People*. New York: Ecco.

Vonnegut, Kurt. 1963. *Cat's Cradle*. New York: Delacorte Press.

Vonnegut, Kurt. 1969. *Slaughterhouse-Five: Or, The Children's Crusade, a Duty-Dance With Death*. New York: Delacorte Press.

Watkins, Basil. 2015. *The Book of Saints: A Comprehensive Biographical Dictionary*. New York: Bloomsbury Publishing.

Watkins, Paul, with Guillermo Soledad. 1979. *My Life With Charles Manson*. New York: Bantam Books Inc.

Watson, Charles "Tex," with Chaplain Ray Hoekstra. 1978. *Will You Die For Me?* Old Tappan: Fleming H. Revell.

Watson, "Tex," with Chaplain Ray Hoekstra. 2019. *Cease to Exist: The Firsthand Account of the Journal to Becoming a Killer for Charles Manson*. Santa Monica: 12AX7 Press.

Webber, Everett. 1959. *Escape to Utopia: The Communal Movement in America*. New York: Hastings House Publishers.

Wenner, Jan S. 1971. *Lennon Remembers*. San Fransisco: Straight Arrow Books.

West, Nathanael. 1939. *The Day of the Locust*. New York: Random House.

White, Hayden. 1973. *Metahistory: The Historical Imagination in Nineteenth-Century Europe*. Baltimore: John Hopkins University Press.

White, Hayden. 1978. "Historical Text as Literary Artifact." In *Tropics of Discourse: Essays in Cultural Criticism*, 81–100. Baltimore: John Hopkins University Press.

Wolf, Leonard, and Deborah Wolf, eds. 1968. *Voices from the Love Generation*. Boston: Little, Brown and Company.

Wyllie, Timothy, with Adam Parfrey, ed. 2009. *Love, Sex, Fear, Death: The Inside Story of the Process Church of the Final Judgment*. Port Townsend: Feral House.

Index

acid   76, 84, 104, 137, 190, 194, 202, 205
   bad trips   104, 107
   the Beatles   12–13
   and depersonalization   184, 211
   dosing water supplies   96, 132–3, 246 n.78
   Kesey, Ken   51
   psychedelic syndrome   26, 32
   religious experiences   19, 25, 42, 67, 215
   rituals   90–1, 107
alternative practices and belief systems
   Drown, Ruth (Dr.)   153, 249 n.31
   Hubbard, L. Ron   64–5
      Dianetics   11, 24, 111
      Scientology   22, 50, 65, 153, 172, 178, 189, 219, 238 n.79
   meditation   20, 31, 57, 59, 65, 82
   Ouspensky, P. D.   20
   Process Church of the Final Judgment   22, 66, 178
   self realization fellowship   20, 51
   Synanon   24

Beach Boys, the   1, 13–14, 55, 76–7, 93–4, 101, 122–3, 179
   Anderle, David   63
   Brother Records   58, 63, 90, 98, 101
   Desper, Stephen   91, 141–2
   Grillo, Nick   141, 164, 250
   Jakobson, Gregg (*see* entry under *commune, hangers-on and/or members of the*)
   Kalinich, Stephen   74, 180, 206
   Love, Mike   57, 63, 90, 101, 142
      "Spiritual Regeneration Song"   59
      and Maharishi Mahesh Yogi   58–9, 77, 91
   Pet Sounds (1966)   13–14
   SMiLE   14, 74, 180
      "Child Is Father of the Man"   74–5, 93

   Smiley Smile (1967)   55
   Wilson, Brian   13–14, 53, 55, 63–4, 74–5, 90, 93, 141, 180
   Wilson, Carl   14, 63
   Wilson, Dennis (*see* entry under *commune, hangers-on and/or members of the*)
   Wilson, Murry   14, 53, 63
Beatles, the   1–2, 12–14, 44, 55, 87–8, 97, 99, 151, 154–5, 160, 176, 189, 207–8
   Apple Records   94, 155, 164
   Beatle George   20, 61–2, 125, 134, 158
   Beatle John   12–13, 52, 59, 191, 208, 210, 212
      and Bagism   169–70, 174
      Chapman, Mark David   75–6
      Claudio, Curt   215
      Cleave, Maureen   108
      Plastic Ono Band   151, 189
   Beatle Paul   9, 35, 52, 66, 94, 146, 189
      untimely death of   158–9
   Beatle Ringo   13, 44, 57, 108, 158
      The Magic Christian (1968)   60
   Martin, George   99, 113, 155
   and Maharishi Mahesh Yogi   13, 57, 61
Beatle albums, songs, and films
   Abbey Road (1969)   151, 158, 160, 163
      "I Want You" (She's So Heavy)   158
      "Maxwell's Silver Hammer"   154–5, 189
      "Sun King"   158
      "You Never Give Me Your Money"   163
   The Beatles (1968) 1–2, 113, 124–5, 127, 129, 157–8, 163, 189, 193, 207, 211, 214
      "Blackbird"   87, 125
      "Cry Baby Cry"   87

"Helter Skelter"   87, 94, 112, 129, 163
"Honey Pie"   88
"I Will"   88
"Mother Nature's Son"   113
"Revolution 9"   45, 87, 114, 125
"Sexy Sadie"   87, 91, 125
"Yer Blues"   113
The Beatles at the Hollywood Bowl (1977)   12
Hot As Sun (n.d.)   155
Magical Mystery Tour (1967)   44, 51, 113, 158, 163
  "I Am The Walrus"   52, 53, 100, 151, 158
Please Please Me (1963)   13
Sgt. Pepper's Lonely Hearts Club Band (1967)   14, 52, 55, 113, 118, 157–8
  and Aleister Crowley   46
  "A Day In The Life"   100, 157
Yellow Submarine (1967)   112
brainwashing (includes *hypnosis*)   1–2, 24, 38–9, 44, 47, 56, 80, 87, 92, 108, 111, 125, 159, 168–9, 178, 180–4, 186–8, 193, 199, 202–3, 212, 214
Bushnell, Horace   77
Cameron, Donald Ewen   132, 133
Pied Piper, the   96, 172, 179, 237 n.58
Svengali   164, 184

Christianity   39, 62, 73–4, 108, 111, 135, 198, 215
The Bible   1–2, 28, 55, 73, 75, 79, 90, 111, 124, 129, 172
  Book of Genesis   28, 237
  Book of Jonah   24–5
  Book of Revelation   72, 93, 109, 111, 122, 124, 172, 200
Jesus Christ   12, 39, 50, 61, 67, 89, 91, 124, 137, 159, 165, 168, 178, 185, 203, 213, 215
and the Romans (literal and metaphorical; includes *police*)   67, 72–3, 105, 110, 158, 163, 182, 202, 204

commune, hangers-on and/or members of the
Atkins, Susan ("Sadie Mae Glutz")   4, 14, 19–20, 28–9, 68–9, 101, 125, 129, 134, 143, 159, 175–8, 183, 217
  Graham, Virginia and Veronica ("Ronnie") Howard   159–60, 164–5, 206
Beausoleil, Bobby ("Cupid")   20–1, 46–7, 49, 51, 53, 79, 124, 136, 143, 193, 216, 247
Brunner, Mary ("Mother Mary")   16–17, 20, 22–3, 29, 68, 91, 109, 169
Charles Watson ("Tex")   4, 80, 83, 94, 111, 119, 124, 128–9, 137–8, 143, 151, 175, 185–6, 205, 214, 240
  drug-dealing with Rosina Kruger ("Luella")   138
  lawyer Bill Boyd   2, 179, 181
Davis, Bruce   55, 151, 155
DeCarlo, "Donkey" Dan   128, 134, 168, 177
Fromme, Lynette ("Squeaky")   4, 17, 21–2, 80, 95–7, 125, 128, 164, 168, 179, 205, 216
Gillies, Catherine ("Capistrano" or "Cappy")   91, 103, 123, 178, 190, 209–10
Good, Sandra ("Blue" or "Sandy")   4, 76, 101, 114, 123–4, 168, 182, 190
Grogan, Steve ("Clem")   82, 91, 94, 96, 112, 117, 123, 128, 143, 173–4, 190, 192, 213
Haught, John ("Zero" or "Christopher Jesus")   178
Hinman, Gary   49, 53, 143, 168, 176, 193, 197
Hoyt, Barbara   32, 190, 205
Jakobson, Gregg   4, 63, 94–5, 97, 115–16, 119, 136–7, 207–8
Kasabian, Linda   88, 143, 201–4
Krenwinkel, Patricia ("Katie")   20, 29, 49, 68, 71, 78, 91, 109, 143, 190, 197–9, 205–6, 211

Lake, Dianne   4, 42, 62, 67, 76, 124, 159, 211
Lansbury, Didi   56
Lutesinger, Kitty   51, 168
Melcher, Terry   93, 96, 115–16, 119–20, 146, 179, 193, 208
  Bergen, Candice   119
  Day, Doris   4, 13, 137
  Deasy, Mike   136–7
  Martin, Deana   119
  Melcher (1974)   216
Moorehouse, Dean   49–50, 235
Poston, Brooks   83, 124, 151, 156, 180, 208, 216
Pitman, Nancy ("Brenda")   54, 56, 123, 151, 169, 190, 216
Ross, Mark   185
Share, Catherine ("Gypsy")   51, 79, 91, 111, 112, 117, 123–4, 169, 190
Van Houten, Leslie   20–1, 51, 82, 99, 112, 124, 169, 175, 188, 190, 197, 205–6, 211, 214, 215
Watkins, Paul ("Little Paul")   4, 56, 58, 66, 95, 151–2, 180, 190, 208
  Crockett, Paul   150–3, 180
  Desert Sun   156, 216
Wallerman, T. J.   111
  Crowe, Bernard ("Lotsapoppa")   137–8, 143, 197
Wildebush, Juanita   123, 151, 169
Wilson, Dennis   4, 14, 25, 63–4, 71, 73–4, 76, 83, 88, 90–1, 94, 97–8, 101, 115–16, 119, 141–3, 164, 179
  "All I Want To Do"   141
  Cafritz, Charlene   116–17
  "Little Bird"   74–5
  Pacific Ocean Blue (1977)   73, 216
commune, investigations and court cases about the
  Bugliosi, Vincent   3, 16, 68, 115–16, 156, 166, 207–8
  and Buckley, William F.   220
  Cielo Drive   116, 119, 143, 146, 152, 186, 208, 219
  Fitzgerald, Paul   199, 200, 208
  Hall of Justice   16, 38, 165, 190
  Hughes, Ronald   199, 202–3, 211, 212, 256
  Judge Older   197
  Keith, Maxwell   212, 214
  Kranarek, Irving   199, 203, 206–10
  Oh! Calcourta! (1970)   188
  Polanski, Roman   53, 89, 92, 152, 201
  Shinn, Daye   199, 204, 214
  Smith, David E.   26, 32, 131, 171
  Smith, Roger ("Jubal")   33, 131, 171
  Tate, Paul   150
  Tate-LaBianca murders   2, 3, 92, 138, 142–3, 166, 189, 204, 219
commune, life and times of
  Barker Ranch   103, 112, 123, 150–2, 158
  Death Valley   1, 45, 103, 114, 116, 161, 165, 185, 188
  Horseshoe Drive   51, 54, 67, 79
  Magical Mystery Tour (MMT)   45–6, 80, 82
  Spahn Movie Ranch   71, 78, 80, 82, 95, 101, 107, 109, 116–17, 123–4, 134, 136–8, 144–5, 163, 172–3, 185, 193–4, 206
  Pearl, Ruby   79
  playacting (*see games*)
  Ramrodder, The (1967)
  Shea, Donald ("Shorty")   150, 216
  Spahn, George   78–9, 111, 123, 128, 168
  Straight Satans   128, 134–5, 143
  Starr, Randy   137, 203
  Spiral Staircase, the   42, 45, 50
  talk-tos   60, 124
  Topanga Canyon   43, 49, 51, 112
  Valentine, Michael   16, 33, 68
  Yellow Submarine, the   123–4
commune, music-making and songs of the
  cover songs
    "Eyes of a Dreamer"   189
    "The Shadow of Your Smile"   29, 37, 66, 80, 238
  desert songs   112–13
    "Die to be One"   125
    "Get On Home"   190

"Give Your Love" (To Be
    Free)   125
"No Wrong"   125
"Ra-Hide Away!"   125,
    129
Helter Skelter Club   128–9
Karpis, Alvin "Creepy"   11
Kaufman, Phil   66, 79–80, 189–90
LIE: The Love and Terror Cult
    (1970)   38, 164, 189
    "Cease to Exist"   90, 93–5, 122,
        179
    "Clang Clang"   54
    "Ego Is A Too-Much Thing"   28,
        95
    "Garbage Dump"   91, 95
    "I'll Never Say Never To
        Always"   122, 123
    "Look At Your Game Girl"   54,
        83, 189
    "Never Learn Not To Love"   101,
        121, 179
    "Sick City"   54, 121, 189
    "Your Home Is Where You're
        Happy"   27, 38, 54
Milky Way, the   54, 128
recording sessions   29, 94–5, 141,
    185, 189–90, 242, 251
    with Stromberg, Gary   37–41,
        66

drugs   1–2, 9, 16–17, 28, 31, 44, 78, 82,
    89, 121, 128, 131, 134, 138, 143,
    159, 171, 202–3
Musa sapientum Bananadine   133

ego (includes *ego death*)   13, 23, 28,
    49, 60, 83, 95, 107, 123, 174,
    176, 183, 185, 197, 198, 210,
    240
experience   5, 9, 16–18, 23, 34, 58, 59, 65,
    67, 75, 81, 97, 98, 105, 118–19,
    126, 135, 162, 192, 220–1, 229
    n.5, 232 n.68

Farrow, Mia   19, 67
    and Sellers, Peter   60
    and Sinatra, Frank   57, 60, 207

games   10, 42, 48, 71–2, 80–2, 125, 153,
    168
    agreements   123, 151, 153–4, 156,
        177, 232
    changes   14, 16, 63, 68, 106, 122, 136,
        151, 180
    scripts   76, 153, 189, 198–9
genre   4, 14, 21, 27, 31, 56, 135, 144, 155,
    166, 179, 197, 200, 202, 222,
    228 n.7
    academic non-fiction   135, 228 n.10,
        240 n.30, 246 n.87
        Earisman, Delbert   25–6, 31, 67
        Goldschmitt, Walter   98
        McLuhan, Marshall   113, 118–19,
            210
        Mead, Margaret   121
        Roszak, Theodore   18
        White, Hayden   197, 202, 229 n.9,
            248 n.7
    conspiracy theorizing   9, 44, 116–17,
        131–3, 151, 181–2, 210
        Allen, Gary   217, 239–40 n.25
        Brussells, Mae   181–2
    counterculture authors
        Freeman, Y. Lee   192–6
        Kandel, Lenore   47, 122, 154,
            202
        Sanders, Ed   4, 22, 45, 62, 71, 72,
            91, 109, 116, 124, 150, 175, 211
    children's stories
        Alice in Wonderland   52, 80, 156
        Wizard of Oz   75
    documentary film   43, 57, 136, 246
        n.77
        Hendrickson, John   185, 190
    fiction
        Calvino, Italo   148, 202, 228 n.12,
            232 n.68, 240 n.30, 257 n.7
        Greenan, Russell H.   137
        Kesey, Ken   15, 51
        Salinger, J. D.   76
        Vonnegut, Kurt   24, 45, 72
    gonzo or "New" journalism   4, 51, 72,
        134–5, 149
        Didion, Joan   48, 201–2, 219, 221
        Vonnegut, Kurt   59, 149–50, 202
        Wolfe, Tom   51

memoirs   3–4, 11, 15, 28, 58, 66–7,
    90, 114, 135, 142, 152, 190–1,
    198, 222
popular non-fiction
    Emmons, Nuel   7, 15, 21–2, 28,
        40–1
    Guinn, Jeff   22, 97–8, 137
psychsploitation   31, 78–9, 96–7, 191
    Wild In The Streets (1968)
    Mondo Hollywood (1967) and
        Robert Cohen   21, 43–4, 46, 48
    Love and Murder in the Commune
        (1970)   191
    Ramrodder, The (1967)
rock criticism   27, 55, 87, 108, 114,
    120–1, 125–6, 160–3, 187, 232,
    250–1 n.60
    Ginsberg, Allen   113–14, 127
    Gleason, Ralph   108–9, 160–3
    Goldstein, Richard   120, 126
    Meltzer, Richard   187
    Wenner, Jann   55, 113, 127, 160,
        212
    Williams, Paul   27, 63
    Zappa, Frank   120–1
rock lyrics and imagery
    Dylan, Bob   26, 42, 52, 86, 108,
        118, 136, 179
    Young, Neil   13, 56, 88, 91
speculative fiction and science fiction
    Brown, Wenzell   92, 94
    Castaneda, Carlos   98, 105, 202
    Cayce, Edgar ("the sleeping
        prophet")   122
    Heinlein, Robert   33, 64, 68,
        210
    Santesson, Hans Stefan   94
self-help and self-actualization
    Carnegie, Dale   11, 65
    Goddard, Neville   106
    Peale, Norman Vincent   11, 24
    Rand, Ayn   19, 57
    Venta, Krishna   109, 111
true-crime   4–5, 14, 53, 97–8, 135,
    136, 144, 150, 156–7, 166,
    190–1, 200, 220
    Capote, Truman   53, 136, 154,
        167
    Gentry, Curt   122, 173
    Schiller, Lawrence   182–3
ghostwriters   29, 58, 122, 129, 165

Helter Skelter, contrasting uses of
    Beatles song   87, 94, 112, 129, 163
    bestselling true-crime book by Vincent
        Bugliosi   3, 14, 67–9, 91, 116,
        146, 156–7, 165–6, 177, 220
    as narrative   1–4, 112, 116, 128, 159,
        165, 170–1, 193, 199–200, 220
    as phrase   165, 177, 206
hidden messages   38–9, 52, 99–100, 108,
    112, 118–19, 125, 158, 176, 181,
    190, 207–10
    Rorschach tests   146–7
    subliminal messages   27, 29, 86–7,
        192

indexing, *see* Kurt Vonnegut, *Cat's Cradle*
    (1963), Chapter   55

John F. Kennedy (JFK)   2, 9, 55–6, 96, 108,
    115, 181, 183, 201, 208, 210

love (universal)   31, 32, 42, 67, 80, 181
LSD, *see* acid

magic (includes *magick*)   19, 25–6, 42,
    76, 115, 117–18, 146, 163, 172,
    180, 185, 196, 211
    Anger, Kenneth   46–7, 202
    astrology   49
        Martin, Steve   127
        Reagan, Nancy and Ronald   48–9
    exorcism   220
    LaVey, Anton   19, 76
    Mephistopheles   19, 187
    mediumship   152, 154
    occult, the (includes: *witches*)   2, 35,
        54, 78, 101, 149, 158, 160, 193,
        196, 203
        Eye of the Devil (1966) 146
        Juanita   66
        Lucifer Rising   46, 50
        Rosemary's Baby (1968) 19, 60, 76,
            89
        Saunders, Alex   146

Tarot, the   18, 26, 148
  Wizard, the   50, 88, 194
mental illness (diagnosed and metaphorical; includes *insanity*)   1, 15, 23, 32, 38, 56, 77, 87, 126–7, 129, 154, 177, 184, 188, 217, 220, 233
Maharishi Mahesh Yogi   65, *see also* entries under the Beach Boys *and* the Beatles
narrative   11, 15, 28, 33–6, 50, 66–7, 71, 76, 80–1, 91, 105–6, 110, 115–16, 142, 145, 147, 148, 166, 182, 186, 200, 220–1, 228 n.12, 257 n.8
  alternative and/or speculative stories   92, 93, 95, 109, 130, 138, 143, 154–5, 187, 195, 206, 208, 247 n.88
  allegory   98–9, 114, 120, 125
  apophany   72, 118, 131, 148, 151, 157, 161, 201
  devices, literary and/or rhetorical   47, 71, 98, 128, 156–7, 177, 192, 213
  dog-whistle   44
  exegesis   4–5, 18, 27, 52, 86, 100, 118, 123–5, 157, 177, 194–5, 207
  figurative language   6, 35–6, 81, 114, 120, 127, 184, 209, 231–2
  foreshadowing   98–9, 169
  propinquity   14, 15, 54–5, 78, 98, 115, 165, 182, 219, 233, 246–7, 252 n.5
  Neurath, Otto   34
  parables   41, 65, 149, 156, 192
  pataphysics   189, 190, 220

non-rationality   52, 98, 104, 115, 118, 121–2, 127, 172, 196
numerology   22, 27, 45, 51, 63, 72, 76, 135–7, 170–1, 215

parents (includes *fathers* and *mothers*)   1, 10, 18, 19, 21, 25, 31, 35, 42, 49–50, 56, 73–5, 82, 84, 85, 88, 100, 110, 120–1, 132, 133, 167, 173, 183, 184, 192, 215
playacting, *see games*

Porfiry, *see* Stovitz, Aaron
psychoanalysis   20, 22–3, 32, 73, 84–5, 121–2, 126, 138, 173–4, 179, 185, 192, 206, 239 n.19

revolution   44, 84, 87, 104, 106, 108, 112–13, 131, 134, 137, 162, 193, 195, 210
rumor   44, 46, 78, 132, 135, 138–9, 146–7, 152, 162, 186, 189, 220, 255–6 n.87

sadomasochism   2, 40–1, 146, 187, 234 n.6
Sixties, the   2, 3, 5, 12, 56, 88, 156, 162, 219, 221–2, 257 n.14
  Alpert, Richard (Baba Ram Dass)   44
  Black Panthers   104, 139, 143, 145
  Buffalo Springfield   91, 103, 118, 209–10
  Byrds, the   13, 120, 208, 212
  Crosby, David   13, 64, 208–10
  Doors, the   31, 42, 97, 126
    The Doors (1967)   27, 29
    Strange Days (1967)   29
  Elliott, "Mama" Cass   208, 210, 211, 255–6 n.87
  Haight-Ashbury   8–9, 17, 23, 32, 171–2, 181, 194
  Hendrix, Jimi   13, 170
  Herman's Hermits   13
  hippies (includes "*hippies*")   76, 92, 96, 105, 131, 149, 164, 172, 179, 184, 187, 191, 204
  Hopper, Dennis   187
  Human Be-In   8, 16
  Jefferson Airplane   29, 42, 120, 163
    Slick, Grace   120, 205
  Donovan   57, 59, 100, 160
    "Mellow Yellow"   133
  Dylan, Bob   26, 42, 52, 86, 108, 118, 136, 160, 179
    John Wesley Harding (1967)   86, 118
  Leary, Timothy   26, 107
  Masked Marauders, the   160, 189
  Monkees, the   46
  Mothers of Invention   46
  Pauleskas, Vito   44
  Phillips, John   210

Rolling Stones, the 80, 135, 189
   Altamont 3
   Jagger, Mick 46, 66, 160
   Weathermen, the 191
   Yippies 104, 204–5, 246 n.78
Stranger in a Strange Land (1961) 33, 35, 64, 210, 219
Stovitz, Aaron, *see* Porfiry

truth games 5, 6, 14, 15, 21, 22, 24, 27, 34, 41, 49, 56, 61, 66–7, 86, 115, 117–18, 132, 135–6, 154, 160, 162, 168, 189, 192, 197, 202, 213, 220–2, 227 n.2, 228 n.11, 248 n.9
timelines, discrepancies within 29, 32, 88, 90–1, 124, 137, 142, 180, 213, 230, 235, 243 n.20
untruths 113–14, 118, 127–8, 136, 168, 197, 213

Zarathustra 118